YOUNG BOBBY

BRIAN BELTON

YOUNG
BOBBY

Volume 1

*The 'Making' of
England's Greatest Captain*

The author thanks Mr Terrance Brown for gifting access to the entirety of the Charles Korr research recordings. These include numerous in-depth interviews with former players and staff of West Ham United, encompassing the entire era this book focuses on.

First published 2022 by DB Publishing, an imprint of JMD Media Ltd,

Nottingham, United Kingdom.

ISBN 9781780916323

Printed in the UK

CONTENTS

FOREWORD BY ALAN CURBISHLEY

Alan Curbishley was involved with West Ham United from boyhood. He joined the Hammers as an apprentice on leaving school in the summer of 1974. After impressing in West Ham's South East Counties League side, he was named as substitute against Everton in August 1974 at the age of 16 and became the youngest ever West Ham player to be named on the team sheet, although he didn't get on the field that day.

Alan made his first team debut in a 1-0 home defeat against Chelsea in March 1975, coming into the team for Billy Bonds who was out with an injury, and in the summer he was a member of the West Ham youth team, alongside Alvin Martin, Geoff Pike, and Paul Brush, that was beaten by Ipswich Town in the final of the FA Youth Cup.

Curbs' (as the Irons fans were to know him) first win with the club and first goal came in a 2-1 home victory over Newcastle in October 1975, in which he had replaced the injured Trevor Brooking in the starting line-up. Impressed team-mates, motivated by Pat Holland, gave him the nickname 'Whizz'.

As an 18-year-old, Alan appeared in both legs of the West Ham's European Cup Winners' Cup third round tie against Den Haag in March 1976. Alan was transferred to Birmingham City in April 1979. Perhaps his chances were limited as for most of his time at Upton Park he was competing for a midfield position with Trevor Brooking, Alan Devonshire, Pat Holland, Geoff Pike and Billy Bonds, but he was to play close to 100 games with the Hammers over his heart. Not long after that move, in 1980, he was selected for the England under-21 side.

Curbs was appointed as manager of West Ham in December 2006. After looking certain for relegation, he led the Hammers to seven wins out of their last nine games, including victories over Arsenal and a 1-0 win at Manchester United on the last day of the season, to keep West Ham in the Premier League.

In 2007/08 West Ham were relatively successful, achieving a top-ten finish despite some critical injuries. That term he brought Scott Parker, Craig Bellamy, Kieron Dyer and Julien Faubert to Upton Park.

Despite West Ham taking six points from their first three games, Alan was unhappy with the club's transfer policy, after key players Anton Ferdinand and George McCartney were sold without his permission.

For me, it was a huge loss to the club when he resigned on 3 September 2008. He was the natural successor to Ron Greenwood and John Lyall, and having 'worn the shirt', he belonged at Upton Park more than his immediate successors Gianfranco Zola, Avram Grant, and the carpetbagging Sam Allardyce

*

One of my first memories of Bobby Moore was when I was playing for West Ham Boys. I'd had a knee injury and Ron Greenwood arranged for me to see the West Ham physio, Rob Jenkins. I got to the West Ham treatment room and Bobby Moore was there being looked after by Rob. I was about 14 at the time, so you can imagine, I was in awe and a bit perplexed as to how to react.

As I was waiting, Bobby needed to be looked after first. Rob came over to me and said, 'We want you to go over to the cafe. Mooro wants a sausage sandwich.' So, I went over to the cafe, that was a couple of minutes' walk away, just over the road from the West Ham ground, and got a couple of sausage sandwiches, with brown sauce as I remember, and a big mug of tea. The people in the cafe put a saucer on the top of the tea mug to keep it warm.

I got back to the treatment room and as I approached, I heard Ron Greenwood talking to Bobby (he often called him 'Robert'). I didn't know what to do, to just walk in with the tea and sandwiches or go and hide. I chose to hide in the toilets. When Ron left, I took the tea and sandwiches into Bobby. He had a right go at me, 'Where you been? The tea's cold!' I tried to explain that I heard the manager, but he said, I think a bit amused, 'Naa! You'd have been all right.' It's probably unimaginable to think of a Premier League club treatment room now with players tucking into mugs of tea and sausage sandwiches.

As a young player, I got a 'green ticket', which was for seats behind the dugout, so I could hear some of the directions relayed to the players and see the game from pretty much the same perspective as the manager. Ron Greenwood laid a lot of emphasis on possession. For instance, he preferred the goalkeeper, if possible, to roll the ball Bobby, although the crowd wanted it kicked quickly upfield. Ron knew possession would be 80 or 90 per cent that way instead of 50 per cent. Bobby was all about possession. If you watch the 1966 World Cup Final for instance, I think he lost possession a couple of times. Like Ron, he understood that possession is the key to the game; if you keep the ball, you deprive the other side of it, so they have less of a chance to score.

Ron Greenwood and John Lyall, like Bobby Robson and Terry Venables, could have managed anywhere in the world. It wouldn't matter if they spoke the language or not. Bobby could have done the same if things had been different. Ron was the start of the 'football intelligence' produced at Upton Park, the 'West Ham Way' if you like; he was behind the couple of generations of successful managers who had started their football at West Ham. It's hard to think of another club that has managed to produce so many achieving coaches and managers.

But there were other special aspects about being at West Ham. I had scored my first goal for the first team in a 2-1 win against Newcastle at Upton Park. I was 17. The ball went up to Clyde Best, who brought it down and laid it off, I controlled it on my knee and half volleyed it. It flew into the back of the net, in the bottom corner. I couldn't believe it. I also made the winning goal for Alan Taylor, so it was a good day.

I went to the game by public transport. I'd walked from my house, in Gainsborough Road, Canning Town, and got the bus on the Barking Road. After the game I did an interview on the pitch with John Motson. Before that John Lyall, knowing I'd come on the bus, asked Frank Lampard (senior) if he'd take me home. Frank agreed and said to me, 'Come to the players' lounge, meet me there and I'll take you home.' I went to the players' lounge; I'd never been in there before. Bobby Moore was in there, he'd been watching the game. He was going for a drink with Frank, so I sat in the back seat, behind Bobby Moore as they took me back to Canning Town.

Just before I got out of the car, they asked me what I was doing that evening, of course I said, 'Watching the game.' As I went to go into my mum and dad's house, Frank opened the boot of the car and pulled out a crate of beer and passed it to me. 'Here, have a drink tonight.' Things like that can mean a lot to a young player. Bobby once asked me if I liked snooker. I didn't play much but said I did. He asked me what my bridge was like. I had no idea what he was talking about. He could have had a laugh about that, but he just showed me what it was. This was a big star player, but he had the time and the interest to ask about a kid's snooker skills!

I grew up watching Bobby either at Upton Park or on the television. He was something very different in football, one of the few players who rarely need to look at the ball, so he could see what was going on during a game all over the pitch. He was an inspiration to anyone hoping to play football at top level.

I'm glad Brian Belton has written about Bobby's life before he became the world-recognised figure, because it gives us all a window on how Mooro used the influences and resources around him to build his 'footballing brain'. His example is useful for us all. Brian also writes about a lot of things that aspiring young footballers, coaches and fans might think about. But as he suggests, watching or playing football, at its best, like the pursuit of excellence in anything, can provide examples of how we might build our own sense of decency, character and attitude to life. However, the game is part of many millions of lives all over the world, so the motivational opportunities of football have the power to inspire endlessly. Bobby Moore's young life is an extraordinary aspect of that potential.

PREFACE

I started writing this, the first of two books, on the early life of Bobby Moore, just over half a century ago. Words have been written, both hurriedly and reflectively. As with all 'labours of love' it has not been non-stop; motivation peaks and wanes, uncertainty, even fear, threatens to betray the pursuit of the ever-elusive truth of matters.

I have gone years without writing a word and gone back to the manuscript to find that great lumps of it were either stupefyingly dull, vaguely incomprehensible, slightly mad or just plain wrong. I'd like to boast perfection, but no biography is the 'finished article'. If that is claimed it is likely the babblings of nativity and/or poor journalistic influences.

As a consequence, there have been more re-writes than I dare to think about and the additions and subtractions would fill at least three other books. But on the whole, I think it has been worth it. I have met some wonderful people and learned likely more than I ever did as I walked the road from Burke Secondary Modern School in Plaistow that took me to City University, the universities of Canterbury Christchurch, Kent, Coventry and Malta, every continent, and almost every major city in the world.

Yet I remain that east London boy I was, the youth worker I became and have never really stopped being. I am pleasantly possessed by my 'home streets' and those of Glasgow, Belfast, Hong Kong, Baltimore and Cape Town, but also mountainsides, forests and lakes, all the places I have worked with and among young people. I am gladly haunted by these lively, funny, often maddening but nearly always intelligent and strong souls, many of whom were football supporters and some part of the great diaspora of 'Hammerhood'.

My collective experiences and others' lives have fed into this book. It is a map made up of the views, thoughts, feelings and lives of players, managers, and supporters. Both books are a report from the front line about a time and times, a place and places, a face and faces, but most importantly people and a person. As is the case with all books, they are also about the writer.

I want to thank all of the spirits that have bled into this universe of letters, these planets of words; some of them welcomed me into their families over years, others donated ten minutes to the cause. But you cannot measure the giving of other people's sharing of their time; their impressions and opinions; their memories and motives – themselves, by the ticks and tocks of the workaday clock. Every contribution is golden.

As you might see from the bibliography, I have also been greatly assisted by many writers, most of them no less able or committed than I might claim to be. Certainly, some are much more gifted in giving the world readable books. The likes of Tina Moore and Charles Korr (how's that for poetry?), coming from seemingly diverse literally genres and habitats, were the shining lights in my library. These are very different books but each beautiful in their own right.

While trying to provide some of the critical analytical craft learned from academic writing over the last five decades, I have tried not to crowd the text with citations, as one is obliged to do in that 'other realm' of prim convention (often for the sake of itself). I have avoided this as it causes paragraphs and pages to stutter and choke in the false service of pointless formality. That said, I want here to acknowledge all those hardworking scribes and thank them for their help. I hope by bringing us all together the picture we paint here might be a clearer, more expansive representation of a life of one we have all respected and continue to admire. My work is indeed less concise than it might be, and I boast no better than the endeavours of others, but the effort to 'cover the ground' does at least provide a broadened vista that others yet to come might improve on.

I have tried, as much as possible, to present each chapter as 'free standing,' to facilitate the episodic reader, but also, in any analytical biography a few central points need to be reiterated in expansion. The reader's patience with this I believe is compensated by the embedding of interpretation.

I have not repeated the same old 'wowwee' stories you have read before – tales wherein everyone is 'great', each warped decision understandable, in retrospect wise, and every achievement phenomenal. Indeed, I have blown apart one or two of these *Roy of the Rovers* tales. I never got high marks for sycophancy, and asking awkward questions is something I'm addicted to – it scares me a bit, but I can't help it. I don't claim to be a martyr for the truth, but I admit to being a slave to logic. The urge to make sense of the senseless is probably a hangover from a confused childhood, but in the land of the mendacious veracity is blasphemy and I've always been seduced by the draw of contrarianism and the accusation of heresy – that said, what's life without a bit of either? In the words of Black Panther, Eldridge Cleaver, 'Too much agreement kills the chat.'

To quote Dave Chappelle, 'The language you are about to hear … is disturbing!' You might also note that, at times, I use the odd word that one might not usually find deployed too much in 'respectable' football biographies and certainly not in academic writing (studies of expletives notwithstanding). You could say this is 'fair warning', although I can't say I've much valued badges of respectability, I'm not going to excuse or justify my sometimes 'colourful' linguistic choices as 'the language of the terraces'; that might have been the case in my football infancy, but it probably isn't so much now. However, it is actually 'my' language and the *lingua franca* of my youth. My own experience and references are populated with these noble invectives of Anglo-Saxon heritage. I can't make an apology because that would be like a signer saying sorry for using sign language. It reflects the philological environment of the 'us' and the 'we' I grew up with and remain part of. The mother who suckled me used it, the grandfather who saved me from alcoholic poisoning used it, anyone who ever loved, cared or was kind to me used it. You probably use it a bit, Bobby Moore definitely used it, and you know what? I fucking love it.

That said, I was brought up to adore words. My mum read to my brother and I every night in bed as far back as I can remember, everything from Enid Blyton to Dickens. When she stopped, we'd listen to the ships down in the docks hooting and whistling our watery lullabies. My dad would take a break from work some days and took the time to read to us. His tastes encompassed Edgar Allan Poe, Denis Wheatley, Bram Stoker and others of that 'horror' ilk that fascinated but also scared the shit out of us – a bit like watching the Hammers in the last seconds of injury time.

The upshot of having these literary doors opened was an intoxication that led to my protracted life in education and I use 'long words' – like often two syllables and more! Indulgent I know, but hey, walk with me, it won't kill you and who knows, you might learn to love it too.

If my words, long or short, profound or profane, offend I apologise in advance, but at the same time you might be thankful that my Gooner brother-in-law or my gasworks stoker grandfather didn't write this book. If you are regrettably upset or hobbled by my much-tempered linguistic propensities, they would most definitely have knocked the tom-tit out of you. But again, calling on Dave Chappelle, 'The hardest thing to do is to be true to yourself, especially when everybody is watching.'

Thank you for picking this book up, even if you put it down again straight away. I like my tea hot, but I understand others don't

Up the 'Ammers!

INTRODUCTION

'West Ham's mascot is a hammer, with a big hammer head, and he goes by the name of Hammerhead.

'A hammer, of course, is a tool that delivers a blow with sudden impact and the heads are genuinely made of steel. The origin of a hammer as a mascot possibly stems from east London's proud shipbuilding history and West Ham's start in life as Thames Ironworks FC in the late 19th century.

'So, a mascot dressed as a hammer is a rather imposing figure, and true to form Hammerhead never deviates from the role he is playing.

'He's as broad-shouldered as he is tall, strutting around the ground with a real geezer walk and I couldn't help but applaud the east London sense of humour. Hammerhead sets the scene for 90 minutes of banter, and I for one loved it!'

Karl Wiggins, *Gunpowder Soup*

Hammerhead wasn't around when I first started watching games at Upton Park and I'm not too sure if he represented the qualities of my manor in the way that Karl Wiggins appears to believe', but I recognise the character of the area he refers too.

In my lifetime, as one might expect, east London has changed, although in many respects, it remains the same. That is the counterintuitive condition for many of us who were born north of the river, east of the Tower up to the mid-20th century. The once mighty docks, alive day and night with booming piping craft, bringing the world to the land of the Cockney, have been gutted, sanitised, and silenced. Dirty dirt has been replaced by cleaner dirt. Canning Town, the district where the ironworks once stood, has been subjected to hygienic depersonalisation and made anonymous, while opposite, Dog Island strains under the weight of faceless corporate nothingness.

And the Boleyn Ground is no more. Yet the eternal abode of the Irons continues to exists in these words I have, as well as in the hearts and minds, souls and spirits of those of us who stood and latterly sat in its embrace.

As before, now still, minutes can change years, and years seem to be gone in minutes. The institution that is West Ham United, its fans, players and managers, even grounds, have been a continuous stream in my life. Who I am is peppered with games played in at Upton Park and my journeys amounting to probably hundreds of thousands of miles following the claret and blue dream (that has yet to fade and die). Speaking to former players, ex-managers and supporters (who are never 'former' or 'ex') has educated, inspired, saddened, angered and enchanted me. Conversations (in-person, electronically and by telephone), the exchange of correspondence, with some marvellously informative and insightful people, have been a rich dialectical experience. At the same time, I have also met my share of idiots and been sent down enough blind alleys and block turnings to challenge my sanity (and lose it at points).

Amazing though it seems to me now, over the expanse of weeks, months, years and decades this two-volume book has been fermenting, I have managed to a grasp something of what happened to one of the hundreds of Hammers who have been good enough to give me something of their time and a few echoes from their lives.

To capture just an essence of the development of the boy, who became the player, who grew to be the man, piecing together impressions from those who played alongside him and those, like me, who were fortunate enough to watch him, could not have been achieved by just be the usual rambling homily or list of results; that would never have done the man justice.

So, I have gone for veracity as told, lived and experienced. As is the way of honesty, it ain't always pretty or easy on the ears or head, but this is east London, and enough patronising bullshit has been spoken and written, serving a multitude of interests, attempting to preserving a catalogue of long-lost and now pointless patronage. I'm at an age that has no time for platitudes and no motivation for sycophancy – although I have hardly ever understood the salivation for the adulation of fools. The time is always right for a little shade to accentuate the light.

Who is Bobby Moore?

Noel Cantwell, who had come to Upton Park in 1952, was alongside Moore from the spring of 1954, just before he turned 13. The intelligent Corkonian was quick to notice the lad had a presence. The Irish international, who led West Ham back to the top level of English football, helped Manchester United win the 1965 and 1967 First Division titles, and captained their 1963 FA Cup Final team, would go on to be one of the most successful managers in the history Coventry City. For this football aristocrat the boy Moore came to him with the remarkable gift for anticipating the warp and weft of the game environment. Noel saw that this could be cultivated to give Moore, and any team he played for, a distinct advantage. Bobby's ability to pass the ball, at first notable, twined with this vision, grew to be, in Cantwell's opinion 'fantastic'.

Noel was to say of Bobby, 'Somehow he knew things were going to happen before they did and he had a knack of freeing himself … from getting into tackles that he did not need to.'

Cantwell saw how Moore become a 'free player at the back, [with] wonderful passing, good control with his left and right foot'. He told how he had no memory of Moore 'having a scar on his face; he would just leave it to us plebs to get involved in the clashing of heads'. Bobby would leave it to others get scarred.

This is the man most of us recognise as Bobby Moore. Cantwell's description feels a familiar, but Jack Charlton, talking about that same person, while making the point that he was 'one of us', struck a chord in me by making the proviso that he 'wasn't like us'.

Likewise, Ken Brown, who played alongside Moore throughout West Ham's 'golden years' of the 1960s, had it that while everyone seemed to like Bobby, and he showed no hint of superiority, he was always 'a bit of a loner'. While he pursued fame in football, part of him to yearned for anonymity. One of the reasons he liked going on overseas trips with the club, especially to the United States, was because so few people would recognise him. He could go to a bar or a club and relax.

John Dick, a senior professional by the time Moore was on the fringes of the West Ham first team, remembered Bobby as a shy lad, who appeared not to 'know what to do with himself' in social situations or make friends easily.

I was fortunate enough to watch most of the games Moore played for West Ham and many of the international matches he was part of. The memory of him leading the Hammers on to the field, punching the ball in the air, with the 'Post Horn Gallop' blaring out of the Boleyn Ground's sound system, will be with me forever, but it was difficult to say that he, for the most part, didn't appear pretty much 'aloof'. As goalkeeper Peter Shearing remembered, Bobby seemed a 'little stand-offish'. He did not seem at all demonstrative with regard to the highs and lows of any game; his reaction to his side scoring or being scored against was practically the same. I did see him show a modest pleasure two or three times on the rare occasions he scored a goal, but most often he'd simply turn away, making a path back into defence, eyes cast down, frowning (although sometimes perhaps with a suggestion of a smile, looking something close to embarrassed).

It's too easy just to say Moore was a paradoxical enigma within a conundrum, premised on a puzzle. As it happens, that's not easy to say at all, but maybe that's the truth. It almost certainly is if the person trying to portray Moore on his pedestal attempts this from the standpoint of a remote spectator – someone who has never in all their puff even considered standing on the concrete of Upton Park, soaked and freezing, watching a clutch of north London footpads, or boggled-eyed Scousers, half-naked Geordies, or a bunch of Manchurian monks going ape-shit with delight as the fickle Irons lose by the odd goal of seven in the last seconds of injury time, the ball bouncing, mockingly over the line, off of Harry Redknapp's left buttock; the mind thus dominated by just one thought, a single word uttered discordantly, 'Fuck!'

The pages that follow reflect on the life and times of Bobby Moore, up to his debut in the elite English game. In this story I look to open a vista on those who peopled the world around the boy, and those who were crucial to his flourishing. I have looked to set his story in its historical and social context – a story without context is not really a story, it's just a relatively colourless catalogue; there are enough of them littering football and Moore's life. Out of this process the figure of the child, the teenager and the developing man is formed, who he was, where he came from, how he was 'built' by this coagulation of his influences and his own will.

Moore emerged from the borderlands of west Essex and east London to be a giant of character in his chosen sport, but he was forged by a context, a place and time, as the spiritual factotum of all the Hammers. The portrait here depicted is set in the landscape of a football club, West Ham United, in the late 1950s. An institution nestled in the dockland district of London, that has a central place in the identity of the communities that arose, arise and shift across and northward the easterly reaches of the Thames, from its bank down from the Aldgate Pump, to the estuary mouth, milking out into the oceans of the world. Included are the club's staff and supporters, as well as the historical setting of 'portside' London, as it started to recover from the ravages of war to enter the first stirrings of the 'liberation decade' and the 'permissive society'.

Thus, the reader will not only track the forging of the man, but also the stuff out of which he was born as a destined icon of the greatest game in history and on earth. The sport that is more than a set of rules and the parameters of a pitch, being more an anchor of personal and communal definition – encompassing defining and desired qualities embracing loyalty, fortitude and perhaps above all, defiance.

All views are formed some time and somewhere. I was never an autograph hunter, but I would often keep my mates company as they waited outside the Boleyn Ground for players to emerge in the hope of collecting a moniker. The reaction to this by the hoped-for signatories ranged from amused compliance, to clearly resentful consent, ignoring completely and telling the pursuers of the illusive 'John Hancock' to 'fuck off'. Johnny 'Budgie' Byrne was nearly always cheerful, if prone to take the piss. One time he asked my youthful companion for his autograph book back as Budgie claimed, 'I've signed me name upside down by mistake.' My pal passed back the book bewildered while Johnny and Alan Sealey chuckled in mischievous delight. On another occasion he signed his name 'Sir

Stafford Cripps'. Bobby was one of those likely just to ignore pleas for autographs. This wasn't always, and now and then he'd take the time to make the day of a line of snotty-nosed nitwits, but more usually he'd just walk by, not changing his usual 'stroll speed' walk, looking a bit cross.

Right though the 1960s the latter demeanour was more or less replicated for those brief news or sports programme television interviews. Moore would have a look somewhere between inscrutable and very serious (at least), speaking in a somewhat affected accent, his sentences a bit stilted, almost rehearsed. This gave the impression he was over-forming his words, deliberately working to get each syllable out in a 'proper' manner. My mum used to sneer at this, saying he was 'putting on airs and graces'. In the days before players were fed 'media training' it was easy to think that, I suppose. Sometimes Bobby didn't seem to like the fans or the limelight very much. But at my innocent and naive age at the time, I think I had a little understanding of his manner. I had seen him in more social contexts, if only briefly, where he was less nervous perhaps, but still often apparently shy and a bit on his guard.

Later, maybe by the mid-1970s, Bobby appeared to loosen up. He looked to be much more amicable with supporters and relaxed with the media. I started to believe his formally, seemingly forced, way of talking had likely been influenced by Ron Greenwood and/or Alf Ramsey. Alf had invested in elocution lessons looking to ditch his Dagenham 'ow's yer farva' accent, and the capacity he apparently had as a defender at White Hart Lane to swear to the extent that might make the proverbial trooper blush. Greenwood seemed to have achieved something similar. Although no doubt a genius in terms of his footballing acumen, Ron, in his first decade at Upton Park, from a distance, probably unfairly and uncharitably, seemed to have something of a Derek Nimmo 'Oh Brother' frisson about him, or a *Carry On* Charlie Hawtrey vicar vibe.

Just a man?

I ask above, 'Who "is" Bobby Moore?' I purposely didn't use the word 'was', because Moore, as has been said many times, 'is' now a legend; he has his own mythology. He might even be described as the first 'saint' of football; certainly the regard for him could hardly be higher in the game. West Ham supporters had, long ago, bestowed the 'knighthood' on him that he surely should have been officially awarded well before his final years. But that's another story, one that I intend to address over the next few years.

It's hard to say that Bobby was just a man, because he really wasn't, else I wouldn't be writing and you wouldn't be reading this book. However, he was once really just another a kid; the pretty ordinary lad who became the adult, who has been made the very stuff of the romantic fairytale of football that has so often been written about.

Thus, what we have is a vision of a figure who lived a storied existence. Moore evolved into a personality, perhaps even a cult of sorts, that will only grow as the past, yesterday and the present become history. This said, as someone who, for the better part of half a century, has been concerned with the growth and development of young people, and been part of the education and learning of many thousands who have gone into the world to devote their lives and careers to the same vocation, it is 'Young Bobby' who most interests me, probably more than the object of fable, although even a survey of his early years has its fair share of parables, the salutary anecdotes that might be thought of as the 'lessons of life'.

What I have sought to do, bringing my writing about the first years of Bobby Moore before an audience expectant of confirmation of his divinity, is to give a bit more than this, perhaps something with extra portion of rationality but also an explanation that tells us more. I've been led by analysis, with the hope of gaining insight into how 'Young Bobby' became Bobby Moore, the personality that, deity-like, has been able to breach the barriers of eternity, to represent part of the spirit of a game. But also more, perhaps 'better' than this, Bobby Moore is a symbol of a place, a time and a world of feeling that has transcended his era and context. This is Bobby's story up to the start of the pinnacle of his fame and achievements, the road that took him to become England's greatest ever captain and the finest, most graceful defender football has known.

Reminiscence is the echo of voices

What I know of Moore, as well as the men who influenced his early development, centrally the likes of Malcolm Allison, Noel Cantwell, Ted Fenton and a little later Ron Greenwood, comes from a range of sources, but I have tried not to rely on the usual 'record of references', that really just repeats itself, painting a picture of Bobby out of sanitised journalistic caricature. This, in the main, amounts to twee/folksy nostalgic ramblings and the biographical equivalent to Chinese whispers.

My endeavour has been to analyse this stuff, critically comparing and contrasting the various accounts. However, looking to make a more sensible narrative, I have called on first-hand recollections and impressions from supporters (including my own and my family's), players and others. With the latter in mind some context of my familiarity with the time and context that Moore was part of before he reached 20 years of age is in order.

In the 1950s to the early 1960s it was fairly routine for a few West Ham footballers and speedway riders to buy shirts, ties and other bits and pieces from my dad. He was a stallholder and for a time a shopkeeper in Queens Road Market, about a three-minute walk from the Boleyn Ground. Dad would buy up anything and everything, stack it high, sell it cheap and swift, largely to fund a robust gambling habit, fuelled by the speed he bought by the van load from a dodgy local pharmacist in the Barking Road (opposite the Boleyn pub), and permissively popped to keep him active in his various businesses around 23 hours a day.

Sometimes, in pairs or mob-handed, these local sporting celebs would come round to our house in Cave Road, Plaistow and pick up some pretty high-quality 'dickies' and (allegedly) silk 'Peckhams' at rock-bottom prices, a quick fix when needed for an unplanned night out and such. At times we had the likes of Malcolm Allison and Noel Cantwell in the living room making their selections. These two men were the clear the 'head honchos', but as we all moved out of the 1950s it was Bobby Moore who began to stand out as the 'leader of the pack'.

My dad was about the same age as Cantwell, with a personality that might have been pitched somewhere between the Irishman's intelligent charm and Allison's confident charisma. He got on well with them, but in different ways. The old man was a good-looking bloke, 6ft 3in, muscular, with his Gypsy mother's dark skin, hair and eyes. He had played in goal for West Ham Boys and as an allrounder for the Essex Boys cricket team. On the nod from West Ham's undercover scout Reg Revins, he had been pursued by Charlie Paynter, looking to entice him to the Upton Park cause, but while my granddad had a lot of time for Reg, and got on OK with Charlie, he didn't really take Paynter too seriously. At the same time the money West Ham could offer couldn't really facilitate Jimmy Belton's ambitions. Thus, dad found Charlie's approaches the stuff of hilarity more than a real prospect. Chas reminded him a bit of Oliver Hardy especially alongside Ted Fenton, who in his younger years could be taken as having more than a passing resemblance to Stan Laurel. However, on a whim Dad nearly went to Highbury, and might have signed if he and George Allison and his County Durham sense of humour been able to accommodate the Canning Town genre, although in truth, professional sport in those days didn't look an attractive financial option for my dad.

Dad, like his father and grandfather, was a committed West Ham man (there was no such thing as 'fans' then) and a student of football, rarely missing a game; the Boleyn Ground was not only part of his social but also his business and gambling life. The comfortable dichotomy between work and leisure we have today really wouldn't have much meaning to many in the immediate postwar decade.

Unlike my grandfather, the terraces weren't for him. The main stand was where he would meet with a melange of the multicultural environment of those days. They had a collective persona that had a whiff of 'made it' gangsters, fringe white-collar criminals, semi-respectable bruisers and 'not dodgy but close' traders and wholesalers. Their names for me were my earliest poetry; Eddie Covosa, Ronnie Chamdal, 'Fairy' Giles, Harry 'Blade' Beasum (a sometime sword swallower, whose party trick was eating razor blades), Henry Blurton, Sammy Wrapp, 'Birdy' Becka, Donny Le Serf, Freddie Fairplay (who didn't), Polly Thoroughgood (who wasn't), 'Boyo' Ollie Doyle, Josh Tishaman, and Stan Flysha to name just a few. These were my dad's role models and friends. The 'boys from the football' were just a nice, if not too flush, kids and if anything, a tad wet behind the ears.

Dad wasn't starstruck in the slightest by footballers, or anybody much. Around our manor he was a bit of a 'face'; everyone seemed to know him (I'm still referred to as 'Jim's son' today). He saved anything like admiration for his 'business associates'.

As a younger man he had worked at the Theatre Royal, in Stratford, just over the road from where the London Stadium stands today. He was involved on the production side. Just after the war many established and rising stars played Stratford, far bigger names than the West Ham playing staff of that era. Jim 'walked out' with a few distinguished actresses of the day – the archetypal 'bit of rough' was the old man.

Thus, celebrity was not something he gave any unusual credibility to. He gave the West Ham lads similar attention and treated them with the same affability as other customers. However, from where I was standing, if anything, they were a little in awe of him. Dad was a good storyteller, and his various tales intrigued and amused the young men. A skilled extrovert, smart dresser, good with words, he could make people smile, but he was worldly, with more than a few quid in his pocket – qualities and resources these 'boys', certainly when Allison and Cantwell departed the scene, lacked.

I recall Dad once, in good humour, telling a little clutch of players, 'I could buy and sell the lot of yer!' and at that time he probably could. As is the way with cordiality, it gets people talking and as he once told me, 'If you get someone to open their heart, you'll be in their head.' Dad was probably even better at listening than he was at talking and had a memory like an elephant on Ritalin.

Now and then, Dad would take a selection of clobber to the now legendary Cassettari's Cafe in the Barking Road, just in front to the Boleyn Ground. This was a place where the likes of Cantwell, John Bond, Allison and Moore would meet, in the main, to talk football. Dad's brief and occasional salvos as travelling salesman were also to encompass a few 'pub runs', such as the Black Lion in Plaistow, Slaters Arms in Romford, and The Retreat on the edge of Hainault Forest, the Moby Dick, in Whalebone Lane, Romford, and later the Blind Beggar in Whitechapel and The Globe in Bethnal Green. This service saved young sportsmen having to troll down to the family stall and shop in Queens Road, which in those days always seemed 'crush crowded' and as such would mean them having to wade through everything from adoring supporters to mouthy traders and gobby costermongers telling them they were 'shit' the previous Saturday (mostly because the Hammers hadn't helped them win the pools). There was also a merry sprinkling of pickpockets, 'genuine' if contradictorily clandestine Rolex sellers and the occasional insurance-risk fire eater.

Sometimes Dad took me with him on his errands. From my infant years into my teens, it was rare for me not to be involved in his various business and 'other' activities of the 'fringe entrepreneurial' character. Even when I was just a little kid, I remember Bobby; compared to the likes of the smooth Allison, and the loud Bond (who was the only potential buyer to try and barter on the price), Bobby, being quiet and blushingly shy at times, hid his bashfulness with an awkward but charming smile, although often seemingly blushing for no apparent reason.

I was not much different to this myself until I got into my later teenage years. I probably covered it up a bit better, being brought up in the markets and put to work on the stall from early on (around the age of four). This experience tended to cause one to develop a practical 'cheeky chappie' front, but inside I was a self-conscious and nervous kid. Bobby perhaps had just developed a different front to mine.

From the time Dad moved out of the market trade in the first years of the 1960s the association with the football boys gradually dropped off. We might see someone like John Bond at our timber yard now and then, but in the main, there were other fish to fry. From the mid-1970s I talked to Bobby a few times over the next couple of decades. Nothing in depth; sometimes the exchange of a few pleasantries, or just the odd line or six of smalltalk. In the first part of that block of time I'd see him at one or two nightclubs and pubs in the Chigwell/Hainault area of Essex where he and a few other luminaries, on occasion, would rock up to for an afternoon session. Once, in the mid-1980s, I happened on Bobby in the car park of Southend United's Roots Hall ground. I passed a few minutes with him. I was always chuffed he remembered my name.

On those brief one-to-one encounters, Bobby never struck me as anything other than amenable and good-humoured, but I wasn't disabused that he was still an essentially a reserved and quiet person. I think his polite modesty and habituated humility was sometimes mistaken for the standoffishness by the likes of my mum and others. Over the years my perception has only been confirmed by what others who knew Bobby best have said and wrote about him.

This knowledge and experience of Bobby Moore forms the foundation of what I have written about him and those who had a part in his emergence to greatness.

See a man in his time, never judge him by it

In his young life Moore was surrounded by some good people such as his parents, relatives and school teachers. At Upton Park the likes of Wally St Pier, Ted Fenton, Malcolm Allison, Noel Cantwell, Ron Greenwood were all, in their own ways, fine and predominantly kind men. There was genius in their ranks and none of them wanted anything but the best for Bobby. I don't for a minute doubt that. Even the people more in the background, Reg Pratt, Charlie Paynter and Len Cearns, were all commendable individuals who played their part in building not just West Ham as the modern footballing institution, but in the doing of that, the English game as we know it.

However, how all these people saw each other needs to be considered, as do the impressions they gave and left with players and supporters; such politics are the making of any organisation, the 'grit' in the works, the tensions of any dynamic. It just isn't true of any social entity, from families to nations that, as Facebook might have us believe, everyone is happy with one another all the time. We tend to kid ourselves that this might not be the case, but to do that is to live a lie and model history on the worst type of quaint mid-1960s situation comedy.

Thus, in these pages there are, what might be for some, uncomfortable perspectives that like all perceptions are partial. No one is perfect, and there really are no saints. If you admire and respect someone, you want to know their strengths and their vulnerabilities – because one is often the source of the other.

I have read and spoken to many people who boasted that Bobby was a friend of theirs. I do believe he had a lot of associates who he received and talked to kindly and politely. However, I'm pretty sure Moore had comparatively few people he might really have thought of as close friends. It is only those uncommon people that might be said to have come close to truly knowing him.

Each of us is made by other people and sculptured by our environment; our brains, in a very literal sense, play out this truth. Areas of your and my 'watch and chain' are stimulated by our early experience and they develop. At the same time those regions that are neglected wither – we actually shed what proves to be unwanted brain matter. Yet we also enter this world with both similar and varying potential capacities, which are honed or abandoned by those around us and so ourselves. The old question asking what is mostly pertinent in terms of impact on human achievement or otherwise, 'nature or nurture', has long been answered; neither and both.

It is the interaction between these considerations that both limits and expands our potential. The narrative of this interplay, for each and every one of us, is the personal biography and the wider story of who 'we', individually and collectively, are or might be, or might have been. Yes, this encompasses our identity, but the examination of any young life, such as Moore's, will add to our generic picture of how the ecosystem of human development works, in his case how the mind can overcome personal and environmental disadvantages. This can mean not giving in to our supposed and actual shortcomings, but using them, turning them into advantages. Not so much about the glass being half empty or half full, it's more 'have glass, will fill'.

Alfie Kohn has had a lot to say about how children learn. He has written, 'To take children seriously is to value them, for who they are right now, rather than adults-in-the-making.'

This is a principal that has guided my work. You see, external force can't make people wise. For sure, you can instruct and indoctrinate, and people will act according to the script they have memorised if they are obliged to. This is the type of learning you might expect of a parrot. But if you can provide the right conditions for people, they will learn what they want to learn and even look to teach others what they have learned. Bobby's young life illustrates that it is this that fosters wisdom. This book is foundationally a study of that process.

The world knows much (or thinks it does) of the feats that would follow Moore's baptism into the elite of football. You, good reader, have maybe seen him play; YouTube and the like facilitate this. Me, I watched him hundreds of times, including all the finals he graced as a senior player and my starting point from that experience is: there's only one Bobby Moore.

That said, I am here writing something more than a biography of the young Bobby Moore. I am (more dimensionally) examining and analysing how 'a' Bobby Moore was 'built' and perhaps can be formed; I'm inviting you to look out on this panorama with me, thinking about how we can and do fashion ourselves, our children, and how people are and might be wrought by their experience of and in the world and what they make of it.

My job as a youth worker is, at base, the cultivation of mind. You, me, all humanity is and always has been a product of our individual and collective minds. This is not the same as brain development, but it is related. How, what and who you are is a reflection of your mind. The cultivated mind shapes attitudes, principles, values and fosters the getting of wisdom, something more than mere knowledge, or mechanistic education. It is this I am looking at in the development of Bobby Moore, how he was nurtured in this respect.

Of course, you can just skip the bits that refer to the development of mind and brain, and how the same impacted on who Bobby was and how he became what he could be. That's fair enough, but I ask you, please don't go all dromedary on me about it. It's what I do. You can take the youth worker out of youth work, but it seems difficult to take youth work out of the youth worker.

West Ham fans are not born,
Nor are they manufactured.
We do not choose,
We are chosen.
Those who understand need no explanation,
Those that don't understand,
They don't matter.
We are never beaten;
We only win and learn.
West Ham 'til I die

1

DEBUT

Bobby Moore's Football League debut saw him literally thrown in at the deep end, running out to face Manchester United, on the Monday evening of 8 September 1958. United would finish runners-up in the top flight, but newly promoted West Ham were doing much better than anyone might have hoped or expected.

The UK music charts looked like this at the start of that penultimate September of the 1950s:

1	Stupid Cupid/Carolina Moon	Connie Francis
2	Volare	Dean Martin
3	When	Kalin Twins
4	Poor Little Fool	Ricky Nelson
5	Bird Dog	The Everly Brothers
6	Mad Passionate Love	Bernard Bresslaw
7	Return to Me	Dean Martin
8	Splish Splash	Charlie Drake
9	King Creole	Elvis Presley
10	Fever	Peggy Lee

Just before the start of the football season *Carry On Sergeant*, the first *Carry On* film, was released in cinemas, while Barbara Wootton, Baroness Wootton of Abinger, became the first female peer in her own right. As *Carry On* star Kenneth Williams might have put it, 'Stop messing about.'

On 29 September, Cliff Richard's debut single 'Move it' was released. The track was to be credited with being one of the first authentic rock and roll songs produced outside the United States and that's where Cliff was destined to remain, outside the United States.

Allegedly unconnected with Cliff's arrival on the popular music scene, the day after his entry into the world of pop saw the start of the Notting Hill race riots in London. Just a week before the game with United the first Cod War between UK and Iceland broke out. An argument with foreigners about fish seems to be something innate to British culture. As this was going on, Britain performed an atmospheric nuclear test on Christmas Island (a big fat 'watch it' to the cod-loving Icelanders!).

A few weeks after Moore's debut for the Irons, BOAC used the new Comet jets to become the first airline to fly passenger services across the Atlantic, while the BBC aired two new programmes, *Grandstand* and *Blue Peter*.

Although he had broken into the reserve side the best part of a year previously (7 December 1957, v Birmingham City), Bobby had imagined how he might fit in and compliment his side playing at the pinnacle of English football. Still a rookie professional, Moore was, at just under six feet tall (1.88m) and weighing in at 12st 12lb (81kg), a solid physical figure. That said, not one of the 35,672 crowd would have been thinking that the golden-haired, good-looking young man would become a legendary figure, not only in terms of the history of his club and country, but in the annals of the global game too. He was just another kid coming through the ranks, perhaps the least interesting player on the field.

Maybe at this distance in time it's hard to see Moore not as the complete article. The model professional to be, built at least as much by his work ethic, intelligence and dedication as any innate talent he might have been bestowed by biology or spirit. But the future icon was on display at an embryonic stage, more open to criticism than praise, more likely to be the object of disparagement than respect (let alone admiration).

Just to up the pressure, the 17-year-old Moore, two years from his school days and only three months out of the bondage of apprenticeship and schlepping ground staff boy status, was stepping into the boots of a giant of a character. Malcolm Allison was revered by both players and supporters, and actively feared by the Upton Park yeomen, the likes of Irons manager Ted Fenton and his predecessor Charlie Paynter, who continued to haunt the stadium like the ghost of some faithful old retainer, continuing in the thrall of the likes of the Bill Cearns dynasty and other board-bound aristocrats such as Reg Pratt.

The club captain who had been central in preparing the Irons to exit 26 years in the football wilderness, Allison would be one of the movers and shakers in dragging English football into the modern era, but he was already a colossus of a personality at Upton Park. Like all bringers of change, he is and was misunderstood. Underrated by the many, while being the focus of suspicion and a threatening presence to those who sustained or suckled on the status quo, Allison was the midwife of Moore's excellence.

Back with the big boys

The Hammers started their 1958/59 campaign at Fratton Park, coming away with a good 2-1 victory in front of a roaring horde of 40,000, including about 7,000 east Londoners. On the following Monday evening the Boleyn Ground saw a meeting with Wolves, the reigning champions. Cheered on by a capacity crowd, the flying Irons turned over Billy Wright *et al* 2-0, Johnny Dick and John Smith on target.

Another Midlands team, Aston Villa, came to Upton Park to be annihilated 7-2. Keeble, Dick and Musgrove all scored twice, with Bill Lansdowne adding to the mix. With the wind of expectation behind them the Hammers were greeted by 52,317 under the floodlights at the 'Krak des' Molineux and came away with a creditable 1-1 result.

Unbeaten West Ham were brought back to reality with a 4-1 reversal at Kenilworth Road, but still in second place, just a point behind Bolton, there was good reason to be looking forward to the next fixture scheduled to be fought out in east London.

Fenton had been able to field an unchanged side for the club's first handful of games: Ernie Gregory; John Bond, Noel Cantwell (captain); Andy Malcolm, Ken Brown, Bill Lansdowne; Mike Grice, John Smith, Vic Keeble, John Dick, Malcolm Musgrove.

But this would need to change for the sixth fixture of the term, which brought Manchester United to the home of the Hammers.

The visitors were in the process of both mourning and rebuilding, just seven months post-Munich, a tragedy that robbed the English and global game of so much, but more importantly took the lives of too many young men, bringing untold grief and loss to their families.

The world of football had been rocked on 6 February 1958 when eight of the finest Manchester United team in history were among the 21 passengers killed in an air crash in West Germany. The accident happened as United were returning to Manchester from Yugoslavia. They had just drawn with Red Star Belgrade to qualify for the semi-final of the European Cup. Their plane failed to clear a fence on take-off from Riem Airport in Munich. Among the dead were the England regulars Roger Byrne, Duncan Edwards and Tommy Taylor. United's manager Matt Busby was also seriously injured. The plane, a BEA Ambassador, was reduced to a tangled heap of wreckage. Driving snow hampered rescue workers.

As such, United's every encounter was being watched and the side willed on to victory by millions of people across the UK and the rest of the planet. The team arrived at Upton Park, led by their still-recovering manager Busby, resolved to keep the spirit of Manchester United going forward after tragedy. Five survivors of the disaster ran out to face the Irons that day: Harry Gregg, Bill Foulkes, Dennis Violett, Albert Scanlon and a 20-year-old who was being posited as the hope of the English game, Bobby Charlton.

Cantwell's call

Most of the West Ham senior squad were at the Boleyn Ground for some light training on the morning of the game. It was then that it was confirmed that the Hammers' regular left-half that season, Bill Lansdowne, was out having picked up an ankle injury in the game at Luton. Andy Nelson and Malcolm Pyke, the men who could have stepped in, were also ruled out. Fenton, looking for a half-back, summoned his skipper, Noel Cantwell, to the manager's office. The Irishman had stood in for the convalescing Allison as club skipper.

Cantwell, saying 'play the kid', advised that Moore be brought into the side despite Fenton having significant doubts about Bobby. It has been said that it was almost certain that had he been forced to make the decision himself, Fenton would have opted to make the United fixture Malcolm Allison's comeback game, sickness having kept him out of the team since early in the previous season. However, it would have been hard to go against his captain's counsel. The folklore has it that Allison had made an almost miraculous recovery from the massive but lifesaving surgery just prior to the Munich calamity.

Malcolm was 13 and a half years older than Bobby. Tall, broad-shouldered and handsome, he was a man; Moore, relatively, was still a boy. Allison could be cuttingly sarcastic (something later Bobby emulated) and while the fedora and cigars were a feature of the future, he was every inch the flamboyant playboy the extravagant manager of years to come would be well known as. Style and panache came in heaps with Malcolm's personality. As would be proven again and again over his career in coaching and management, he had a gift to detect embryonic greatness and it was that he had nurtured in Bobby from Moore's early teenage years.

Had 31-year-old Allison not been sidelined by illness, he would never have been out of the first XI. Although there was no love lost between him and Fenton, it is true that Ted understood Malcolm to be a quality act, and would hardly ever go for youth over experience. For most of 1958, while Bobby had been fighting to get out of the reserves, Allison was striving to pull himself back into a shape that would give him a shot at playing again. Bobby was knocking on the door to his future; Malcolm was trying to prove he could still cut the mustard after months in hospital, followed by a stay in a sanatorium recovering from tuberculosis. Yes, Moore was getting England youth recognition, but so were other young players. For all his amazing fightback, and that in his opinion he was ready to return to the first team, Malcolm had played just a couple of reserve games and had significantly reduced lung capacity.

For all this, West Ham's goalkeeper Ernie Gregory was to express the reaction to Moore's selection for that game,

'It was a shock to everybody when Bobby was picked ahead of Malcolm ... Big Mal had been a huge influence at the club ... Bobby was going to develop into a class player, but his promotion to the first-team came earlier than any of us expected ... at that time he was a bit of a wild card.'

Certainly, most of the first team might have wanted Allison on the field in preference to someone who many of them would have, at that time, seen as little more than a child, but (as I will explore later) the majority were aware he probably wouldn't. But fittingly it was Bobby who became one of the first significant graduates of Fenton's youth policy to break into the Hammers' first team.

West Ham United: Ernie Gregory; John Bond, Noel Cantwell (captain); Andy Malcolm, Ken Brown, Bobby Moore; Mike Grice, John Smith, Vic Keeble, John Dick, Malcolm Musgrove.

Manchester United: Harry Gregg; Bill Foulkes (captain), Ian Greaves; Freddie Goodwin, Ron Cope, Wilt McGuiness; Colin Webster, Ernie Taylor, Dennis Violett, Bobby Charlton, Albert Scanlon.

Preparations

The arrival of the patched-up United certainly provided an exciting atmosphere for Moore's initiation into First Division football. As the 7.30pm kick-off approached, tens of thousands of home supporters, locked out of the full-to-the-gunnels Upton Park, packed Green Street and the roads and alleyways surrounding the stadium, looking to share the ambiance and interpret the roars of those who had been fortunate enough to get a view of the game.

The notion of pre-match entertainment hadn't really evolved in the late 1950s. Right up until my late teenage years, pre-Hammerettes, with David Bowie in his pomp, for fuck knows what reason it was thought the crowd might be enamoured by the various mediocre to passable brass bands of east London, although K Division Metropolitan Police Band and the British Legion Band were pretty 'hot' in the heady metallic aerophone world. I do however recall actually hearing the latter once, playing 'The Stripper' of all things! One of their number actually started shedding his togs. I'm not sure how that might have gone down with the likes Lord Kitchener or Field Marshal Bernard Law Montgomery, 1st Viscount Montgomery of Alamein.

My usual perch as a youngster was the 'shelf' in the old North Bank, latterly and colloquially known as the haunt of the 'Snipers', the infantile Hammers supporters of yore. For the most part, in that place (and most other places at the 'fortress of the Irons') amid the singing and chanting, you couldn't hear a note of the determined blowers on the pitch. On that warm and noteworthy evening in 1958 the stoical Leyton Silver Band (probably the best of the bunch locally) were on parade in front of the players' tunnel, puffing for all they were worth.

Regardless of sinfonietta identity (or quality), 'Bubbles' was always the last number, and likely the only one anyone took a blind bit of notice of – unless you were right at the front of the West Stand, where I guess the dulcet tones might have been hard to avoid. It would be just before the players ran out that the band would deliver a rendition of the 'Hammers' anthem', mostly coming out as a dirge, akin to the 'Death March' or sometimes like a jaunty cover of the theme from *The Archers*, 'Barwick Green' (occasionally a mix of both). Invariably the crowd would join in, with different sections, following various timings, tempos and even lyrics. However, remarkably, perhaps miraculously, it nearly always came together by the time we got to 'PRITTEE BUBBELLZZ YIN DE AAAAYR!'

Fenton told Bobby to keep close tabs on Ernie Taylor, seeing the diminutive forward as 'the general'. Bobby wasn't too sure about that perception or instruction, but had a good idea what was needed to harness little Ern.

In the arse-end of the 1950s there was no such thing as an onfield warm-up as such. While a few, the likes of Noel Cantwell, might have a brief stretching routine, for the most part, other than a bit of hand-rubbing, and trotting on the spot during the coin toss, players would run out on the park and a couple of minutes later be at it.

Moore's dressing room preparation was as it always would be. Shirt on first, socks pulled up, lace boots, while downstairs his modesty was covered only by his jockstrap, the best the Co-op East Ham sold. Not that they had an eye-popping selection of nut-buckets – you had to go to Rathbone Market in Canning Town for that. Well, you could still pick up a 'Mizpah No.44' (the 'pejazzle' of its day) from the haberdashery stall ran by Solly 'Two Stoves', and cholera if you hung about too long.

Bobby never shaved before a match. He did give it a try when he started to develop a beard, but this (predictably given his fair skin) resulted in soreness to the extent of being a distraction. So, he took to shaving post-match, plugging in his electric razor so that he wouldn't chance any hint of being unkempt in lieu of any celebration (that by the mid-1960s at West Ham would be alcohol-soaked and take place whatever the result) or merely going home to his family.

In the early 1960s Bernard Joy, the great Arsenal centre-half, was a leading football writer. He told Moore before a big game that he looked scruffy and 'could do with a shave'. Bobby told the former Highbury hero that he never took a razor to his mush until after a game. Apparently the Arsenal players of Joy's era had the same routine.

Moore always left his shorts to the very last moment, looking to avoid creasing or staining from the horse liniment players were accustomed to spreading all over themselves then. Some brands of the embrocation seemed to be radioactive; if I inadvertently got even a scintilla of the stuff on the sacred Niagaras the burning sensation, and so the eye watering, despite brutal and sustained attacks armed with school kitchen strength carbolic, persisted for days! I was once told the 'recipe' for the stuff started out as a chemical weapon during the Boer War – that might be bollocks, but saying that I can see the irony (or poetry).

The sound of a loud buzzer was the players' call to the pitch. Pre-war and for some time thereafter, for no apparent reason, this call-to-arms was known as 'Mrs Richards' – I think it might have had something to do with Dick Richards, an Irons stalwart of the early 1920s. Later in life he turned to acting, most famously being stunt double for Brian Glover in the film *Kez* – probably Ken Loach's best work.

The buzzer was the cue for Bobby to stand, tuck his shirt in his shorts and move toward the field of play.

A couple of minutes prior to the 7.30pm kick-off, as the Leyton Silver Band finishing their set, Bobby jogged from the players tunnel on to the pitch (at that time he chose to be last out – something he was later to reverse as skipper of the Irons). It was a humid evening as he trotted out to take his bow at the very top of the English game. The warm air was slightly rippling from the roar of the close-in, tightly packed Boleyn Ground. For a moment Bobby felt encased in the noise and slightly claustrophobic, with the waves of people almost pushing at the edges of the field. Upton Park was a 'cosy' ground, if feeling the heat of the collective breath of the rolling sea of people might be thought of in that way. Moore once remarked after a few lagers, 'West Ham don't have fans, they have a horde of warrior pilgrims.'

Ernie tamed

From the opening whistle West Ham put their visitors under pressure. Harry Gregg was obliged to earn his wages, foiling both Malcolm Musgrove and John Dick in the early minutes.

In truth, United were pinned down in their own half for long chunks of the first period, the hosts looking to have more than the measure of the game.

Bobby's first significant act in League football was to tackle Ernie Taylor. The wee Scot jinked to the right, Moore went with him, then he swerved past Bobby on the left. The young Hammer was made to look naive and feel bit stupid by this veritable highland fling. It was a simple, predictable rouse, but executed with alacrity and the kind of panache that speaks for itself, but also the traditions of the Caledonian game. However, the next time Ernie tried the same trick Moore was ready for him. He went right, Bobby went left and they crashed into each other. It was the teenager that came out of the collision, pushing forward with the ball, making a swift pass to Musgrove on the West Ham wing.

I have read descriptions of this initial clash which have it has a very late challenge on Moore's part. Again, perception is always relative, but in a clear and definite manner, Moore was letting the United man know he was around. For all that, a predictable if brief rebuke from referee John Hunt (a perennial victim of Cockney rhyming slang) and a free kick for United followed.

Some have argued that as a younger player Moore demonstrated a belligerent streak. I think this makes the mistake of comparing different eras. All tackling in those days would look like the work of an executioner on assassin's wages on today's cosseted pitches. The Premier League has become a stage whereon grown men crumble and writhe at the merest whiff or a challenge, as if they have just arrived from the catwalk, expecting to do more posing than battling. The only snowflakes seen at Upton Park in the immediate postwar decades were those that fell with the first winds of winter, which in those 'post-Greta' years stretched from the start of September to the first buds of May. Those of us who slept with ice on the bedroom walls for half a year, when central heating was something regarded as close to a vice of upper-class dandies, might be forgiven for quietly welcoming global warming – not all climate change sometimes feels like bad climate change to some of us (but no, I don't want my grandchildren to fry – just in case you thought I might be up for that).

Bobby was later to tell of how senior players advised him to 'get stuck in' to various opponents. This was likely because few defenders prior to the mid-1960s would have much idea about 'style' in the sense of Moore's eventual application to the game. So, for sure, the 17-year-old Bobby Moore might have looked to have a few rough edges in relation to the 1970 model, but in all reason, what else might have been the case? The ilk of gorgeous Cristiano Ronaldo would have been lightly buttered toast in those studs-up, demolition tackle days – fed like Little Red Riding Hood to a pack of ravenous, raw as the artic, plebeian wolves

For all this, Bobby slotted into the team with at least some ruinous intent, predicated on a man-marking role, as tough right-half Andy Malcolm fired the Hammers' engines. The former Hornchurch schoolboy, built like a butcher's horse on steroids, put in an admirable performance, particularly as he was playing with a sore throat, replete with matching temperature, busting the mercury out the end of assistant manager Bill Robinson's army surplus thermometer. With Malcolm's muscle at the rudder the Irons dominated.

Ultimately, Moore didn't see much more of Taylor, the Pictish munchkin having been assigned to lie deep in United's half, gathering balls that came out of their goalmouth to instigate attacks from inside his own half.

'Fenton's Furies'

In the eighth minute, right-back John 'Muffin the Mule' Bond unleashed his right peg. Bond's Irons colleague Jimmy Andrews had taught Bond how to kick the ball so hard it earned him the nickname of 'Muffin', a reference the popular children's TV character 'Muffin the Mule'. With England manager Walter Winterbottom in the crowd, the Dedham howitzer sent the ball 60 yards up the field and into United's area. It rebounded off Fred Goodwin to John Dick, West Ham's Scottish inside-left, a player also possessed of the strongest of shots; he scored his fifth goal of the season with a clever but powerful drive.

Seven minutes before the break, an adroit flick from Vic Keeble set up John Smith to put the home side two up. The 19-year-old midfielder blasted a 20-yard drive that spun off Gregg and the Irons walked off at the break 2-0 to the good, with the supporters going ape-shit.

The second period started as the first had finished. Dick probably should have put the game beyond United, but his shot ballooned, sending the ball out of the ground, and as fable had it, inflicting both shock and concussion on a drayman's horse loitering outside the Boleyn pub.

The Irons seemed to be less than fortunate with regard to the sympathies of the referee when Malcolm Musgrove was hacked down in the penalty area. However, the volume went up to 11 when Musgrove added to the woes of the travelling Mancs, making it 3-0 to the Irons. Winning the ball and cutting in from the left wing, the future assistant manager of the Red Devils smacked in a mighty effort from the edge of the penalty area through all of seven defenders, leaving them (each respectively) aghast, agog, appalled, apoplectic, angry, awed and apparently apologetic.

For 70 minutes the match had been all 'Fenton's Furies' as West Ham were being called in the press. It has been reported in later years that the supporters were, at this point, chanting, 'We want six.' That however is probably journalistic license or a trick of memory, as repeated mantras of that type were something more of the mid-to-late 1960s than the last gasp of the smoggy 1950s. As is the case with winkle pickers and kipper ties, things have their time and fashion, and people repeating this type of fantasy just appear painfully twee or a tad dopey to those of us who were around at the time. It isn't (for instance) the kind of thing you might hear at the London Stadium, or much outside the National League, these days. But it is true that on that Monday evening long ago, the hosts appeared to be strolling toward a comfortable win and the Upton Park congregation were revelling in it.

United seemed dazed. Wilf McGuinness pulled a thigh muscle and appearing all but out of the game, the heavy strapping on his leg seeming about as helpful as a bowler hat might have been. These were the good old days when the idea of substitutes was akin to an act of gross cowardice and players played on without a head if necessary (I've heard it said, harshly perhaps, that Harry Redknapp frequently played without a brain). In the eyes of traditionalists, the Football League went flaccid in 1965 allowing the three parts dead to be replaced by fresh legs.

However, as might be said to be typical of West Ham culture, on the hour, concentration flew from the home side's purview like a crazed bat might from a starving dog. With 22 minutes to play, Welsh international and alleged Druid Colin Webster, always likely to take advantage of a 'leaky' defence (see what I did there?!), was allowed to head the ball home from a 'hoppy' McGuinness cross.

Andy Malcolm's health appeared to start to impact on his tackling. It seemed whatever had been in the injection he'd been given before the match (high-grade diesel perhaps?) was wearing off. As a result, the main source of West Ham's resolve and punch was muted. The midfield was wavering as a dandelion might in a Martian sandstorm, and the tussle Andy had been winning with Charlton was turning in the favour of the Ashington lad (who still had a lustrous barnet at that juncture).

In the 78th minute McGuinness, who seemed to have risen Lazarus-like, scored the visitors' second. The 20-yard looping shot arched over the helpless Gregory as might an avenging rainbow (if such a phenomenon might be imagined).

The last part of that game will be all too familiar to West Ham aficionados down the ages – what is colloquially known along our stretch of the river as 'shit yer pants time', when opposing sides not only draw level but score winning goals in the last 14 seconds of way-too-extended injury time. Fenton and Robinson were popping up and down in their dugout like Sooty and Sweep on crystal meth. If panic might be endemic the pair would have been super-spreaders.

West Ham were now on the back foot as Taylor started to push into and find room in midfield, creating problems for the Irons with some smart passing.

Charlton was charging at the Hammers' rearguard with a deal of power and determination, twice going close with forceful long-range efforts that the world would come to expect of him and fear.

Cantwell stopped what looked like a goal-getting shot, Freddie Goodwin nearly levelled matters with a solid header and Ken Brown (as was his wont) nutted danger away from practically under Gregory's crossbar with earnest Ernie nowhere.

It looked as if West Ham were about to piss away their advantage totally when Violett's head connected powerfully, only for the ball to sail just over the bar.

Still the storm wasn't over and Gregory did well to hold the ball at the feet of the 'Hulme Hurricane', Albert Scanlon.

What was being played out was to resonate when Moore later said that the second half of his debut had taught him a very valuable lesson: Manchester United do not have a tradition of admitting defeat.

It's an ask for a side having taken what has to feel like a winning lead, having dominated a game, to hold its nerve when their advantage has been all but snatched away. It is even more exacting when, in the dying moments of a match, with a packed house making an avalanche of noise in the tight Upton Park atmosphere. The mighty Mancs were in full flight, pouring forward, backs up, in all-out attack mode, with the spirit of Duncan Edwards driving them on, demonstrating the fighting soul that was to take them to that year's FA Cup Final.

However, in the illumination of the Upton Park floodlights, which sent a glowing halo high above the haunt of hope that was the abode of the Irons, the Hammers managed to hold out to send the crowd home sitting atop of the First Division by a clear point, taking a 3-2 victory to hang over the mantlepiece.

Half a dozen games in, the Irons had polished the winning teapot four times.

'You were great, lads. You won well,' said Matt Busby, addressing the entire West Ham side in the communal bath (I don't think Matt was actually in the bath, but who knows, he was a miner from Lanarkshire after all?).

This made a great impression on Bobby, certainly given the stress the United manager was surely suffering after the fatal crash in the snow of Munich, fighting to find his own health and to hold his side together as a force in the game. The gesture he made to Bobby and the rest of the West Ham team that day was the kind of action that made Busby one of the most respected and loved figures in the football; a true 'special one' who would never have had the narcissistic temerity to claim such a moniker. The likes of José Mourinho will never be fit to stand in that man's shadow, just as he was never big enough to fill the dimensions of an Old Trafford overlord.

The class of the likes of Matt Busby was perhaps more likely to be wrought in a two-roomed pitman's cottage in the Lanarkshire mining village of Orbiston than out of a comfortable, middle-class setting in Setúbal (a suburb of Lisbon). Moore, to his, West Ham's, England's and football's advantage, was to take a bit of the Busby spirit into his own attitude to his sport and profession.

Booing Bobby

During the match Moore was consistently booed by the home crowd, particularly when he, too regularly for them, passed the ball back to Ernie Gregory, something that irked the long-serving keeper and was generally disapproved of by most supporters in those far-off days. This might have betrayed a lack of confidence on the part of the 17-year-old, although he would have had it drummed into him by Allison that 'possession is all'; you can't control a game as well without the ball as you can when you have it.

Nevertheless, Malcolm Musgrove, was to tell how for him, '[Moore] played in the game as though he'd been in the side for years. I was a lot older than Bobby at the time and I was still a novice, nervous as hell. At the kick-off Bobby stood in the left-half position just looking round. He had an unbelievable temperament. Lots of players have ability, but they haven't got the temperament to make them go even further, as far as they might want to go – Bobby had that temperament … There was no way he was never going to get as far as he got.'

Musgrove was the only player who played that night to retrospectively talk of Moore's debut at any length. What the newspapers reported was never going to focus on Bobby's performance, unless maybe he had made a dreadful mistake or scored a phenomenal goal. He was the least-known player on the pitch and regarded by most as something of a makeweight. The supporters were always going to give him a hard time as he was, in their eyes, stepping over not one but three of the men responsible for getting West Ham promotion. Moore was predictably critical of himself both at the time and after – that's what he did, who he was. No, if we are looking for something of an accurate and objective assessment of Bobby's debut, I'd counsel listening to 'Muzzy' – no one was to know the West Ham side of that era better than him, or be in a position to assess the side's performance on the field better. I think we can take it Bobby did a bit better than OK.

Andy Malcolm had been playing for West Ham for five years when Bobby came into the side. He was eight years senior to Moore, but detected the lad had something of an 'aura' and 'class' about him; always looking like he had the makings of a quality performer, being keen to learn and improve his performance

Moore had won a place in West Ham's first XI relatively quickly by the standards of the time, probably just a bit too soon for the taste of many. Bobby didn't want to be understood as precocious young upstart, with any sense of entitlement, but top-end football against Manchester United was no time or place for humility. To his credit, the youngster held his poise, he didn't let the negative reception get to him and was not provoked to somehow take risks just to prove himself.

As West Ham had come away with a positive result much false criticism of Moore would have been avoided. Most who were present that day would have seen his performance, even if grudgingly, as pretty solid.

The newspapers the next day wrote of West Ham being 'carried by a roaring flood tide of Cockney enthusiasm' and the tale of how the 'injury-stricken' Hammers had 'swept to the top of the First Division'. A dramatic image of Ernie Gregory diving to save a shot from Charlton certainly summed up the last part of the game.

One publication praised the efforts of West Ham's right-half and Malcolm's prospects for an England call-up. The most notable mention of Moore was the pointing out that Fenton had been obliged the play the youth international 'who had never faced the demanding rigours of the First Division'.

Dubbed 'hell-for-leather heroes', the Irons were depicted as leaving the field with 'sweat-drenched bodies' and everyone seemed excited by what had been a classic example of the English game at its best.

The Reds got their revenge when the Irons visited Old Trafford at the end of September. The encounter drew a huge attendance of over 53,000 and proved not the best of debuts on this northern stage for most of the West Ham players. Many felt like one of the players who might have played instead of Moore against United at Upton Park. Bill Lansdowne recalled, 'I didn't do well at Old Trafford. Ernie Taylor tortured me.' A hat-trick from Albert Scanlon went most of the way to giving Manchester United a 4-1 victory.

In early October, Blackburn Rovers were beaten 6-3 at Upton Park. Vic Keeble scored four goals and skipper Noel Cantwell got his first of the season. He had a good weekend. The following day he scored both goals in the Republic of Ireland's 2-2 draw with Poland in Dublin. Recognition for two other Hammers came when John Bond and Andy Malcolm played for the Football League against the Scottish League at Ibrox.

In with the new

In the same month, Malcolm Allison retired as a player. A testimonial match was played at Upton Park in November. It drew a somewhat disappointing 21,600 crowd, but they were treated to 13 goals (West Ham got seven) and a splendid evening's entertainment by some of the country's greatest talents. Stanley

Matthews, Tom Finney, Jimmy Scoular, Ray Barlow, Brian Clough, Don Howe, Peter Brabrook and Bobby Charlton were in the 'All Stars' team against a West Ham XI. An injury to Sheffield United's England international Graham Shaw resulted in young John Lyall being called upon to deputise for the All Stars.

At the end of the campaign, Manchester United would finish second on 55 points. West Ham would be just seven points behind in sixth. It was a more than respectable start in the top flight for the Irons.

At the time of writing Bobby is still the tenth-youngest debutant for West Ham, at 17 years 149 days. In 1958 he was the third-youngest; only forwards Billy Williams (1921) and Robert Allen (1914) were younger, with defenders usually emerging later. The programme of 20 September 1958 v Chelsea carried a report of Bobby's first-team debut,

'The selection of Bobby Moore as left-half proved justified by the display which foreshadows a grand future for the 17-year-old called upon to make his debut against one of Europe's leading sides.'

The result against United at Upton Park that season was a big one for the West Ham players. Many, such as John Dick, would see the beating of Busby's side as a high point in their careers. Bobby was typically modest when looking back on that seminal point in his professional journey, 'I just hit a couple of balls straight. Nothing really.' He was to recall, years later, with his usual masterful understatement, that his initial impact was 'not great'.

In fairness, Bobby knew then and later that his League debut wasn't seen as a dream start to his first-team career. A local newspaper report confirmed his assessment and Andy Malcolm's stoical contribution, commenting while Moore had made a 'promising start' the 'home fans mutter their thanks that fellow wing-half Malcolm passed his fitness test to play his customary blinder'.

Bobby had nearly not made his debut game at all, however. On his way to Upton Park the whole of Barking and East Ham appeared to be moving in the same direction as Bobby, clogging up the few miles to Boleyn Ground from his family home in Waverley Gardens[1], Barking. Standing in the seemingly endless bus queue he'd all but given up hope of making it to the ground before half-time.

---

1   This is the address almost universally reported to be the place where Moore lived until his first marriage, in June 1962. However, there are references to him having moved as a baby to Ivyhouse Road, Dagenham, where he was said to have lived until moving to the Hainault Estate at the age of nine. However, he is recorded as only attending one primary school, Westbury Road, which was in Barking, close to Waverley Gardens but more than three miles from Ivyhouse Road and not an easy route via public transport now or in the 1950s. Tom Hood Technical School in Leyton, Moore's only recorded secondary school, was a difficult commute for Moore, more than five miles from Waverley Gardens. Hainault was over nine miles from Tom Hood. Although Moore's birth was registered in Ilford, Essex, about four miles from Waverley Gardens, Moore was never to contradict the generally accepted knowledge that throughout his young life he was resident, with his parents, at Waverley Gardens

He was fortunate enough to squeeze himself on a crushing upper deck, but on making it to the top of Green Street he found the stadium was encased in a huge mass of people. The gates had been locked more than half an hour before the game was due to start. The Hammers' compact stadium was packed out with in excess of 36,000 supporters, leaving what felt like about three times the same number outside to mill around the darkening streets.

At first Bobby couldn't find a way passed the police lines that were surrounding Upton Park's main gates. Luckily, he was able to get the attention of a steward, who literally dragged him though the line of coppers who refused to break ranks.

That steward, whoever he was, pulled Bobby Moore into sporting history.

Early the following season Bobby remembered going to White Hart Lane and watching his team play. He recollected, 'Noel Cantwell was left-back, Noel Dwyer in goal. It was the best display of defending and goalkeeping I'd ever seen. They drew 2-2 but without the two Noels it would have been Spurs by a distance.'

He was keen to be part of what he saw. He was excited at the possibilities, in many ways watching his dreams being made real. How football might be played with class and a touch of majesty.

2

ROBERT FREDERICK CHELSEA MOORE

Robert Frederick Chelsea Moore, son of Robert Edward and Doris Joyce Moore (née Doris Smaggasgale Buckle), was born on 12 April 1941. Family and friends knew Doris as 'Doos' and after the birth of his son, Robert's father was pretty much universally referred to in their neighbourhood as 'Big Bob'.

Why was Robert given the name Chelsea? This is an oft-asked question by many a West Ham aficionado. It has been mooted that it wasn't about any affiliation to the blue bridge dwellers of SW6, but an affectionate nod to paternal uncle. But Chelsea would have been a very unlikely name to hang on a child of either gender in the 1920s and '30s. When it became more common in the 1970s it was, in the main, a name given to female children. I have been told a few times that the name was motivated by Dick Foss, a professional at Stamford Bridge in the 1930s[2] who was born in Barking and who played a part in getting Big Bob a job at Barking power station. Apparently, Doris had rejected the idea of calling her only son 'Dick'.

Robert never pretended that his spiritual affinity was with the Hammers. In an August 1969 interview with *Shoot!* magazine, Moore described himself as a boyhood Charlton Athletic fan. He did say it had been a toss-up between the southerly Addicks and indomitable Irons, but he preferred the former crew as, at that time, they were in the top flight of English football (West Ham weren't). At the same time, it was easy enough to get to 'Mordor SE7' via nautical means (the Woolwich ferry). The Valley dwarfed Upton Park as a sporting arena; the record attendance of that temple of sport all but doubled the capacity of the Boleyn Ground. But as so often in life, less is more, small is beautiful and envy is unattractive.

Big Bob would turn 28 twelve days after his son was born. Doris, born in Romford, Essex, was five months younger than her husband. Doris had three sisters, Dora Gladys, Ena and Beatrice Ethel Lilian Buckle. Ena recalled being at work at a building society in Ilford, maybe a 20-minute bus ride from where her sister and her brother-in-law lived, when Doris went into labour. Their mother,

---

2   Before signing for Chelsea, Foss played for Thames FC, a side that briefly played out of West Ham Stadium in Custom House, less than three miles from Upton Park and the east London home of speedway, greyhound racing and baseball (see Belton 2007).

Beatrice Elizabeth Louisa, together with Big Bob's mum, Mrs Cooper, were with her during the afternoon. The midwife was popping in and out.

Big Bob had experienced a tough childhood, sharing with my paternal grandmother the trauma of losing his father in the First World War. The records show Big Bob's parents to be Robert Moore and Rose Hetty Sipthorpe, so it seems likely Mrs Cooper was Rose, and Cooper was her name from a subsequent marriage after the death of Robert Moore. Big Bob had a brother, George Moore; Bill Cooper was his stepbrother. They all worked at Barking power station, where Big Bob was known as a 'thorough gentleman'.

Getting to the Moore family home, 43 Waverley Gardens, Barking, after leaving her work at 4.30pm, Ena found that her sibling had been placed on a stretcher in the hallway. Doris, who had spent the previous night on a bed that had been moved downstairs, had been unable to give birth at home, so an ambulance had been called. Mrs Cooper went over the road to her house to get her coat and accompanied Doris to the hospital. Doris was taken to Upney hospital. Mother and child (who Doris would almost unfailingly address as 'Robert', although everyone else knew him as 'Bobby') were to spend just one night in hospital before being sent home. Hospital beds were at a premium in the wartime conditions.

Robert was brought up in Barking, on the border of west Essex and east London. His home was a long free kick from the busy main route between London and Southend, the A13. The modest house still stands just a few miles away from where England's 1966 World Cup-winning manager Alf Ramsey was born in Dagenham.

The Moore home had a front fence where Big Bob chained his bike. It was a decent but ordinary place, albeit close to an industrial estate. The relatively small street, with its 68 houses, remains today, remarkably, comparatively quiet. Built in the 1930s, the terraced houses feature shallow, arched brick entrances over the street-facing doors, pebble-dashed walls, and triangular gables over front bedroom windows. Now the three-bedroomed former Moore home has a blue plaque that marks out the end-of-terrace house as the abode where Robert grew up.

Robert's aunt, June Cooper, the wife of his dad's half-brother Bill, who lived at 20 Waverley Gardens, the house opposite the Moores, remembered that her nephew would invariably be seem with a football. Often, heading home from school, he would visit and she would make him some chips (he liked his chips). She was never surprised by his success. Robert had shown his footballing talents from his earliest school days.

The Moores had several relatives as neighbours in Waverley Gardens. Like many streets in the east London area of the time, family members often lived in the same road or round the corner to each other. Families didn't tend to move too far from each other then. It was understood as a positive thing, reflecting the stability of a family. However, in the days before the welfare state the support systems were within families and neighbourhoods. Outside of that, apart from the church, the individual was alone.

The street was the extended family and the social security system. Hence there was no propensity to want to 'get away' from parents and families; that notion was born in the 1960s for the majority. The extended family regularly went on holidays. For my family it was hop-picking in Kent; in the case of the Moores vacations were often set in Devon, even with teenagers in tow.

Unlike my family of labourers and costermongers, the Moores were what we in mid-century east London might call 'respectable' and 'quiet'; the latter meaning they kept themselves to themselves, unlikely to be involved in too much gossip, showing a dislike or even distaste for 'fuss'. Young Robert would follow his parent's example in these respects.

Marking Barking

I was born some 14 years after Robert. On a typical weekday, my family home is about a ten-minute drive east from where he lived. My mum, like Big Bob, was from Poplar (her family resided on Dog Island – a place very much set within its own culture). My paternal grandmother grew up in Barking. In her childhood years Barking still had something of the fishing village it once was about it; a meadow or two more than semi-rural.

By the time Robert first saw the light of day, urbanisation had encroached on the district, and the power station, where Big Bob worked, was part of this. Not least because of the coming of the Ford plant in Dagenham, which in 1941 was moving into its second decade. This development brought people and services flooding into the area like never before, along with the infrastructure of an industrial suburb. In October 1931 the first vehicle was churned off the production line – the Ford AA van. Half a dozen years later the plant was producing 37,000 vehicles a year, a massive number for the time.

With the coming of war the plant produced large numbers of vans and trucks, along with Bren gun carriers, a multitude of 'special purpose' engines, and agricultural vehicles: at one stage, the Fordson tractor made up 95 per cent of UK tractor production. The factory and the surrounding district (where most of the workers lived) from the earliest wartime air raids was a natural target for the Nazi bombers.

When I was growing up, Barking was certainly viewed as a 'better area' than Dagenham. Likely, generally speaking, the demographic might have been seen as 'doing OK' (but a bit short of affluent) working class. Dagenham was a bit like 'Canning Town in the Essex', a tad down-at-heel compared certainly to the East Ham district down the road, which encompassed what we took to be the 'made it' areas (moving from lower to higher) Upton Park, Forest Gate, and Manor Park. The Navara of east London, Wanstead, was more a place for afternoons out than hopes for residence.

My father's family were, as we used to say, 'out of the old town', the 'rough' river/dockside locales of Canning Town, Custom House and Silver Town, but they got all upwardly mobile following one night during the Blitz that saw their council house home in Custom House flattened (at the back of the grand old West Ham Stadium – famous for its speedway circuit and greyhound track).

Homeless, my father and his mum – my grandad was fighting overseas – wandered into an empty house in Plaistow and that area was where we stayed until relatively recently. Thus, I was born and brought up less than a five-minute walk from West Ham's Upton Park home, straddling the hotly contested boundary betwixt West and East Ham. In the early days of spring my brother and I would sit in our prams outside the council house in Sampson Street, E13 to be lullabied by the 40,000 choir just beyond the house tops in Green Street. My earliest words included 'day fry zo I' and 'for-effa bowin' blobbles'.

No fuss

Although my maternal grandad knew Big Bob (George was a member of probably the most radical socialist council in Poplar's history), we don't know too much about Doris and Big Bob; certainly no one got very much about them from their son. We can, I think, be pretty sure that suited them. They would never look for a moment to bask in the glow of their son's reflected glory and were ultra-careful to avoid the limelight. For instance, during an England game at Wembley, the Moores were watching their son from an area of the stadium reserved for the players' relatives. Robert by that time had about five dozen caps to his name, and was the long-time captain of the side. For much of the first part of the game a bloke had taken to standing up, blocking Bob and Doris's view. Big Bob civilly asked the 'jerk-in-the-box' if he could try to stay seated. The fella spun round and brusquely asked Moore senior, 'Do you know who I am?' and let him know his son was playing. His lad was winning his third cap. Big Bob, who was 'big', probably could have flattened that knobhead with both hands tied behind his back, but he just smiled and said absolutely nothing. That was characteristic of the couple's nature. Irrespective of the situation, they refused to use their Robert's name to their advantage.

I was to experience the striking unpretentiousness of Big Bob and Doris when they were invited to a local community centre for a showing of a film of the European Cup Winners' Cup Final, which West Ham won in 1965. I went with my mum and brother to see that same recording. They were clearly agitated and perhaps embarrassed when public attention was drawn to them being in attendance. I remember asking myself why people just didn't let them be.

I had been in the close to 98,000 crowd for that first all-English team's victory – they were in every tie – at Wembley. My dad had got tickets, but for some reason, I can't recall why, he didn't accompany me. I used his ticket to take a mate, Sadiq Khan – no, not the eponymous mayor of London, although he was however to reach similar heady heights. After starting work with the Egg Marketing Board (as I believe an 'egg counter') he made the natural progression (?) to became a coalman. However, the last I heard of 'Genna' (his nickname, derived from 'Genghis' – 'The Great Khan') sometime ago, he was heading up a chain fish and chip shops around Guangdong, China.

I've never seen anyone who could strike a football more powerfully than Genna. He once scored a goal, on a mud-drenched pitch at Southern Road, Plaistow, reminiscent of the worst days of the Somme, with a shot about ten metres out from our right-of-field corner flag – if there had been an actual corner flag, which there wasn't, only in spirit, sort of. The ball (circa 1923) had long forgotten what bouncing might be, being a creature of ancient porous leather, capable of soaking up several gallons of foul, pitch surface fluid.

Replete with rock-hardened laces, although it had become addicted to the gravitational pull of the planet's inner core, Sadiq drove the ball's resisting arse to send it, discernibly shocked, into the mad-grey skies, above the dizzily morose east London skyline. Reaching the top of its sluggish arch, the crusty orb plummeted, meteor-like, beyond the opposition keeper's impressive impression of a Peter Bonetti swallow in flight, into the top left-hand corner of his astonished net; the ground palpably shook as the dazed spherical monster returned to earth.

Like mother, like son

Doris was an attractive woman, who in her late teenage years had won a district beauty contest, so it's likely Robert inherited his looks from her. She was recognised as a good person, genuine, modest and generous to those she cared for, often giving away things that she thought people needed more than her. However, as a typical Scorpio, she would, like my mum (a Gemini), not give up on a grudge. Should anyone say anything derogatory about her boy there was no way back for them: blanked forever.

Tina, Robert's first steady girlfriend and later to be his first wife, recalled that whenever she dined at the Moores' family home, Doris would use an ice-cream scoop to serve mashed potato in precise half-moon shapes. For Tina this seemed to epitomise Doris's neatness. But Bobby's mum wasn't alone in that practice at that time and that place. My grandmother used the same implement for the same job, as did my mum when working in school meals. But Doris was very much a perfectionist with a feeling, perhaps a drive for detail.

Doris also passed on many of her personal traits to Robert. He was good-mannered, but there was a side that could be something more than guarded, if slightly less than repressed. He often dealt almost silently with anxiousness for periods of his life. This manifested itself on the pitch, where he would rarely show any sign of being pressurised, although over long periods West Ham was a club that found itself in or on the edge of disaster. Watching himself in action during an interview with famed commentator Brian Moore of *The Big Match*, the long-serving ITV presenter asked Bobby if he was as composed as he looked on a recording of him passing the ball around the penalty area. He replied, with a little laugh, that he was more composed in that situation than he was at that moment watching himself. That comment tells us more about the man than a good proportion of the millions of words written about him.

From an early age everything about Bobby had to be impeccable. Like his mum, Robert was very self-disciplined, probably stricter with himself than with others. While Doris was an abstainer when it came to drink, in later life, even when pissed in the small hours, Robert would take a clothes brush to the suit he had been wearing before going to bed. As a football player, he exemplified his up-brining; his pristine hair was always neatly combed, he was the epitome of 'clean-cut': neat and tidy, socks pulled up, shorts ironed, shirt tucked in.

While Big Bob cleaned Robert's muddy boots on the Saturday evenings following a match, his mother would painstakingly wash and iron her son's kit, including the laces of his football boots, scrubbing and bleaching them with a nailbrush to make sure they stayed sparkling white. They were subsequently ironed again before every schoolboy game. Football kit notwithstanding, Doris made sure the collars and cuffs of her Robert's shirts never failed to be as smooth as silk. Her ironing was both an art and a labour of love, part of her painstaking desire to see to her son's every need.

As a child Robert made sure his books were shelved and his toys discretely and appropriately stowed. This sort of proclivity has, by any number of writers and others, been portrayed as exceptional, and to an extent Robert was. But he was born into a world of chaos in wartime conditions, and the one way many families coped with that was to stick to a domestic order.

This was the environment Robert was brought up in. Thus, to a significant extent, he reflected what might have been taken as a respectable working-class family life, there being a place for everything and so everything needed to be put in its place. I certainly recognise this from my own upbringing; my grandparents and parents having had life-changing experiences during the often frightening pandemonium of war, including evacuation, dodging bombs and fighting around the globe.

Like Robert and Doris, my dad and his mother chose not to be evacuated out of London during the years of conflict. They lived through the Blitz and that experience was carried by them and others into the peacetime world. My mum was evacuated, sent to remote North Wales as a lone four-year-old, which had equal and perhaps more detrimental consequences for her. Most of any memories she might have had were blotted out. Knowing the abuses and horror many evacuees went through, her unconscious self-protection is probably not surprising.

So, it's easy to look at Bobby and those like him and suggest that they are in some way 'pathological' or 'abnormal', but understood in another way, it would be more perverse if they were disinclined to seek out and impose order on their world.

That was the foundation of Moore's overall elegance, which became a symbolic marker of his dignity as a player and leader of men. When Robert had become the Bobby the world knew, Doris proudly told how she never had never been obliged to clean up after him as he was always neat and tidy. That summed up Moore as a player, but perhaps more meaningfully, this was the part of the very grounding that was to make him the footballer he was. Moore's team-mates were hardly ever burdened with the task of cleaning up after him, but he made the task of cleaning up not only after, but before them, the hallmark of his genius.

Thus, at least in part, perhaps we have the Luftwaffe and fat-boy Göring to thank for Moore's drive to sculp order from chaos; the man who was at the centre of German defeat in 1966. Oh, history is ironic.

It would be simplistic and unfair to portray Moore's childhood years as restrictive, or even see him as subjected to over-protection, although his parents did want to be seen to look after their boy well and do the right thing in terms of his upbringing. In this respect they were again like a lot of parents of the time and place the family occupied.

My grandmother was the matriarch of my family. When we talk of 'gender equality' nowadays it is as if men were always and everywhere the rulers of every facet of life, perhaps in particular the domestic realm. Being raised and majorly influenced by strong women, I can't help but feel this is less than the whole story. In my early life, certainly in my immediate and extended family, men seemed pretty much to live and act at the behest of women. As such, Doris being the dominant figure in the Moore marriage and Robert's childhood, and him being surrounded by a nexus of female influences, feels familiar.

Like my grandmother and my mother, Doris was fiercely protective of her offspring; in her eyes he could do no wrong. When he came near to erring it was hard for her to fathom. Once, desperately needing a leak, with no toilet to hand, Robert was obliged to make use of a milk bottle. On finding this out Doris was amazed, unconvinced that the fruit of her womb could do such a thing. Thus, her Robert would have been very much aware of 'standards', 'manners' and what was required of him in terms of decorum.

For all this, Doris might not be easily taken to be a conformist; she had a rebellious streak in relation to her family's values, including a background of commitment to Salvationist principles. As is the way with the Salvation Army, they, as 'God's troopers', would be out every Sunday with their Bibles, bonnets on and singing hymns. Doris's faith upbringing, which was always kept quiet and rightly personal, might well be understood as one of the cornerstones of Robert's personality. Later, perhaps she came to the conclusion that it wasn't for her – she was fiercely independent – but the culture, as cultures do, persisted. Doris and Big Bob were very respectable and God-fearing. Typical of the Salvationist ethic, neither drank alcohol or smoked; indeed the domestic environment precluded both 'vices' from the hallows of the family home.

I grew up with the sound of the 'Sally-bash' brass bands as a constant. They were big in east London and Essex. They even followed us to the hop fields in the long (sometimes) hot summers of the late 1950s and early 1960s. Their tradition of working in my easterly manor goes back to their first murmurings. The very base of their schtick was the value of truth and decency. Think what you will of them, but on Sunday morning, marching down the road, banners flying, music blaring out 'Onward Christian Soldiers', you couldn't help but admire this mob. They really nailed their colours to the mast without apology, inhibition or fear. Wear your courage with modesty, and keep a straight bat and your chin up. Robert grew into those boots. I have sometimes felt a touch of a similar 'faith' in the crowd at Upton Park:

'Gates of Hell can never,
Gainst the Church prevail.
We have Christ's own promise
And that CANNOT fail!'

I love the defiance. Somewhat contradictorily, the opening lines of a ditty we used to sing on the North Bank during my mid-teenage years reminded me of the Sally's bold adherence to their truth. It was sung to the tune of 'Everything Is Beautiful', a song written, composed, and performed by Ray Stevens – it got in the top ten for a time. Ironically perhaps it was adapted from the hymn, 'Jesus Loves the Little Children':

'We're the boys in claret and blue.

Who the fucking hell are you?'

Doris and Big Bob were the kind of 'salt of the earth' people who enabled Britain to move into an era comparative luxury of the 1960s. Their generation was the foundation of the 'permissive society', but counterintuitively not of it. Neatness, minimal swearing, decency, tidiness, order and an insistence on politeness were the considerations that got people through and won the Second World War, particularly those who shared backgrounds like those of Big Bob and Doris. At the same time the maintenance of these values and behaviours constituted the foundational rationale for fighting that war, as well as the recovery from it.

It is perhaps no wonder that Robert grew to epitomise that sort of 'Englishness'; a social being somewhat better than the 'keep the aspidistra flying' attitude to be found in the British middle classes of mid-20th century Britain. While this type of atmosphere might cultivate modesty or humility, it was short of what might be seen as introversion. As a boy Robert could hold down a conversation when called to, although he wasn't what you'd think of as a 'chatty kid'.

Robert's parents had tied the knot during September 1939, just weeks into the war, in Ilford, then just beyond the easterly edge of east London. In that place and at that time, you didn't even think about honeymoons, and even if you did, financial restrictions would have kept you not too far from home. Like many of their era, including my grandparents, and for others sometime after, they got the bus home following their marriage vows. They were obliged to 'keep it simple', but probably that's what they might have chosen anyway. As Robert was to personify, there is a complexity to simplicity, a frisson of nobility, and a facet of true courage.

There are not too many images of Big Bob and Doris; she didn't like her photograph being taken. She would do what she could to turn her back on any camera pointed at her. The spotlight was not for her. Big Bob was a mild person, fun to be with. He had a vibrant but gentle sense of humour, wearing daft hats and so on. Prematurely bald, he often joked about that and other things at his own expense. But he wasn't ostentatious, having a quality of humility that allowed him not to take himself too seriously. He was thought of by most as a nice, polite, regular, kind man with a twinkle in his eye. For all that, he was always frank and would let someone know if he believed they were 'in the wrong'.

Unlike many men of his time and station, Moore senior wasn't one for going down the pub with his pals. Home and family were at the centre to Big Bob's world, and Doris was his queen. Thus, it's likely that Doris had the last word in the size of the family and her hubby would have gone along with that. He, coming from the older part of the East End, was much more Cockney than Doris, who like her Robert (and me) had that more gentle lilt to her voice, indicative of our part of the world. The faux enunciation that predominates on the dark pantomime that is the BBC's *EastEnders* has never really featured (everyone sounds like they come from 1930s Peckham!). The inflection I am referring to is a sort of return ticket between the Aldgate Pump Cockney and Colchester, via Burnham-on-Crouch East Anglian; Hereward the Wake meets John Keats (someone who referred to 'warta' rather than 'water') sorta vibe.

Hammers and Heinkels

The day before Robert came into the world West Ham had hosted Clapton Orient at the Boleyn Ground in the London War Cup (Group One). The teams entertained a crowd of 7,000, a respectable gate in the context of wartime restrictions. An exciting game provided eight goals, West Ham's George Foreman and Jackie Wood getting a couple each and Scotsman Corbett the other

Like so many other places in Britain, given the threat of aerial bombardment, during the first part of the 1940s Barking had to be blotted out after dark. Little Robert had not yet reached his first 100 hours when the vibration of the Blitz rocked his family home to the foundations. Windows broke and ceilings cracked as the Luftwaffe sought to destroy the Ford factory and put Barking power station, down by the river, out of the game.

Working at the power station, Big Bob's workday started with the ten-minute bike ride to the Thames-side plant. A mile or so peddle to work had been a boon before the war, but as the bombs began to fall, one of their prize targets was way too close for security, let alone comfort.

Work in power then was not what it is today. My grandfather, Jim Belton, was a stoker in Becton Gas Works before war broke out. Like Big Bob, by the end of a shift he'd return home black with coal dust. As soon as he could he volunteered for the Royal Engineers.

Reserved occupation

Both Big Bob and Jim, at the start of the war, were in jobs known as 'reserved occupations'. In April 1939 the Military Training Act was passed, under which men aged 20 and 21 were conscripted to complete six months of military training.

At the outbreak of war, the National Service (Armed Forces) Act made all men between 18 and 41 liable for conscription into the armed forces. However, in 1938 a Schedule of Reserved Occupations had been drawn up, exempting certain key skilled workers from conscription. Australia and New Zealand introduced similar schemes. The government was determined not to repeat the mistakes of the First World War, when the indiscriminate recruitment of too many men into the military had left major war production schemes short of the necessary workforce.

The reserved (or scheduled) occupation scheme was a complicated one, covering five million men in a vast range of jobs. These included railway and dock workers, miners, farmers, agricultural workers, schoolteachers and doctors. Ages varied. For example, a lighthouse keeper was 'reserved' at 18, while a trade union official could be called up until the age of 30. Engineering was the industry with the highest number of exemptions. After November 1939, employers could ask for the deferment of call-up for men in reserved occupations, but outside the reserved age.

The government frequently reviewed the situation, as its need for men to join the armed forces demanded. As the men went off to fight, women began to fill some of reserved occupations, for example working in munitions factories and shipyards and driving trains. Such jobs acted as incubators for women's football, as the women's works teams developed, marking the beginnings of the women's game gaining more recognition and respect (although the journey had initially started in the First World War and continues even today).

Some men in reserved occupations felt frustration at not being allowed to fight, while many of those in the armed forces envied them for not being conscripted. Appreciable numbers of those in reserved occupations joined civil defence units such as the Home Guard or the ARP, which created responsibilities in addition to their work.

I've never been sure how Jim ducked under the wire. He joined up pretty quickly in 1939. Like his father before him, he was keen to kill fascists, so may have slipped through the subsequent net, allowing him to spend the war terrorising Nazis in a way that perhaps only a Canning Town gas works stoker might. It's hard to feel sorry for a Nazi, but with bareknuckle, 6ft 2in, 18st, rock-hard, street-fighting, muscled Jimmy boy coming at 'em in full flight, it is difficult not to feel a shiver of fearsome empathy.

Like many of his generation, Jim never talked much about his wartime experience, although his single-handed assault on a Norwegian farmhouse occupied by a handful of the brutal SS Ski Jäger Battalion was a family legend. Having gained access his rifle jammed, but he made impressive impromptu use of a weighty but apparently adaptable Dyker's hammer he happened on, screaming 'Up the 'Ammers' as he went about the slaughter. As was his wont in life generally, no prisoners were taken.

It's fair to say that most of the reserved occupations were often far from a soft option. Jim would work 12-hour shifts in an underground hell of flame and dirt. Such was the heat, the stokers laboured naked, apart from steel boots, drinking from vats of salted milk to replace the loss of fluid and minerals. Going on killing rampages alongside the Norwegian resistance likely equally suited Jim's gib.

Most in the reserved occupations looked at long hours, often working in difficult and dangerous wartime conditions. Most places where reserved workers were needed, such as power stations, factories and dockyards, were prime targets for enemy bombing. In addition, if you were in a reserved occupation, you could be transferred to another location anywhere in Britain if your skills were needed. For example, dockworkers were moved from Southampton to Clydeside in Scotland.

Coal mining suffered a severe shortage of labour. In December 1943 the minister of labour, Ernest Bevin, decided to select men of call-up age for the mines by a ballot. One in ten men aged between 18 and 25 were to be selected – only those who were on a list of highly skilled occupations or who had been accepted for aircrew or submarine service were exempt. These conscript miners were known as 'Bevin Boys'. They came from all backgrounds and worked alongside experienced miners, doing the less skilled tasks such as unloading coal from the tubs.

Some 21,800 young men became Bevin Boys, alongside 16,000 who opted for coal mining in preference to the forces when they were called up. The scheme lasted until 1948.

Bombs, bombs and more bombs

The number of Luftwaffe aircraft sent against London and other British cities in the first months of the Blitz averaged 200 to 300 bombers per raid, some flying multiple sorties. This rose to over 400 in individual night raids from October 1940, to over 600 (London, 16–17 April 1941) and to more than 700 (London, 19–20 April 1941).

During April 1941, the government estimated that over 6,000 British civilians had been killed in air raids. Further very heavy night raids on London took place on 16–17 April 1941 (890 tons of high explosive and 151,000 incendiaries dropped with 1,000 killed) and on 19–20 April 1941 (1,000 tons of high explosive and 153,000 incendiaries dropped with 1,200 killed).

The present is made from the past

My mum's dad, George, had fought in the First World War, rising to the rank of a non-commissioned officer. He was over conscription age in 1939, but he joined the Auxiliary Fire Service. His distinguished military service and qualities of command naturally led others to look to George for leadership and him taking on more responsibility as London burned.

A while ago I received a letter concerning that time in the East End. I include it here as I think it gives some dramatic insight to the nature of the blitz and what was at stake.

Dear Dr Belton

I hope it is OK getting in touch with you, but I dearly wanted to contact you.

On the evening of 15 September 1941, a street in Poplar, east London, had been set ablaze after being struck by heavy incendiary bombing. The firefighters had done their best, but such was the fury of the flames, they had all but given in to the conflagration.

A group of women were struggling to prevent a young woman from going back into a blazing house, she was crying hysterically and screaming 'MY BABIES, MY BABIES!' A fire officer, who had led his men's retreat from the blaze, approached the group to be told that twin one-year-old girls were in a back bedroom of the house.

The officer looked at the distraught woman, and then strode hurriedly back to his men. He pulled a scarf round his face, ordered the other firefighters to douse him with water and took a fire axe from one of his crew. Soaked and dripping he jogged back toward the group of women, still wrestling to prevent the mother from going to her certain death in an attempt to save her children.

The officer pulled out his own hatchet, and with an axe in each hand, as the firefighters and the women froze in disbelief, he ran, head down, into the roaring house. All eyes were fixed on the inferno, as the street was lit up brighter than day.

Elongated seconds grew into painful minutes. Over a seeming eternity, what little hope there had been all but evaporated in the unforgiving heat.

Then, out of the frantically mad flames, a blackened, smoking figure staggered into the street, in each arm he held a small, sooty, screaming child.

The women rushed forward to grab the babies, as the fire officer fell, face down to the road. He was quickly surrounded by his men, spraying their hoses on their smouldering leader.

Dear Dr Belton, I was one of those children and the fire officer was your grandfather. I have lived a full and happy life. I have three wonderful children, six grandchildren and great grandchildren. My twin sister, Victoria, has lived in Melbourne, Australia, since the early 1960s. She has two children and four grandchildren and five great grandchildren.

You probably know your grandfather was decorated for his bravery during the Great War. He must have been quite a human being. Over the years, on and off, I did bits and pieces of research looking to trace his relatives to let them know how thankful my family and I are for his bravery. We of course owe him everything. However, just before lockdown [in 2020], my great granddaughter, who is training to be a youth worker, showed me a book authored by you in which you write about your grandfather and from there I was able to 'track you down'.

We never got the chance to thank George. Mum even had trouble finding out his name during the war. The brigade did not encourage any contact with their people, but she met one of your aunts who was serving with her dad and was at least able to pass on our gratitude via her.

I understand that you are something of a legend in your own work all over the world. I know your granddad would have been very proud of you. I am confident you are proud of him.

Thank you!
Yours very sincerely,

Emely

Black Monday

The Nazi bombing of London had kicked in on what came to be known as 'Black Monday', just eight months before Robert was born. However, on 16 April 1941, a Wednesday, Hermann Göring, Luftwaffe commander-in-chief and all-round fat bastard, properly let the population in and around London's docklands have it. It was ferocious and undiscriminating, probably one of the most awesomely barbaric air raids in human history at that point.

By the next day at least 1,000 Cockneys had been slain, many thousands more were injured and tens of thousands made homeless. Despite the pleading wrath of Labour harridan Barbara Castle for the Tory government, which had been in power since 1935, to create mass shelters when war seemed imminent and throughout the 'phoney war', the public had been left wide open and vulnerable to the inevitable carnage from the skies. Such was the magnitude of the resulting inferno, my firefighting material grandfather was, on dark winter evenings, to tell how the night-time streets were as 'light as day and as hot as hell'. The roads and vehicle tyres melted into hot and dangerous magma. East London was, in parts, transformed to the inside of a volcano.

As might be expected, the Cockneys fought back the best they could. The Barking Park and Wanstead Flats anti-aircraft barrages (where several West Ham players were stationed) answered the assault from the sky with all the thunder they could muster, but in what we used to call 'Barking Town', at Blake's Corner, a popular shopping area, Killiwicks furniture shop was wiped off the face of the planet, effectively closing off much of that area.

Arthur Harris took over as the commander-in-chief of Bomber Command in February 1942. He was promoted into the position after the British realised how woefully inadequate the response had been to the Nazi bombing terrorism. Harris was brought in to fix this. He was to state at the beginning of his tenure at Bomber Command – speaking under the glare of a 'bomber's moon', reflecting in the silvery Thames, the river George and his crew had drawn on to douse the savage flames of terror,

'The Nazis entered this war under the rather childish delusion that they were going to bomb everyone else, and nobody was going to bomb them. At Rotterdam, London, Warsaw and half a hundred other places, they put their rather naive theory into operation. They sowed the wind, and now they are going to reap the whirlwind.'

Britain's answer to Hitler was indeed ruthless and brutal. Looking back, it was horrifying. But if you were in the Nazi line of fire, if you were flung into the furnace they ignited, like my dad and grandmother, Emely and Victoria and the likes of Big Bob, Doris and baby Robert were, you might be forgiven for hearing the words of 'Bomber Harris' differently than we might at our safe distance.

History tells us: Wounded Albion will injure with a greater wound.

Bobby bombed

For Robert's mum the Blitz, at its height, was as it was for everyone, both a frightening and bewildering experience. When the bombing started Big Bob and his mum laid across the baby and Doris to protect them. However, when it became unbearable, with Doris fretting for the welfare of her child, Big Bob tried to get an ambulance to take him and his new family to his in-laws' place, a couple of miles away, where they would perhaps have been a bit less vulnerable to the death raining down from above. But there was no way that was going to happen given the need to evacuate and tend to the injured.

As it turned out, a very British exercise in commandeering came to the rescue. In the first minutes of the new day, it was Barking's Mayoral chauffeur and the alderman's limousine that finally evacuated the Moore family across Barking to 110 Faircross Avenue.

The raid was so bad that Ena couldn't risk attempting to get back to her own home in Ilford, so she had gone to stay at her parental home. Around midnight, while making a hot water bottle to take into her parents' air raid shelter, the Moore family arrived. Big Bob all but banged the door down. The moment Robert's aunt Dora (Doris's younger sister) responded, England's future captain, swaddled in a huge blanket and blissfully oblivious, was placed in her arms.

Fred Buckle, Doris's dad, carried his daughter into the house. Fred was a huge man, weighing in at 17st. His wife Beatrice (senior) had taken the precaution of sleeping downstairs, so Big Bob, Doris and little Robert could be lodged upstairs. The hot water bottle was given to Doris, and Robert got a chest draw for the night, not an uncommon crib for east London tinies at the time.

That night of terror was not the last of the bombing. It was six weeks before it was thought safe for the Moore family to return to Robert's childhood home. For those six weeks Ena got the job of washing the future World Cup winner's nappies.

Back at Waverley Gardens the next day, a neighbour rose at 6am to find out how mother and baby were. She got no response when she knocked at the door of number 43. She later found out that when the 22-year-old midwife, Josephine Lawson, arrived at the Moore home, Big Bob returned at the same time and told of how he had taken Doris and little Robert to his in-laws' place.

The same former resident of Waverley Gardens remembered baby Bobby as 'a dear little soul', and later as a small boy, unfailingly to be found kicking a ball in the road. That ball found its way into her garden regularly, causing her to instruct or plead for him to take it somewhere else. But she recalled Robert as a good lad and always polite.

She went on to say that the Moores were seen as an 'ordinary family' and Robert really was the archetypal boy next door – he gave the impression of never hurrying but seemed to glide down the street whenever she saw him.

Today we remark on, and see as an exception, young Robert's good-mannered behaviour, as a small boy saying hello to people and asking how they were. But such politeness was something taught to his and my generation from the cradle. We can rightly be perplexed as to why this doesn't appear to be the case now. Robert was uniformly remembered as being very respectful to everyone from early on, and no one ever had any complaints about 'Doo's boy'.

War Hammers

During the Second World War, football and West Ham United adapted to the conflict in what proved to be ingenious ways that kept the game alive.

I have written in detail about the Hammers' response to football in both world wars, its consequences and meaning (Belton 2006c and 2015), including how football provided a stage on which many players built and extended their careers. More than a few players would never have had the chance to play for professional teams had the conditions been 'normal'. Many of those who would have got a game or two in peacetime had protracted wartime careers and consequently a playing CV in the postwar football job market. At same time, war robbed many of their best years in the game.

For West Ham, and many other clubs, both world wars also cemented a relationship with supporters. Players and fans experienced war together; they got each other through.

A lot of players turned out for several clubs, all over the country. This provided unique opportunities to experience different management and organisational conditions. Most significantly, particularly during the Second World War, this movement created a dialogue between players on a scale never before known. This is not to be underestimated with regard to the organisation of players as a workforce after the conflict. The latter led to the abolition of the minimum wage and ultimately a complete revision of the way football was organised as an industry. In fact, it is probable that the war obliged the boardrooms of professional clubs to move more swiftly towards becoming mature business enterprises, which included industrial relations.

This transition was to ultimately displace the cultural fiefdoms that many clubs were, ruled over by the owners, often a petty bourgeoisie cabal of local builders, brewers and shopkeepers. Thus, the war years were to shape the future of football clubs and perhaps West Ham more than most.

The years of conflict altered and moulded new attitudes and motivations of the most perennial aspects of West Ham's human resources, in particular the character of support and the nature of the board.

As a child who came to the Hammers just a decade after the war, who played on bomb sites, and whose parents, grandparents and teachers were shaped by and in the war, I was something of the product of the wider social changes that encompassed football, not too differently from the young Bobby Moore. The players who formed his and my vision of Upton Park and the Hammers, those who played in the first games I was to attend at the Boleyn Ground, which included Moore, were products of the postwar organisation of football, itself something that had been recreated from 1939 to 1946.

While the First World War played a crucial part in changing West Ham United, altering the class dynamic of the administration of the game (following the 'football class war' within the war – see Belton 2006c), the Second World War saw the further development of the sport as a commercial endeavour. The conditions demanded that the final blow be delivered to the practically feudal system that pertained in the game, complete with despots and patriarchs, with delusions and pretensions of being the 'betters' of the playing staff. This 'class' had dominated the organisation of the sport at every level, although there were regional differences in this respect. Moore's formative years in football took place and were part of this transition.

The war created the room and need to modernise, not only the playing of the game, but also the running and administration of clubs. At board level, West Ham's Reg Pratt was perhaps the first to see the need for what was eventually to be a revolution of sorts. To his credit he probably transformed his own approach and attitudes in the first instance; not an easy task for the best of us. While Leonard 'Len' Crittenden Cearns (the third-generation chairman of West Ham, who ruled the roost for 31 years, starting in 1948) did as much as might be expected of him to back Pratt.

For all this, West Ham remained on something of a plateau, even going into decline after the 1960s. It was only in the Terry Brown era that the next change of gear happened. For the first time an actual supporter, someone who had stood on the terraces of Upton Park, took a controlling hand in the club, and it was Brown's administration that brought a final end to the dynastic character of the West Ham hierarchy.

Before the coming of war, one would have more chance of an audience with the Pope or a pint in the Boleyn with Xi Jinping (both Hammers supporters, of course) than a meet with Bill Cearns (Len's father) or his dad round at their drum on the fringes of the Royal Forest of Epping. Although 'of' and 'from' them in origin, Will had little to do with the 'great unwashed' who stood on the terraces at Upton Park. The wartime football culture, while not ending that sort of courtly regime, did much to undermine it by way of the shift in power from boardroom to players, which continues up to the current period; this revolution of sorts was a 'war baby'.

Football enlightenment

Where we are today started with the coming of war. The years of attrition and real and oppressive austerity; something more than extended paid leave and being asked to wear a flimsy fabric face covering (not a suffocating gas mask) as we were asked to do during the many months of the pandemic, the period when this book was written. In those bleak and fearful times of the 1940s, football brought moments of illumination and much-needed distraction. It did something of the same job as the empty but televised pandemic stadiums of Britain.

During the dark days of the Second World War, as the Nazis were raining down fire and destruction on the place that was the Moore family home, the area I was born and brought up in, West Ham brought a breath of optimism and a shaft of light. Football was more than just a game to the Moore boy from Barking; it was, as it was for wartime supporters everywhere, an enterprise of hope – or as Sir Geoff Hurst has put it 'a game of tomorrows'. Bobby's discovery and use of the game is a tale of light.

The postwar story of 'Young Bobby' is of a child growing and becoming a young man in a time when the Irons of east London came home from war to shape football, with its promise of the next goal, the next game, next week, when Saturday comes, into a future that offered an escape from grey reality and the psychological exhaustion that follows the alleviation of constant threat.

Escape is different from escapism (which is perhaps what football is today). We need to face or escape danger; perhaps facing it and escaping it come to much the same thing, but football, West Ham and Bobby Moore helped with that. For kids like me, amid the destruction and slow rebuilding of our dockland home, and the working people who were and are the fans, the game, the 'results', the personalities coming out of our own, like Bobby, mattered and they continue to matter. Hope happens by way of the match still being or to be played in the place we know as our home.

During the time of war, for the precious, illuminated length of a game, there was light and hope for the future. As the docklands of London emerged from the veil of war as I was growing up, young blonde Bobby personified that hope realised.

3

THE BOY ROBERT

Local memory in Waverley Gardens had it that Robert Moore started to kick a ball around when he was about four. A neighbour recalled him, about that age, knocking on the door asking for her son, who had a football. At that point Robert didn't, so if the lad wasn't up for playing Robert would borrow his ball. A little later it was rare for him to be seen without a football at his feet.

Early most Sundays, as a small lad, Robert could be found kicking a tennis ball against a wall while waiting patiently to get called into a game with local older kids, more than a few of whom would make the professional grade. He would watch games intensely from the touchline, hoping for a moment when there might be a place for him to fill. When he was finally summoned to the field, despite what he lacked physically, he'd hassle for every ball, being a regular pain in the arse for his opponents.

Robert, like most of us to some extent, was a reflection of his generation, and was very much a product of his time – an infant of the war years, growing up in the immediate post-conflict era, in a Britain that was pretty close to skint. This was a period where you had to make yourself or really not be very much at all. The idea of teenagers looking for or being provided with 'support' was something of a contradiction in terms: the strongest, healthiest most energetic group were understood to need to give support to the elderly and infirm members of society; to respect their elders more than look to be dependent on them. It would have been thought ridiculous if they or others suggested that they were in some way more 'vulnerable' or less well off than the aged or sick.

Now, in the UK, we live in a time where personalities in music, comedy and much of sport, for example at Olympic level, come from relatively privileged backgrounds. It's surprising how many of these people are ex-public school children and denizens of Oxbridge. After the war, these occupations and sectors were largely the province of working-class young people. For instance, the Goons, the Monty Pythons of their day, were all boys from relatively humble backgrounds, and none had the chance or expectation of university. However, unlike the 'footlight fodder' the Pythons were – who really tried to ape the likes of Sellers and Milligan (you didn't notice because they failed so badly) – the Goons were both original and funny.

Unlike the privileged posh grammar school kids, the likes Jimmy Carr and Jack Whitehall, most of the young people who made it to celebrity from the late 1940s had striven to get away from the factories or the offices of the living dead – read their biographies; few did not have to fight and draw on the stoicism that was necessary to survive in the not-so-well off 1950s. Moore was of their ilk.

A family thing

Even before he was born and certainly as Robert grew, he was his parents' reason for being. His mum was involved in everything her boy did. Doris, and when work allowed, Big Bob, were unfailingly, rain and shine, hot and cold, present, from his infancy on, supporting him as he turned out for the teams he played for. From every touchline they gave him encouragement (never calling him anything but 'Robert'). It was not unusual for the Moores to be accompanied by a group close relatives, supporting 'Doo's boy'. His aunt June was to recall how, at the age of ten, as a matter of routine, Robert would play in defence for the first half of a game, then join the attack in the second half. She said that even at that tender age he seemed to control games. But what stood out most was that he was never 'flash', being 'a genuinely caring young man.'

Later, Doris could sometimes be less keen to watch her son. During the 1966 World Cup she found herself unable to view much of the tournament. She went to two of the early games, but she had a superstitious streak and became anxious when her Robert was involved in the biggest matches. A worrier by nature, her apprehension worsened watching her son carry such a load of responsibility. When England progressed, she refused to watch the matches at all, although Big Bob went to all the games. During the semi-final with Portugal, Doris found herself jobs to around the house, while her nephew kept her apprised of the televised situation.

As the World Cup Final was being played, Doris spent the entire afternoon in the garden trying to remain preoccupied (it was a nice day weather-wise in London). She only came into the house when the game was done. She did watch the Queen presenting her Robert with the trophy, attempting not to cry. Doris gave little away of the pride she would have certainly been bursting with; she didn't celebrate. Her Salvationist culture clearly ran deep; pride is a sin, but this attitude was not untypical of working-class people in the east London area at that time. Yes, we are stereotypically thought to be 'swaggering', but you 'give it loud' when met with prejudice and discrimination – you get put down, you either go down, or big yourself up – that's a suite of understandable defence mechanisms kicking in.

When the World Cup Final and all its pomp and circumstance was done, Doris simply turned to her nephew and said, 'Let's go for a walk into town and do some shopping.' Doris coped by keeping herself occupied. As I often advise (preach to) students, 'Do something, anything, but whatever you do, don't do nothing.'

In the era and place I grew up in, between family, neighbours, friends, boasting or even accepting positive affirmation was akin to how profanity or blasphemy might be received in other communities or cultures. At one of the few school open days my dad attended, a teacher who took responsibility for the institution's very poor football team, told him I was a pretty good defender. I did once, admittedly during a measles epidemic, play for the City of London Boys – the side was short on the evening of the game and made a public appeal for anyone in the crowd with a modicum of skill and of the appropriate age to step forward. I was the only candidate. I kept the shirt until it fell to bits. My father, no slouch as a player for West Ham Boys, told the teacher, 'He ain't no Bobby Moore!' In truth he was right. Robert had an exceptional passion for sport; it was for him an outlet through which he expressed himself. I had other distractions; smashing windows, attempting to chase girls, being chased by coppers, fantasying about being chased by girls, experimenting with a disturbingly heterogeneous range of at best questionable substances, and a myriad of moneymaking enterprises, few of which were entirely legal, healthy, or advisable and often not terribly lucrative.

Doris liked her sport too. She had a keen interest in popular spectator events in east London during the years between the outbreak of peace and the release of Disney's *Lady and the Tramp*. Her favourites included greyhounds, speedway racing, and boxing (a sport that Bobby was always ready to talk about). She also had an enthusiasm for the theatre that was professional wrestling in the UK at that time – a sometime attraction at the Granada, East Ham.

Fat boy Bobby – sticks and stones and staying on your feet

Prior to his teenage years few would see a 'natural athlete' in Robert. His left foot was, in the main, for standing on; he more lumbered than ran, and he couldn't jump in an era where heading was a big percentage of any footballer's arsenal. Young Moore, for the most part, confined his contact with the ball to his right foot. He was really something of a conundrum. As a child other children nicknamed him 'Tubby', 'Tubs' or 'Fatso'. A memory that stuck with Moore was going into a cafe following a school match. There were some lads in there from another school. One of them asked his pals, 'Is that Bobby Moore, the fat one?' As a mature professional he looked back and remarked, 'Nicknames can hurt a boy.' The telling thing is, though, that these kids knew about Bobby Moore – he already had a reputation.

Now, in a time when anyone without 'mental health issues' is considered mentally unhealthy, it is a taken that we need to outlaw such disparagement, fearing for the psychological wellbeing of young people and the risk of 'trauma'. This is understandable – who wants to see anyone suffer, least of all our children? We are naturally fearful that they might be scared or even destroyed by insinuation and cruel remarks.

That said, one doesn't need to look too far to conclude how often subsequent insecurities, from experience of early derision, prove to be the stuff on which we build the determination and motivation to work hard at our hopes. One powerful desire might be to prove such nastiness wrong. We create for ourselves a carapace, crafted out of our supposed and actual deficiencies and they are what, not unusually, become the means of developing our most useful strengths. We don't really know the consequence of totally disallowing exposure to being, albeit crudely, told how other people see us, 'warts and all'. If I think I have a marvellous singing voice and am forever protected from the sad truth, that my supposed dulcet tones are less than ordinary, firstly I will be unlikely to find much motivation for improving my warbling and ultimately, I will continue to be prey to, and carry the consequences of, the worst of all deceits – self-delusion.

Despite his plumpness, Moore described his boyhood self as always being a 'footballer in fact', like it was somehow 'in' him. He read the biographies of the great Scottish players and how they learned the game on the tough, tenement-lined streets, supposedly unlike southern lads, having the game coached out of them. But all of Moore's early football was played in the streets of Barking, the local park, or on patches of waste ground, some of which were ankle deep in trash. It was the same for me and all my mates. Perhaps one of the handiest resources was the debris-strewn bomb sites, which were still around when I was a kid. I loved them – urban wastelands full of curiosity and possibility. The young Moore built the foundations of his play on the unforgiving surfaces these places offered, whereon 'on-the-ground' tackling was a hazardous business and simple survival instincts taught one to play football on your feet.

Noel Cantwell was to correctly point out that for most of his career, '[Bobby] was never dropped from the team and he never sustained any injuries and I don't think he ever broke anything. What's more, his shorts were never dirty because rarely did Bobby Moore have to make emergency tackles. He was always standing on his feet.

'The theory that it might have been from his days playing in the streets, when you would cut yourself if you dived in, could be correct because he was always standing on his feet. He would never be falling all over the place because his tackling would be timed so well.'

Well, in football as in life – if you know that if you fall you're going to fall in the shit, you better learn to stay on your feet, but keeping upright means developing awareness, the bedrock of intelligence.

During his childhood, Robert, almost certainly at first, quite unconsciously, started to cultivate a capacity to read and foresee the course and patterns of play. This kind of foresight and insight is at first developed via observation of 'actual' situations and events. That's not quite the same at seeing something recorded or televised. Noises, smells, multidimensional perspectives and even the use of the tactile senses help in the process. Consequently, Robert's anticipation and sense of positioning, allied to with inborn strength, a power to remain firm in action, and an endurance to pump skill to gird his talents, were to give him the makings of not only a remarkably rounded and accomplished defender, but also a player who alone could transform resistance into offence in one gliding movement.

Moore's lasting strength was his towering, special intelligence and an ability to see the direction of play as it was happening and in emergence, although he didn't inherit some of the physical and biological traits one might want if one was going to build a top footballer, he did have, seemingly, some genetic predispositions that better 'muscle-blessed grunts' usually lacked. This, and the situation and family he was born into, were the strengths he built on.

Adaptation, endurance and perseverance

Moore would flower into a sportsperson of magnificent ability from a foundation laid even before the street games; the kick-arounds with his father and uncle on Greatfields Park, not far from his boyhood home provided the first stimulation and germination of his talents. He was to recall these first years as the bedrock of his feeling for the game,

'We had a little park nearby, but we used to come home from school, dump the books, get a ball and go out in the road and start and play football or walk over the park to play.'

Robert's first school, Westbury Road Junior, was situated on Ripple Road, Barking. It was opened in 1904 and reorganised into infant, junior boys' and junior girls' schools in 1931. The institution was later to become Ripple Road Primary. Westbury Junior is where Robert first started to formally develop the essentially 'informally' built skills he had picked up from casual, impromptu and improvised park/street kick-arounds. The best of our humanity uses what resources we find around us – we are, at our finest, and closer to the beings we are, in the process of adaptation. As a species it's what we do. The more you get what you think you want on a plate, the less it is what you actually want – what we want is established in the course of adaptation.

Although Robert's basic skillset was not in those initial years brilliant, the foundational 'sense' had been put in place. Thus, through determination and hard work enhancing this budding awareness, he was able to break into playing in his school side at inside-right. Around the age of nine he was also taking part in Saturday morning football, turning out for South Park Boys, who were part of the more than respectable Ilford League.

If it doesn't kill you

Robert's endurance and perseverance led to him lift his first silverware. Having been selected to play for the Barking Primary Schools team, he won the London-wide under-11s Crisp Shield; his side was to take the trophy two years running. In his second year he was made captain and found he enjoyed the responsibility. Later in life Robert was to speculate that being captain might have compensated for being called 'Fatso'. So, one could venture that this harsh appellation was at least part of the motivation to achieve and be recognised as a leader; without it, maybe, no captaincy, and no Bobby Moore as we came to know him.

Famed psychiatrist and psychoanalyst Carl Jung reckoned that people will do anything, no matter how absurd, in order to avoid facing their own souls and that one does not become enlightened by imagining 'figures of light', but by making 'the darkness conscious'. Despair, frustration, unhappiness, worry, distress and boredom are feelings that all of us, at one time or another, and perhaps often, encounter in our lives. These moods and inclinations are common to the human experience. We all have highs and lows in our personal journeys. They maybe relate to, or be about jobs, family, relationships or the state of the world around us. But for most people, most of the time, perhaps these 'natural' clouds will usually dissipate over time and/or be accommodated in our experience and learning about ourselves and our lives. Mostly we'll 'get by with a little help from our friends'.

Of course, deep despair will sometimes haunt some people, and they may find their moods and feeling limiting their lives, but this is the case in relatively few situations. For most of us, learning to cope, calling on or discovering our own resources, is valuable; it is how we learn to live and control our lives, giving us the means to find out our own strengths and resilience. This can build not only self-confidence, but motivate the 'life treasure' that is hope.

For sure, we can relate the feelings we have as manifestations of, for example, 'poor mental health' (what in other times and places might be called 'madness' or 'insanity') and be assigned to a 'practitioner', and so exposed to various 'techniques' to rid us of what we might be persuaded is a 'malady' to be 'cured' or 'fixed'; we can be 'normalised according to some standard not of our making. The pain or frustration can be (so we are told) short-circuited or repressed, although the latter might be more eroding of the soul than the free expression of unhappiness – the path to anything we might get to know as happiness.

However, I do doubt if the categorisation as, or designation to 'madness' (or any euphemism for the same) and 'intervention' en masse, does less good and more harm.

Learning to walk is difficult. It's frustrating and it hurts. But a baby, with no help at all, will persistently struggle to make herself (and so learn to) walk – pain and failure will not stop her. She will marshal her inner resources, she will strengthen her will; she WILL rise, she WILL stand, she will, unaided and unfettered, WALK!

Of course, adult appreciation and applause of each step will likely be assuring and perhaps motivating – we all like (to give and get) a bit of 'positive affirmation', a pat on the back for our achievements, the overcoming of adversity. We deserve to celebrate life's little victories. So, we are not saying to toddlers, 'Yer on yer own, kid.'

But imagine if we prevented that pain, if we 'intervened' in that frustrating struggle, say with the help of braces or chemical strictures/stimulants. What if we saw the striving as a drive that was 'dangerous', so obviously not 'healthy' (learning to walk isn't 'safe').

Again, a small minority of infants do need more or less help in walking, because of birth or genetic defects and conditions, but certainly, applying such 'treatment' to the majority or even a sizeable minority, would have damaging social, mental and physical consequences. We really do need our pain, as much as we might our joy.

Something different about the kid

The Crisp Shield looked about as big as the dimpled Robert in the local newspaper photo of him holding it. He was becoming a 'face'; even at this early stage Moore's name was well-known in London junior football. Those involved began to see something different about him. He wasn't tall for his age, and you would probably kindly call his build 'stocky', although, in the current era of childhood obesity, his build would have looked distinctly average. As such, his stature didn't have much similarity to the physique he would build in his adulthood. He had not acquired more than a hint of the elegance he was to demonstrate on the football field later on.

South Park Boys was run by Len Lilley, with a mate who lived in the same street in Dagenham, Bonham Road. This was the street where Ken Brown and Dickie Walker lived, both West Ham stalwarts. Spurs star Les Allen and brother Dennis, who played for Charlton, also hailed from Bonham Road, as did Terry Venables, who lived opposite the Allen family.

Robert played at centre-half in the old-fashioned sense. Len was to recollect that Robert's team-mates saw him as 'quiet' and 'keeping himself to himself'. Despite his physical disadvantages in his pre-teenage years, Len was to confirm that Robert was recognised as good player. Much as was the case throughout his career, Robert ran with a straight, stiff back, head up. On the floor and in terms of ball control, including his passing ability, he seemed better at what was asked of him than his young team-mates.

Len used to have the kids round to his house to play snooker (the half- and quarter-sized tables were quite popular – it was on such a home-based table that I learned the game) and there he'd choose the XI for the Saturday game. This might be thought of as the primal 'academy' which would, a decade on at the Boleyn Ground, create much of what we know of the modern English game.

The likes of fabled Hammers scout Reg Revins and others have told me that Len had a sharp sense of, maybe an instinct about, what youngsters were good at. He had the foresight to give them the time and space to express and so develop those skills. This is something I took into my own practice as a coach. What I found is that as young people become better at what they are good at, other areas of capacity start to flower; they seem to have more scope and opportunity, perhaps confidence, to extend their capacities. This seems logical; a platform or a foundation is needed for anything we might want to grow or build.

South Park played a distinctly 'open' game, with an emphasis on attacking football and mobility. This made the team a fun and attractive option for kids. Promoting a dynamic approach. Len made drills enjoyable, pressing the point that in defence no one should be standing still, and that defending needs to be taken as a platform for a side's next attack, so everyone was moving all of the time. This demanded players to be both observant and thoughtful, which kept every player engaged in the game. If you know anything about chess, South Park's play might have reminded you of the Evans Gambit[3]. Not quite the 'total football' of the great Dutch sides of the 1970s, but maybe an embryonic incarnation of the same. The idea however was to allow kids to develop rather than create according to adult ambition, the sin of so much youth football.

Casting his mind back to the young Moore coming into his side, Len remarked that like most very young kids, at first, Robert used to follow the ball like iron filings might be drawn to a magnet, constantly diving after it – seemingly on the ground most of the time. But he was ultimately to lose that habit. Even in the roughest and dirtiest of situations, after being ruthlessly downed in the mud, he

---

3   The Evans Gambit is used to keep the black king from castling (defending itself and setting up a potential line of attack) and overwhelm black with very active pieces in the centre

would hardly say a word. He just got up and got on with the match, apparently engrossed for every second of the game.

It was while playing for South Park that Robert found himself up against Jimmy Greaves for the first time. Jim was also playing in the Ilford League, as midfielder for Huntsman Sports, out of Hainault, Essex. The team was based in the same street where the Greaves family had moved to from Dagenham. A bit like Moore, and most kids at his age at that point, Greaves wasn't too fond of passing. Of course, Jim become adept at knowing when to let go of the ball and where to be to pick it up, the very essence of his genius was that 'sense'.

It has to be remembered that during the early 1950s Britain was in postwar recovery mode, with rationing just starting to ease off. Most of the country's cities still bore the physical, emotional and spiritual impact of war. Rugby in east London was unheard of until I was in my mid-teens, hardly anyone knew much about golf, while athletics was more punishment than anything else. In winter it was football and summer it was cricket, even if only using a dustbin as a wicket. That was pretty much what 'sport' was. Yes, there was table tennis if you could stand the suffocating, brown and dirty beige atmosphere of youth clubs, but that was a bit like snooker; 'ping-pong' was considered by most young people as closer to a board game than a sport.

The pull of alternative sports was almost non-existent. Football in east London was king; its only rival was boxing, but the noble art wasn't as accessible and a good deal more painful (certainly for the likes of me!).

Robert was clever and liked winning, be it games or tackles. He had a knack of getting the ball and passing it effectively. South Park had a couple of teams; he played a year in advance of his age, but would also turn out for the younger side as captain for cup ties.

With kids his own age Robert was dominant, winning everything. Moore left South Park after three years, focusing on his school side and representing Leyton Schools. But the Ilford League had done its bit and South Park had been the bedrock of greatness

Only child

Like Moore, his team-mate at West Ham and with England, Johnny Byrne, was an only child. He once told me,

'Bob and me, we pretty much thought of each other as the brothers we never had. Neither of us put it in those words, you wouldn't, but while we looked completely different personalities, we had a lot in common.

'Playing football for a decent club and internationally, a lot of people want to be your mate. You fall for that a bit when you're a kid. I mean, it's great ain't it?

But it doesn't take too long to see most of these people are hangers on … they just want to stand in the light with someone. A lot of people aren't too patient with that, but I never really saw Bobby angry. He'd rather walk away than have a row. That's not saying he couldn't get a bit annoyed now and then, but not losing it ever … He could read people and he was never anything but decent with everyone, pretty much whatever … there was a thoughtfulness and a kindness in that.'

Traditionally, in the UK and worldwide, only children have been comparatively uncommon. But around the time Bobby Moore was born, birth rates and average family sizes got smaller over a short period of time. Increasing costs of raising children, personal preference, family planning, physical/fertility health issues, time constraints, women working outside the home, fears over pregnancy, and more women having their first child later in life were among the reasons for this. At the time Bobby was born, in the British context, the women of his mum's age were having fewer children than would be the case a couple of decades or so later.

There have been indications that only children can sometimes be more likely to develop precocious interests (perhaps a consequence of spending more time with adults) and to feel lonely. It has been thought that they can compensate for the aloneness by developing a stronger relationship with themselves or creating more active life of the imagination than kids with siblings, 'world building'. You might understand this as a sort of foresight.

John Lyall, after he had left football, was to tell me,

'Bobby had that rare thing, you hardly come across it in any situation, of being able to see, or understand what is going to happen in the next moment. How things would be as they are taking shape. You could almost hear the cogs turning when he had the ball, but no one can imitate that, it sort of grows into you. I've heard it called "awareness" but it's more than that. It's a kind of intelligent imagination.

'He always seemed a bit cautious, thinking before he spoke. I don't think he did much what wasn't considered. But that didn't make him hesitant. He didn't think about the pass as he picked the ball up, or at least that was the impression. He'd been thinking about that pass well before he got the ball. I think that was pretty much the same in everything for him. I did pick up on a bit of that sort of thing myself in management. It's not a bad habit.'

You can perhaps see that a practiced imagination, combined with a deep consideration of experience, would be basic to the qualities Lyall was talking about.

In our society, only children can experience stereotyping, being seen generally as 'spoilt' or 'selfish', 'aggressive', 'bossy', 'lonely', 'stand-offish', 'aloof'. In China these collective traits have been called the 'Little Emperor Syndrome': in short, a maladjustment. At one time, the likes of the American psychologist G. Stanley Hall said being an only child was 'a disease in itself'.

While only children might logically have more access to attention and resources that might advance their development, as a group it is not altogether clear that they are generally overindulged or come out of childhood too differently to those with siblings.

Some research has suggested younger only children can have issues developing interpersonal skills, although the disparity seems to disappear later in childhood. Some studies have shown only children to be brighter, more autonomous, better behaved, and overall, more mature than those with siblings.

Cinema, soap operas, theatre, literature all have a tendency to give the only child an uncooperative persona, particularly in traditional domestic situations. The lack of competitors for the attention of adults is portrayed as causing them to develop a sense of entitlement. Alongside pop-psychology and urban myth this can negatively impact their understanding of relationships with others. Added to this, there is a popular belief that only children experience more pressure by way of parental expectations, and that commonly, only children are perfectionists.

Bobby's parents seemed mostly focused on their boy growing up as a polite, clean and ordered person. From a distance that feels more like socialisation than pressure. Things fall out of that maybe, respect for oneself and others, an outlook on life that self-organisation, discipline even, might be the foundation one's needs to get things right as one moves into the world.

This focus on the self as an individual presenting in the world as an autonomous person perhaps gives the only child less of a determination to change others and more of an inclination to adapt to environments and circumstances; building a view that in this world, much of what you do yourself dictates the nature of your experience. This attitude can be understood to mirror the solid notion of the respectable working class, 'You only get what you work for.'

At one time the 'only child syndrome' was widely accepted in psychology. This notion (that some continue to adhere to) had it that only children have less in the way of social skills, or developed them more slowly than other children. At the same time, they were thought to maintain some antisocial dispositions from childhood. Moore could not be said to be an introvert in any severe sense. He was shy though, and humility was second nature to him. But if he had been antisocial, it would have been hard, perhaps impossible for him to excel at a team game. However, later analysis has indicated that peer relationships might compensate for any lack sibling relationships; a team of course is a group of peers.

Related to the latter, currently in the field of child development, there is a strong argument that has it that only children excel in the building of capacities to interact with others relative to those with siblings.

Another observation about only children is they seem to have a propensity to mature quicker. When Bobby moved to secondary school he felt, at first, socially isolated. That really was the reality of his situation for a while, but he was able to find a path through that, principally via football. That shows him to have had considerable social, perhaps survival skills of sorts, as well as maturity one might more expect of someone older than 11 years. Then as later, he adapted, pulling on his own resources and those he would pick up (being coached, watching and reading about football, it's clubs, players, international dimensions and so on).

This autonomy is a sign of budding adulthood. However, the greatest homily to Moore's ability to make relationships with others was the respect he commanded from his team-mates and the awe he inspired in his opponents. This might not rate as rabid sociability, but it demonstrates social intelligence. It was, perhaps above all, these earned responses to his self-made qualities that demonstrate Bobby's social skills. This marks up something deeper and more profound than the ability ingratiate oneself via smalltalk or negotiating a position by way of guile and/or sycophancy, attributes often mistakenly called social confidence – if anything such behaviour betrays the opposite, indicating the archetypal self-doubt of puberty.

A 1987 study found only children are, on average, likely to attain higher levels of achievement and the motivation to achieve. This was put down to only children likely getting a better level of parental resources, expectations, and scrutiny, opening them to more rewards, and more of a possibility of punishment/disapproval for failure. Another analysis revealed that only children (along with children with just one sibling, and first-borns) scored higher in tests of verbal ability than later-borns and children with multiple siblings.

Other slightly earlier research, looking at relative intelligence, adaptability, and relationships with peers and parents, found that only children bettered others in each category apart from children who were in similar situations to them, for instance first-borns. Another finding indicated that parent-child relationships were positively stronger relative to children with siblings.

On the other hand, it has been argued that only children, during their lifetime often become more aware of their only child status and are very much affected by society's stereotype of the only child, whether or not the stereotype is true or false. This view has it that growing up in a mainly 'sibling society' impacts only children and that having no sibling relationships can have an important effect on the how they see themselves and others and how they interact in the world.

The 'Five Factor Model' (or 'the big five personality traits') has it that firstborns and only children are more conscientious, more socially dominant, less agreeable, and less open to new ideas compared to later-borns.

Today, the trend in the UK is for smaller families. This is becoming the norm and generally speaking across all developmental outcomes, only children seem indistinguishable from first-borns and people from small families, but all of these family make-ups do better than children from large families.

Some recent research findings suggest only children often feel a slight awkwardness with children of their own age. This, in part, is probably because in the case of only children these encounters usually happen in a supervised setting – nursery, or school, for instance. They start in the less-than-easy formal settings that are often subject to regulation. So, the only child doesn't get the same opportunities to read other children, thus their growth in this respect might be a little slower, but the likes of the children of family friends and cousins can compensate.

However, the apparent 'two sides to the story' continues. A survey of Spanish teenagers found only children experienced higher rates of peer victimisation, while a more recent study in China concluded that only children were more flexible in their thinking, and therefore more creative.

In a lot of cases, it is probable that the only child's domestic world can be predominately populated by adults, which makes the home experience usually relatively organised and comparatively tranquil. This might mean that the only child may not be accustomed to more disorganised or chaotic situations, and work hard to organise and control situations in later life. You might see something of this in Moore's behaviour and habits.

I would argue, that if there was the 'typical' only child of the mid-20th century then Bobby Moore was it – although I'm disinclined to think that anyone is 'typical'. This said, much of who and what Bobby was, the 'why' and the 'how' of the way he turned out, had much to do with his childhood situation and the relationships these circumstances, to a certain extent, dictated. Hence, given the task of this book, these need to be considered.

The same is true of all of us of course, although I shy away from crass and crude Freudian determinism. The adult is more than the stuff of the child. Flawless predictability in terms of child and human development is more a fantasy than a fact. That said, it would be a fool who dismissed any period of life as failing to have an impact on at least the perception of the whole of a life lived.

So, I wouldn't go so far as to say if you were looking for another Bobby Moore that you would do well to focus your search on only children, because so many other factors were involved in his 'making'. However, this factor of our common experience (you were either an only child or you weren't) indicates perhaps quite a lot about the manner in which Bobby responded to and operated in the world. The same analysis will equally apply to me and, of course, you.

The position of the only child has changed a lot since Bobby's childhood. As more recent research has indicated, there are often much more opportunities for compensation; what might have been the situation of the only child in the 1940s will not totally or necessarily pertain to kids in the same position today. Nevertheless, many 'traditional' ideas about the character of only children ring true in Moore's case. As a child he started out as something less than ordinary in any physical pursuit, but he applied himself. Another West Ham youth international, the first black player to wear his country's colours in football, John Charles, told me that after the marathon drinking sessions that typified part of West Ham's and wider football booze culture during the 1960s, the next day Moore, 'Was out sweating it out, while everyone else was nursing their big heads. He was what you call determined … He would often be training on his own, kicking balls at a bucket 50, 60 yards away, never failing to hit it, even putting the ball in it. He was all "practice makes perfect" and when everyone else was fed up, he was still at it!'

Bobby did things on his own, not always, but maybe more often than his peers in football of his day. He did things alone because he could.

Transition to peace

All in all, the war years had been a relatively successful time for West Ham. Perhaps in the leagues they contested, Arsenal and Tottenham fans might argue that those sides came out better in terms of results, but they did not innovate and modernise to the extent that the Hammers did. Hence, within two decades Upton Park had caught up with White Hart Lane and was on Highbury's tail. That the club lost ground after that is another story, part of which I have told elsewhere (see Belton 2013a, 2013b).

West Ham held the English wartime record for the longest unbeaten run on the road: nine games between 16 September and 11 November 1944. In Great Britain only the mighty Glasgow Rangers with ten had done better.

The biggest wartime crowd had been 139,468 at Hampden Park to watch Scotland v England on 13 April 1946. The 1945/46 season had been a term of transition for football, although the Football League decided to stick with the regional format for the last time. The 'normal' game, the kind interrupted by Hitler in 1939, would pick up the pieces on 31 August 1946. It already seemed an awfully long time since spectators had first been told what to do 'in the event of an air raid'.

The years from 1939 to 1945 set the scene for the greatest period in the history of the Hammers; the 'golden' age of Upton Park. With the move to the London Stadium, it's pretty safe to say – the wonders of David Moyes notwithstanding – that the era, which had started with the development of Bobby Moore, the coming (and going) of Ted Fenton, the push of Malcolm Allison and the executive maturing of Reg Pratt, and concluded with the best days of John Lyall, would be the greatest the Boleyn Ground had ever known.

As suggested by the idea of transition, the football authorities did not go directly back to the way of things prior to the war. The season of 1945/46 was organised to give clubs a chance to adapt and normalise their affairs.

Many players remained in the services, and this would be the case long after hostilities ended, particularly for those who were stationed in the Far East. Although there were few modifications, the organisation of the season was obliged to adapt. The First and Second Divisions had been put in mothballs after the first few games of the 'normal' 1939/40 season. The clubs that had started that term were grouped together and divided into north and south competitions at a point approximately between Stoke and Derby. Newport County were the only club in the League South that West Ham had never met in the Football League or Southern League. The Hammers' longest journeys would be Plymouth in the south, Swansea to the west and Nottingham and Derby to the north.

The Iron's first game of the League South campaign took them to St Andrew's, where a crowd of 30,000 saw a penalty from the boot of Charlie Bicknell beat Birmingham City, who had no retort. This was followed by four consecutive Boleyn Ground matches, resulting in just the one win.

The Hammers were more roofless than ruthless as Upton Park continued to bear the scars of a V1 attack; West Ham's first home game against Arsenal was referred to in the programme as 'the Roofless v. the Homeless' as Highbury had been requisitioned by the army at the start of the war. The will and the money were in place to put Upton Park back together, but this wasn't possible because of a shortage of skilled labour and the necessary materials.

In November 1945 a meeting of players from 53 clubs voted in favour of a strike; it took a lot of hard bargaining before the Football League agreed to compromise on the pre-war maximum of £8 a week – change was on its way. As with many workers, the conflict had given footballers a clearer picture of the worth of their services, the war conditions having facilitated a much wider conversation between players than had been the case previously.

The rebirth of the formal organisation of international football was heralded by the FA's agreement with secretary Stanley Rous that England should have a team manager. Walter Winterbottom was later to be given the job. Walter wasn't going to be allowed a totally free hand though – there was still something of the Olympic 'Chef de Mission' to the role. The FA reformed its pre-war Selection Committee, and its new members insisted on touring the country and voting for the professionals who, in their opinion, most accorded to their amateur standards; it was from among these individuals that the England team would be selected. The old guard seemed to have some fight left in it.

In May 1946 West Ham finished seventh in League South, trailing champions Birmingham by ten points. But the Irons bettered Fulham, Spurs, Chelsea, Arsenal and Millwall – these clubs trailed behind in that order.

At the Football League's annual meeting on 1 June, it was decided that the normal programme would start in 1946/47 under a new wage structure: players would receive £10 a week in the winter and £7 10s in the summer (before the war this had been £8 and £6 respectively). Player benefits were upped from £650 to £750. Things had never been better.

4

DREAMS OF ENGLAND

From the age of about ten, winter Saturdays would see Robert on his bike making for the Woolwich ferry and thence to The Valley, home of Charlton Athletic. Some of the local boys his age were more inclined to get the bus to Upton Park, and he occasionally went with them, especially the floodlit games, one of which saw the Irons thumped 6-0 by Milan.

South of the Thames offered a vista on some of the best practitioners of football on earth. The Valley was one of the stages for the men who would become Moore's first footballing role models, in particular West Brom's thoughtful and composed Ray Barlow and Duncan Edwards of Manchester United, a beefy midfielder with a striking intelligence in terms of positioning and passing. For Moore, Edwards was, 'The Rock of Gibraltar at the back, dynamic coming forward. There will never be another player like him.'

Moore was to tell how, in his formative years, the England team bristled with legends. The side included the likes of Stanley Matthews, but there was no one in the team young Robert idolised like Barlow and Edwards. He also rated Ronnie Allen (another WBA man), Johnny Nicol (during his years at Chelsea), and Frank Dudley (Leeds and Southampton). But for him Barlow's poise and cogent approach to the game made him, 'A great left-half. So calm, played it so easy, just knocked it about. Don't talk to me about Wright and Matthews. How often did Ray Barlow play for England?' Moore saw Barlow's single cap, against Northern Ireland in 1955, as 'diabolical' and typifying of the staleness of the selection system.

While Matthews was past his best when he faced Moore as a Blackpool player in September 1960, Bobby blotted him out completely.

Robert would go to exceptional lengths to develop his football insight, such as going so far as to skip school to study Edwards on a day when he scored twice at White Hart Lane; Doris would have done her nut!

England calls

Big Bob was an adherent of his local side, Barking, and the team's supporters' association. In 1934/35 the Blues won the Athenian League title. Following the Second World War, they were victorious in the 1945/46 Essex Senior Cup.

Barking was a tidy enough team that commanded a not unimpressive following locally. It was in 1952 that Barking switched to the Isthmian League.

Canning Town-born Jack Leslie, after playing for Barking Boys joined Barking (then known as Barking Town) in 1919. Jack represented Essex and during his time with Barking helped the club win Essex Senior Cup in 1919/20 and, in 1920/21 the London League and the London Senior Cup.

Leslie moved to Plymouth Argyle in 1921 and it was in October 1925 that the then Argyle manager Bob Jack told the player that he'd been selected to play for England. However, when the squad was announced his name was not included, apparently because officials from the Football Association had realised he was black. Jack told a 1978 interview with the *Daily Mail*,

'Everybody in the club knew about it. The town was full of it. All them days ago it was quite a thing for a little club like Plymouth to have a man called up for England. I was proud – but then I was proud just to be a paid footballer … They must have forgotten I was a coloured boy.'

Leslie returned to Barking as trainer in 1938, and during the 1960s he joined the boot room at Upton Park, remaining with club until his retirement in November 1982. In 1980 Leslie had told me he had followed Bobby's career from his boyhood days and remembered Bobby's dad being a regular at Barking's games, often with his little boy and wife. Leslie also remembered Big Bob being active with the supporters' association. Bobby would often ask Leslie about his opinion of games and players. Leslie recalled, 'Bobby hardly ever talked about himself. He wanted to know how others thought about and saw things. He'd nod, as if thinking about what you said, and then ask another question. He was a quiet person but always a gentleman.

'Bobby always wanted to play for England. After Ramsey got in that was really his team. I said to him once that I hadn't seen him turn right round when he played. He seemed not to think about turning his back on someone who was trying to get the ball off him, now and then trying a full turn. You can do that. It can confuse the other chap. Not spinning, but turning your whole body. He started to work on that and got quite good at it. Bobby always listened. That's how he got good.'

The seed of the 'dream of England' was planted early in Robert. He had been first taken to games while still a baby, in Doris's arms. Later, home and away, Big Bob would take his little boy to a range of matches. However, the pair were among the privileged 99,000 to be at Wembley, a record crowd for an England game at the stadium at that time, to watch the 9 May 1951 encounter between England and Argentina.

Big Bob had got the Wembley tickets in the hope that his son might witness the talents of the peerless Stanley Matthews, but the Blackpool virtuoso, who had originally been chosen to play at outside-right, had sustained a bruised foot. Tom Finney swapped sides and Vic Metcalfe was called on to replace Matthews. Bill Nicholson was also sidelined having picked up a leg injury playing for Spurs in a friendly against FC Austria.

The 1951 international had been part of a Festival of Soccer, which had been organised by the FA as part of the celebrations of the Festival of Britain. It took place throughout May 1951. The associations of Scotland, Ireland and Wales were asked to support the plan.

The Wembley match programme greeted the South Americans in English and Spanish,

The Football Association extends on behalf of all British sportsmen a warm welcome to our visitors from Argentina – to the players, the officials, and to the number of enthusiasts who have made the long journey from Argentina to be present on this historic occasion in Association Football.

'The Argentina footballers come with the reputation of being among the greatest Soccer artistes in the world, and we look forward to a most entertaining afternoon.

'It is the sincere hope of all British sportsmen that our visitors will carry back to Argentina pleasant memories of this afternoon's match, and that they will visit this country again in the near future.'

John Graydon, author of the popular *Soccer Enquire Within*, wrote an article titled 'Welcome Argentina!'.

'WEMBLEY STADIUM! The name of Britain's premier football stadium is treated with respect – aye, and awe – in every country where association football is played. All over Europe, and in South America, I have heard many of the world's greatest footballers express an ambition to appear upon Wembley's soft and perfect Cumberland turf in a full international match.

'This afternoon the soccer elite of Argentina, all of them achieving a personal ambition in facing England, will also set up a rather unusual record. They are the first footballers from abroad to play in a full international match at Wembley.

'During the past year we have heard a good deal about South American football, the World Cup finals, held in Brazil, focusing the eyes of soccerdom upon this part of the world.

'When British colonists first played football in Latin America, and later qualified coaches went to South America to pass on their knowledge, I doubt if they visualised what a grip the game would eventually have upon the sports-loving citizens of the various republics. Today, association football is the major sport of South America, and in Argentina, Uruguay, Chile and Brazil, to mention but four of these countries, the aim of everyone is not just to play soccer, but play the game well.

'Last June and July, when I accompanied the English team to Brazil, I often found myself intrigued in watching youngsters either on Copacabana beach, or in a park, performing tricks with a football few top-class players in Britain can equal: and all the time was conscious of the burning ambition of every youngster to become a "maestro".

'In the World Cup Final, Uruguay, it will be recalled, defeated the much-fancied Brazilian team, but Argentina did not compete in the competition and many sound South American judges were of the opinion they would have won the Jules Rimet Trophy.

'At home in Britain, I had heard many colourful stories of South American football and the excitement which goes with it but found just the opposite to what I had been led to expect. On the field of play the sportsmanship was splendid: the crowds although perhaps a little more excitable than we expect in England – they release fireworks when our fans prefer rattles – were most orderly: the standard of football was of the calibre which would have delighted even the sternest coach and purist of the old school'.

'South Americans concentrate upon the classical. Many of their combined moves rank among my greatest football memories. There was a sleekness about everything they attempted which invariably impressed.

'Teamwork was all the time put before individual brilliance, and in my view the nearest approach in Britain to the soccer we saw served up by South American teams is that provided for us by Tottenham Hotspur, the champions of the Football League. During the past few years, the Argentina FA has gained in power and prestige: in an effort to still further raise the standard of refereeing have engaged officials from Britain, and reports suggest their presence has had the desired effect.

'The First Division of the Argentine Football League consists of 17 clubs, while the Second Division is formed of 18 teams, the system of promotion and relegation being worked on our lines. When one remembers that the world record soccer attendance of 200,000 was set up in South America, during the World Cup finals in Rio de Janeiro, it is not surprising to discover that in Argentine they have a large number of beautifully constructed grounds.

'Most of them are equipped with floodlight equipment. Two of the biggest, and most luxurious, belong to the Racing Club, which accommodated 118,000 spectators with ease, and River Plate FC, who have had attendances of 95,000.

With soccer enthusiasm so great in Argentina, clubs find no difficulty in filling their stadiums.

'With these facts placed before you it will be appreciated that our friends from South America will this afternoon prove most worthy opponents.

'In England we are very proud of our record of never having been beaten in front of our own folk by a foreign team. We can depend upon Billy Wright and his colleagues putting everything they possess into preserving this magnificent record. Win, lose or draw, however, I am certain everyone will enjoy watching the Argentinians to whom we all say "welcome" on this historic occasion which marks the forerunner, we hope, of many England-Argentina matches.'

The highly respected journalist and author and sports editor of the *Empire News*, Harold Mayes, also chipped in, looking forward to the game, '

Form reversals in Rio de Janeiro and Belo Horizonte in last year's World Cup series staggered the football-minded public, so used to the unexpected happening, probably more than anything else in soccer history. For one reason – because England, the teachers and the master, were on the receiving end.

'What change had taken place that the representatives of the old world should have to bow the knee to those of the new world? Well, England's temporary eclipse was largely due to the fact that the timing of the series was such that we had to face it with a team in the transitional stage – a team which sought to capture the mantle of the great wartime side in which such as Tommy Lawton, Raich Carter, Frank Swift, Joe Mercer and Stanley Matthews sparkled. They did not succeed.

'That, however, was but one of the reasons for failure. As we have found in so many sports, overseas performers are good pupils, because they apply themselves diligently to every game they tackle, and having acquired the knowledge, they employ every means to turn it to account in competitive play.

'The average English follower of the game was shocked at England's decline, and more than mildly surprised at the emergence of Uruguay as world soccer champions. They began to wonder what type of football was played by teams from the South American countries that they should be able to stand so far above our own.

'Today they have the opportunity of making the comparison. Not Uruguay, but Argentina who did not compete in the Rio series, provide the opposition in the first of the Festival of Britain Internationals.

'Do not regard the test as any less severe because of Argentina's non-participation in the World Cup. Representatives of the visiting country have learned the rudiments of the game very thoroughly, and play at a speed which prompted one knowledgeable England soccer authority to refer to them as the "racehorses of world football".

'If we are inclined to be over-critical of our own teams, it is only because of a desire to see them on the pedestal of unchallenged supremacy, and the England representatives charged with the task of winning back prestige today are certainly fully conscious of the responsibility which they have to carry.

'Should they be beaten, the victory would be acclaimed everywhere outside Britain as a major triumph in the sporting struggle between the old world and the new. Should they win, the men who do it will not receive from so many quarters the congratulations which will really be due to them. It will, in fact, be regarded as "just one of those things".

'That would be grossly unfair, for there is no doubt at all about the strength of the opposition. If England triumph today, regardless of any other circumstance, we shall rightly be able to say that the old country's soccer is on the way back.

'There is one other important factor which must be considered outside the battle between old and new. As yet, no England team has ever been defeated on home soil by a team from outside the British Isles.

'Twice in recent history overseas invaders have come close to taking away this cherished record. Italy did everything except win at Tottenham 18 months ago, when only an inspired exhibition of goalkeeping by Wolverhampton Wanderers' Bert Williams kept them at bay long enough for the forwards to earn a late victory.

'Then, last November, two goals by Bolton Wanderers' Nat Lofthouse earned a draw against Yugoslavia. Can today's team keep that unbeaten certificate intact?

'All of us hope so. The responsibility is a heavy one, the task indeed is not light. Good luck to them.'

The skipper that day was Billy Wright. Although it is probably football sacrilege to say as much, Moore grew to be no great fan – like myself, he saw little exceptional merit in the podgy Salopian. With the hint of 'man boobs' during the latter part of his career, he reminded me more of Ted Molt or Harry Corbett (you've got to be a certain age for those names to mean anything) than, say, Augusto da Costa or Carlo Annovazzi. But let's not go into that. The match was graced by a bevy of immortals of the postwar game, the likes of Stan Mortensen and Jackie Milburn. Not such a big name was playing at right-back that day: the intelligent, skilful, but also tough, uncompromising and physical Tottenham defender, Alf Ramsey.

Unlike today, the age of the internet and a world shrunken by access to information, most of the people who rocked up to Wembley, including Big Bob and Robert, would have known little or nothing of football beyond the shores of Britain. South America was in every sense still the 'new world' and another world when it came to 'soccer'. An article by W. Anderson was included in the programme and looked to explain some of the cultural features of the *Argentinos* game, 'To the English soccer fan little or nothing is known about the superb quality of Argentinian football. 'Due to some differences with the Brazilian FA, Argentina did not send her representative team for the World Cup at Rio de Janeiro last year.

'Thus, perhaps, they missed winning the championship, which went to their neighbours, Uruguay.

'It was obvious that with their absence, the World Cup lost a great deal of interest, and, with it, the value of Argentina's football could not possibly be judged.

'Football in Argentina is not so "modern" as is generally thought. Paradoxically, the origin of football in Buenos Aires came through cricket.

'In 1860, a group of *Argentinos* and Englishmen founded the cricket club in the capital. During the periods that cricket was not played, football took its place on the same ground. So, in May of 1865, a handful of soccer enthusiasts conceived the idea of forming a football club, and the Buenos Aires FC was created. On 22 June of the same year the first official football match in Argentina was played.

'During the course of the years the English sport was outstanding in the sporting calendar of Argentina. That famous sportsman, Sir Thomas Lipton, donated the Lipton Cup, a handsome trophy presented to the winner of the annual Argentina v Uruguay match. During the years this international game was played, Argentina won eight times, with six matches lost and eight ending in a draw.

'The most famous clubs in Argentina still boast their English names, or mixed up with Spanish: River Plate, Newell's Boys, Banfield, Boca Juniors, Velez Sarsfield, etc. Perhaps the two greatest teams in all Argentina are Boca Juniors and the River Plate.

'The *Argentinos*, though in their liking for everything in relation with soccer, prefer the annual championship of the league to that of the cup. In any local "derby" match in the league, the enthusiasm of the crowd is so great that any Arsenal v Spurs match is quiet in comparison with this "feast of soccer" in Argentina.

'It is necessary to expound the actual abyss that separates the English methods from the *Argentinos*. "Here in England," it is said, "the players are more or less slaves of a system: they do everything in their power to prevent opponents from scoring. The improvisation and individualism is being slowly killed."

'In Argentina, soccer is considered more of a sport than a spectacle. The player is educated in the task of becoming a star, to consider football an art, and so to be the supreme artist in his position. Therefore, the Argentinian player is sought by nations which believe in this education. In the past season, more than 180 players have been "exported" to Colombia, Uruguay, Spain, Italy, France, etc. Some of the players are being paid fantastic sums with a two-to-three-year contract.

'The speed of the Argentinian player is phenomenal, as you will see this afternoon. You will be considerably impressed by the terrific speed and ball control of the Argentina players. It is a mistake to think of them only as nippy striplings chasing a light ball on a hard ground. On the contrary! They make the ball do the work, with accurate passes two and three yards ahead of the player, and they are also masters in the art of dribbling.

'I am certain that the Argentina players today will fully uphold the traditions and sportsmanship associated with the game of football in their country.

'We look forward to a most entertaining afternoon and may the better team win.'

Robert had just passed his tenth birthday; the game was to prove to be a seminal moment for him and perhaps marked the first stirrings of his footballing enlightenment. The legendary players fighting to the finish, undefeated within their own fortress, presented a prospect that was exciting and inspiring, but it was the Argentineans' quicksilver, short passing that lodged in young Moore's imagination and memory. In particular, it was the play of the South American number six, Boca Juniors man Natalio Pescia, that was to have a lasting impact. A legend as a player with *La Mitad Más Uno*, Pescia performed with a cool panache and artistic craft.

The hosts started with a resolute charge, but were to have a fight on their hands as the game progressed. The Argentinians had based their training at Highbury. Those who observed their routines were impressed by their speed and rapid interplay and it was this that perplexed and threatened England for much of the match. Doug Lishman, the Gunners' inside-forward at the time, told me,

'The Argentinians nipped around like whippets. They moved the ball about like lightning. Unlike us, the whole of their training sessions included the ball and they seemed to be shouting and laughing all the time. We'd not seen anything like them before and you couldn't take your eyes off them.'

Looking to bring something new to the England side, the selectors gave a debut to 33-year-old Jim Taylor, Fulham's centre-half, who had been part of his nation's World Cup squad in 1950. The match was the first of his two caps.

The encounter was the first meeting of England and Argentina; the South Americans were only the second country, after Scotland, to play England at Wembley. Another first was the hosts wearing red shirts (with white shorts, black socks with white tops) under the shadow of the twin towers.

The visitors had not been part of the World Cup the previous year, although in the mid-1940s they had won the South American Championship over three consecutive years, and overall had best record in the history of the competition.

A novelty for the England players, with regard to their club experience, was the FIFA rule that a substitute could replace an injured player prior to the 44th minute, and a goalkeeper at any time. Not that England were ever going to indulge in such a lightweight and unmanly shindig. The only player to leave the field of play would be a dead one, and then they'd need to be headless.

The Argentine coach, Guillermo Stábile, sent his team out in a 2-3-5 formation, mirroring England's setup. This is one of the oldest base structures in football. It can be thought of as inflexible incarnation of the more familiar (to modern sensibilities) 'pyramid' formation. The 2-3-5 became widely deployed in football the world over after its development in Britain. Wrexham favoured the formation for their first Welsh Cup win, in 1877/78, but by the start of the 20th century it was the most commonly used formation in top-level competitions, with three major variations, all of them associated with major successes. With just two in defence, half the outfield players were pushed forward. The central half-back role was to move between offensive and defensive duties, if and when the situation necessitated. This was the only position with any real latitude; otherwise it was a pretty rigid system, with each player devoted solely to defence, construction or attacking phases, depending on the position. Uruguay adopted this formation in the 1930 FIFA World Cup, as well as in the Olympic Games of 1924 and 1928. From there it became pretty much the default setup, taking off like the 'Black Bottom'.

Guillermo had been the top scorer in the 1930 World Cup. At club level he had won two national championships with Huracán and had experience of playing in both Italy and France. As manager, he would, in all, lead Argentina to victory in six South American Championships and Racing Club to three league titles.

Forward Henry!

The indomitable Henry Cockburn was swift to stamp his authority on the game and soon Miguel Rugilo, in the visitors' goal, was obliged to make a string of agile, if unconventional saves from Mortensen and Milburn. Baptised post-match as 'Tarzan' by fans and press, Rugilo was the source of some mirth, swinging from his crossbar and seemingly playing funambulist throughout the match, as he demonstrated a range of extravagant moves. But he did the job, repeatedly foiling the English forwards.

The Argentines, in what would become their familiar sky blue and white broad-striped jerseys with white collars, black shorts, pale blue socks, constructing their play around their quick, short passing, scored the opening goal of the match, in the 19th minute. It was the result of the visitors' first dangerous attack; the head of Mario Boyé did the damage from six yards out.

The reversal started with a midfield error by Billy Wright. The South Americans worked the ball dazzlingly. Labruna killed Rugilo's lengthy clearance effortlessly, and sent the ball to Lostau. Beating Ramsey for pace, the outside-left tempted Williams from his goal and chipped the ball up to the head of the outside-right who nutted it beyond England's goalkeeper. Wembley had hardly seen anything to match the exuberant celebration of the Racing Club forward. Unabated joy understates it.

From that point, up to the break, England were dominant. Milburn connected with a Mortensen pass but was denied by Rugilo's courageous dive at the Newcastle United man's feet. A lightning drive from the boot of Hassall and a couple probing headers obliged the Argentine keeper to make a trio of saves as the hosts turned the screw, backed by the mighty 'Wembley roar'.

The pressure was however to no avail. As the whistle signalled half-time England continued to trail their talented and spirited guests. The home manager Winterbottom dived down the tunnel to commence his half-time lecture before the players reached the dressing room. He was still giving it as the players took to the field for the second period. Former Southport lorry driver Bill Eckersley, in the England line-up that day reputably admitted to not understanding a word Walter had said. It is widely recognised that Winterbottom introduced a deal of strategic thinking and tactical ideas to the England team, but he was occasionally less than successful in communicating them to some players. Although Winterbottom came from modest origins, it has been suggested that his later educational and other influences disallowed him to 'effectively instruct, much less inspire, working-class footballers'. I'm not sure who that depreciates most, but there can be no doubting the commitment and knowledge of England's first manager.

At the start of the second 45 minutes England, apparently replicating the opposition's play in the first half, were passing more and at greater speed; this appeared to have a positive effect. Wright's support of Finney improved, while Milburn found space in the Argentines' hard-tackling defensive shield.

England had the visitors under sustained fire for quarter of an hour. Allegri had come on for Colman ten minutes from the break, following some 'payback' from Metcalfe, and it was the Vélez Sársfield centre-back who pulled off a balletic scissors kick clearance to keep the score at 1-0. This was followed by Milburn hitting Rugilo's right-hand post twice.

With the unforgiving seconds passing, Williams remained an onlooker as he had for the vast majority of the match. The clock showed that 79 minutes had ticked by as the tsunami of noise from the Wembley hoard drove England forward, and it was Mortensen, surfing the roar, who took to the air to convert Finney's corner (England's 14th of the game) with a solid header close to the goal line.

There were four minutes left when Milburn connected with Mortensen's header from a Ramsey free kick. As the ball zoomed across the goalmouth 'Wor Jackie' thumped it in from a couple of yards. He had scored two for Newcastle on the same pitch in the FA Cup Final in March of that year.

England effected the first 'great escape' (without Steve McQueen).

The Teams
ARGENTINA

Rugilo, Miguel Ángel   Vélez Sarsfield

At the age of 28 he was an experienced international goalkeeper who had been outstanding in the private trial matches held shortly before the party left by plane for Britain.

Colman, Juan Carlos (off 35th minute)   Boca Juniors

The most expensive player in Argentina, at nearly 25 years of age, was a right-back with a reputation for constructive play. Difficult to beat in the air, noted for the supply of regular of streamlined passes to his forwards.

Filgueiras, Juan   Huracán

A strong left-back, noted for his powers of recovery. Rated as one of the steadiest full-backs in Argentina. Quick on the turn and a tenacious tackler.

Yácono, Norberto A.   (captain)   River Plate

A powerful right-half with terrific stamina, close to Pescia as an all-round wing half-back. A first-time tackler and a fine distributor of the ball.

Faina, Ubaldo R.   Newell's Old Boys

Youngest member of the party at the age of 21, he appeared to be on the threshold of a great career. Argentina's centre-half, he was able play either an attacking or defensive game. The game was his introduction to representative soccer. Colombia offered £30,000 for his transfer.

Pescia, Natalio A.   Boca Juniors

Said to have been the 'Billy Wright of Argentina' this left-half had proved himself as a model footballer and sportsman for thousands of young Argentinians. Had a remarkable resemblance to Johnny Carey, the Manchester United skipper.

Boyé Auterio, Mario E.H.   Racing Club

A much-capped right-winger, apart from being speedy, he had built a reputation for one of the hardest shots in Argentinian soccer. Had experience of playing in Italy.

Méndez, Norberto D.   Racing Club

One of the most colourful footballers in South America, and a real artist at inside-right. He had helped his club win the league championship in 1949 and 1950. Apart from making openings, he was also a proven goal scorer, a dazzling dribbler, possessed of 'quite a crack in either foot'.

Bravo, Rubén   Racing Club

Recognised as one of the best centre-forwards in South America, he had been prominent in the Racing Club's run of success. Bravo was seen as a 'general ' and was a prolific goal scorer. He had a habit of wandering, so upsetting well-planned defences.

Labruna, Ángel A.   River Plate

One of the best-known inside-forwards in South America. He had played in over a dozen games for Argentina at inside-left before the Wembley game. The speed of his dribbling was well known; he was also renown as a master of the defence-splitting pass. Had been ten years with River Plate.

Loustau, Félix   River Plate

This top-class left-winger/outside-left had turned out for his country on several occasions. Small and speedy, with outstanding ball control, possessed of a powerful and accurate shot.

Substitute:
Allegri, Ángel N.   Newell's Old Boys

On in the 35th minute for Colman. A full-back, who like Colman, was a very constructive player. Adept at keeping the ball on the ground, he was making his first trip with the representative side.

Other squad members:

Hector Grisetti – goalkeeper. An all-round athlete who won many high-jumping contests. This 24-year-old was a spectacular but safe keeper who played for the Racing Club.

G. Perez – full-back. New to representative football, this player had an outstanding season with the Racing Club during 1950. Particularly noticeable for his powerful clearances. A big future was predicted for him.

S. Maurino – central half-back. Like Faina, who was a year younger, Maurino was a newcomer to representative soccer. For the Banfield Club, he had proved an outstanding figure. He was one of the greatest pivots Argentina had produced up to the early 1950s.

A. Lombardo – half-back. Had been prominent for Newell's Old Boys. Versatile, able to play on either flank.

Ernesto Gutierrez – half-back. Playing for Racing Club, he had appeared on several occasions in Argentina's international team. Small but powerful. He had an outstanding positional sense.

Santiago Vernazza – forward. His form for Platense saw him hailed as the best outside-right in Argentina. Speedy, and clever, he was noted for his accurate, quick centres. In the early 1950s he was seen as a winger for whom any club would gladly pay a big transfer fee.

J. Benavidez – forward. Playing for San Lorenzo, this 26-year-old centre-forward was seen as one of the finest dribblers in the game. Although not quite so deadly in front of goal as Bravo, he was also known as an accomplished leader.

Juan José Pizzutti – forward. A classy inside-forward who had a big future forecast for him. River Plate paid half a million pesos (nearly £11,000) for his transfer that season.

Llamil Simes – forward. One more star from the Racing Club, and another who had shown extreme promise.

Ezra Sued – forward. One of Argentina's greatest stars, this 25-year-old left-winger occupied a place in the South American game comparable with that of Stanley Matthews in England. Playing for the Racing Club, he had established a reputation as an elusive and brilliant player with phenomenal ball control.

ENGLAND

Williams, Bert F.   Wolverhampton Wanderers

The £3,500 paid by Wolves to Walsall in 1945 for this agile keeper was to be money well spent, particularly in the light of his many outstanding performances for Wanderers. More than once after he took over as England's regular last line in succession to Frank Swift, Williams often stood between victory and despair, but his most memorable performance was against Italy at Tottenham. Not surprising, since he so often demonstrated that he took delight in outshining the acrobatic continentals. But this Bilston-born player was safe as well as being spectacular.

Ramsey, Alfred E.   Tottenham Hotspur

England's right-back was generally regarded as being responsible for the transformation which made Tottenham the team of the previous two seasons, during which Spurs had achieved the feat of winning the Second Division championship and then the First Division. Moving to White Hart Lane from Southampton in 1949, and in addition to the calm, almost casual way he displayed his ability on the field, he was known by his closest associates as one of football's most thoughtful students. He had twice captained England prior to this match, against Wales and Yugoslavia earlier that season.

Eckersley, William   Blackburn Rovers

At left-back Bill was smaller than average height for a defender at that time, but compensated for his lack of inches by speed and intelligent sense of anticipation, which meant that he was seldom found out of position. Joined Blackburn in 1948.

Wright, William A. (captain)   Wolverhampton Wanderers

Even though he was essentially an attacking player, playing his 35th international, taking the right-half role, he never ducked his duty in defence. Captain of Wolverhampton Wanderers' FA Cup-winning side in 1949, he had been on the Molineux staff since he was 14.

Taylor, James G.   Fulham

A tireless worker, centre-half Taylor came to top representative honours slowly. He was a member of the touring party to Canada the previous summer, and was one of those called upon to join the World Cup party in Rio without appearing in any of England's three ties.

Cockburn, Henry   Manchester United

Diminutive, but a tireless ball of energy, the left-half had represented his country on numerous occasions without ever becoming a regular. A member of Manchester United's 1948 FA Cup-winning side, he had been almost ever-present for the Old Trafford team, which had consistently challenged for honours in the postwar period.

Finney, Thomas   Preston North End

Playing outside-left against the Argentinians, Preston's skipper was known for his sparkling displays. He had played a significant part in his club winning the Second Division championship that season. At that point he had scored more goals than any other England player in postwar internationals. He was just as adept and deceptive with his ball control as Matthews, and his record proved that he packed a scoring punch as well.

Mortensen, Stanley H.   Blackpool

Inside-right and leading First Division goalscorer that season, he was equally at home either supporting or leading the attack. Probably the most courageous of all the players in the game in his era, he never gave up fighting and chasing, whatever the odds against him. The marksman really responsible for Blackpool's two FA Cup Final appearances in recent years prior to the game against Argentina, he scored goals with head or foot with equal facility, and was amazingly quick off the mark.

Milburn, John E.T.   Newcastle United

This Ashington-born member of a famous footballing family was probably the speediest player in the game in those days. Although a frighteningly powerful centre-forward, he had played in every position in Newcastle's attack, and opinions were divided as to his best position. But they were not divided about his ability, which delighted FA Cup Final crowds that season when he scored the two goals which took the trophy to Tyneside. He had twice competed in the professional Powderhall Sprint.

Hassall, Harold W.   Huddersfield Town

Hassall had recently scored England's first goal against Scotland within the first half-hour of his initial international appearance. A schoolmaster and a qualified physiotherapist, England's inside-left was born in Lancashire

Metcalfe, Victor   Huddersfield Town

A natural left-footed player and his position at outside-left was essentially unchallenged during his 12 years of postwar football at Huddersfield. He was known for his pace and shooting power and above all for the accuracy of his crosses from the wing. Representative honours for wingers were hard to come by in the days of Matthews and Finney. Metcalfe only managed two caps – the other was against Portugal also in May 1951 – in both matches his club colleague Harold Hassall played at inside-left.

Other squad members:
Stanley Matthews – Blackpool (outside-right)

A player about whom more superlatives have been written than many. With every other honour the game has to offer, he had the misfortune to appear twice in losing FA Cup Final sides at Wembley in the space of four seasons, although at 36 showing better form than he has done at any period of an illustrious career, his time would come in that competition.

Ted Ditchburn – Tottenham Hotspur (goalkeeper)

Born at Northfleet 28 years previously, he played for the local side until the end of 1939, when he turned professional with Spurs. In 1943, while in the forces, he was posted within easy reach of White Hart Lane, which gave him a season's regular football, and he played for England against Scotland in 1944. His first full cap was against Switzerland in 1948. He was a member of England's World Cup party.

William Nicholson – Tottenham Hotspur (right-half)

Joining Tottenham in 1936, Bill turned professional two years later. Made his debut in January 1939 after 'guesting' for several north-eastern clubs during army service with the Durham Light Infantry. He settled down at Tottenham in 1947. He was chosen for the FA close-season tour two years previously, and was the only member of the 26 players in the party who did not play. Appeared in a B international against Switzerland at Sheffield in the 1949/50 season, and was also a member of England's World Cup party.

Stanley Pearson – Manchester United (inside-left)

One of the most outstanding successes in postwar football, Stan was a member of Denis Compton's touring side while serving in the army in India. He made the international grade for the first time against Scotland at Hampden Park in 1947. He was a member of the FA party which visited Italy and Switzerland during the close-season of that year. Was only 17 when he made his league debut before the war.

Nicholson was replaced by Harry Johnston (Blackpool) on 9 May. Nicholson's fellow Tottenham player, Ted Ditchburn, was brought into the squad as reserve.

England had only just avoided losing their proud unbeaten home record against overseas opposition. The team travelled to Buenos Aires the following year. That match had to be abandoned after 21 minutes of goalless play due to torrential rain. The sides would meet again in the 1962 World Cup, where England would include Bobby Moore in the starting XI for that encounter – his third cap. Argentina returned to Wembley in 1966 for the World Cup, and that, oh yes, is another story.

There's lovely Sandy

The match referee on that day in May had been Benjamin Mervyn 'Sandy' Griffiths, a teacher by profession. It was he who 'rattled the pea' in the 1953 FA Cup Final, forever remembered as the 'Matthews Final'. His decision, with two minutes remaining, enabled Stan Mortensen to equalise from a free kick from just outside the penalty area, and ultimately Matthews was finally able to claim an FA Cup winner's medal with Blackpool.

Sandy, representing Wales, officiated at the 1950, 1954 and 1958 World Cups. In the first of these he appeared in the opening fixture, and in the second he took charge of the semi-final between Hungary and Uruguay. He ran the line for the distinguished English referee William Ling in the final. In the closing minutes of that match, and with the score at 3-2 to West Germany, Griffiths flagged probably Hungary's greatest ever player, Ferenc Puskás, offside, just as he beat Toni Turek in the German goal. Ling was famously lumped by Hungary's Gyula Grosics immediately after that game.

Sandy was the first Welshman to referee an international at Wembley, the first from the principality to referee an FA Cup Final, and, at the time, the only Welshman to officiate in a World Cup Final.

Our Alf

Sandy's linesmen on 9 May 1951 were E.P.L. Grieg (yellow flag) and Alfred Bond (red flag); Bond would also be the referee in the 1956 FA Cup Final. He was born in Silvertown, local to the Thames Ironworks, the firm West Ham United grew out of. He was a former right-half for Danes Athletic in the South-West District League and would ultimately serve as that club's vice-president.

Bond lost his right arm at the age of 19 when working in a rubber factory. He learned to write and perform other tasks with his left hand. He tried to resume playing but found that his 'balance had gone' so he decided to take up refereeing instead. Promotion came via the Corinthian League, the Football Combination and the Southern League.

Alf was the proprietor of a newsagent's business in Fulham. He commented on being selected to officiate at the FA Cup Final, 'It's a grand feeling to know that you have gained this honour.'

Bond controlled his first league game in 1948 – a Third Division South match. He officiated at the 1954 FA Amateur Cup Final at Wembley between Bishop Auckland and Crook Town and also refereed four international matches. He died on 1 July 1986 in Wandsworth aged 75. He was reportedly interned with his sterling silver match whistle in his jacket pocket.

'Tribuna Natalio Pescia'

For Robert, entering the most receptive, impressionable and life-forming stage of his existence, the experience of that Wembley day would have been massive. Each event within the game would have been magnified, to be etched into the memory by the impact of the totemic personalities ranged before him and the magnitude of England's mighty, tumultuously vociferous support.

This was a time before television made football the wallpaper it has become, making us blasé to monuments like Wembley Stadium, gargantuan crowds and the giants of the game. In that swirling caldron of incarnated fantasy, watching the 'field of dreams' made real, how might the spark of ambition to one day play for his country not have been struck in young Bobby?

That game, packed with 'firsts', was Moore's first England match. The breeze of his kindled ambition was not something he would readily share with anyone. Even just entering his 11th year, he recognised this as a dream, but we are animated by our dreams, the best of our reality is made of them.

In a touching symmetry, following the death of Natalio Pescia in 1989, as West Ham honoured Bobby Moore by naming an Upton Park stand after him, Boca Juniors paid homage to their great number six, the man who ignited ten-year-old Robert's dreams, giving the title 'Tribuna Natalio Pescia' to one of La Bombonera grandstands. We are joined in the game.

5

EDUCATING ROBERT

In life there is probably one thing harder to learn than how to win and that's learning how to lose. Moore once recalled, as a 12-year-old, losing a cup final for the first time. He sped back to Waverley Gardens to his dad and mum sobbing as he mourned the 3-1 defeat. Although his parents were able to get him to see that although the result was a disappointment, it wasn't the tragedy he had thought it to be; he learned from the reversal. He had seen the loss as his failure and his responsibility. His dream was to play for England, so it's likely he might have seen the defeat as a dent in that reverie and nothing hurts a child more than bruised hope.

For all this, Robert began to grasp that we build and realise our ambitions out of the pieces of our broken dreams. He started to understand that the only answer to not doing as well as you might want was to try harder to do it, and in this way, he continued to get better. We are defined by the way we turn disadvantages to our advantage – they educate us. An example of the purposeful way Robert put this into practice was how, on occasion, he would play bare-footed while both team-mates and opponents kept their boots on. This gave others an advantage as well as a chance when opposing him. The advantage Robert got was that this made him think more about his game.

Relatively few working people could afford private vehicles in immediate postwar Britain – looking back on my childhood, my father's car looked rather lonely in Cave Road, E13. The lack of cars parked in the roads facilitated endless street games of cricket and football that Robert would invariably take charge of. However, when all the other kids went home, or the snow was thick on the ground as it was regularly in mid-century winters in east London, after school he would practice endlessly each evening. One routine was to kick a tennis ball upstairs and as it bounced down and back to him, he'd trap it. That's not easy – give it a go.

Robert passed the 11-plus, the exam that dictated where one would be placed in the 'tripartite' educational hierarchy of grammar, technical or, in the basement, secondary modern school. His success meant the door opened for him to attend a school somewhat better than the secondary modern the likes of myself was assigned to (I hadn't been allowed to sit the 11-plus because of my questionable behaviour – what the world missed!).

On 9 September 1952, Moore started to attend Tom Hood Technical High School in Leyton, now Buxton School. This was a stereotypical Victorian two-storied institution (another floor was plonked on top during his time there). He had been expecting and hoping to go on to the South East Essex Technical School in Barking, where some of the boys he knew were sent, but he was told he should be interviewed at Tom Hood. All he could later recollect about the interview was being asked about his interest in sport and then being told that he was to attend that seat of learning.

Robert's initial couple of months at Tom Hood proved to be an exacting experience for the 11-year-old. No one else came from his area. At that time, Leyton, on the border of Wanstead, would have been thought of as a comparatively well-off district, relative to much of Barking, so one might guess Robert would have been looked down on by some as result, or at least he might have felt that to be the case. This was a time when the UK was still very much a society divided by class (it still is, we just don't talk or think about it as much).

Robert felt a nagging sense of isolation on arrival at his new school. Coming to Tom Hood as a rather more introspective kid than most, his neatness, which caused him to stand out somewhat, demonstrated his self-consciousness. He was a well-behaved boy, from a straight-laced home, with a strict but loving mother who hated attention and fuss. He was accustomed to having people he knew in close proximity, but his school seemed like a different world and culture to the one he had that far inhabited. You don't have to work your imagination too hard to grasp how uncomfortable he might have been surrounded by strangers in a strange place.

As a scholar Moore saw himself as average, although he was probably better than that. His worst subjects were French and music. He was to recall what he saw as his worst day at school. In his first music lesson at Tom Hood, he was obliged to sing the national anthem, standing facing his class-mates. He was mortified. Talking about it years later, he could still feel the hot flush of awkwardness. The sense of being humiliated was always to stay with him. His embarrassment of course made his rendition worse; the words came out in a half-hearted drone. Such experiences for a perfectionist child were likely to embed the need to make every effort not to be caught off-guard again and take care to be prepared for such eventualities.

Later he found a way to get through music class without revealing what he saw as his 'terrible ignorance'; he drew the chords he was supposed to learn on his fingernails.

Robert was also to be haunted, like most of us who were fat kids, by jibes about his weight. He was to be a life-long weight watcher, for example taking the trouble to count the portion of 12 peanuts he allowed himself.

These types of considerations aside, getting from Barking to Leyton meant a 7am rise for Robert to make his solitary journey; the bus from home to Barking station, to catch the Wanstead train, then waiting for the trolleybus to Leyton, followed by a long walk to school. It was a protracted and lonely day; he wasn't getting home to well after 5pm.

Unsurprisingly this made Bob ill, but in that period, there was no solid concept of relative childhood mental health as it might be understood today. Visits to the GP involved trying to get Robert into any school nearer home. Eventually a diagnosis of travel sickness meant he was given the dispensation to move to a more local school. But in the same week as he got his sick note Moore was selected for the Leyton district schools football team. He looked back on the day he went into school with the letter from his doctor in his hand, and being informed that he'd been selected for Leyton under-13s, and how this information miraculously cured his travel sickness. The letter forever remained unread.

'If there is no struggle, there is no progress' – Frederick Douglass

Today we devote a lot of time and resources to our children's mental health; in modern times Robert would have likely been assigned by his GP to a therapist of some sort for 'treatment' (too often another word for 'correction'). One wonders what the outcome of that might have been. Treatment and cure have become the recourse of childhood malady, the period of our lives when motivation, inspiration and expectation have the greatest traction. We likely, as a society, pay a heavy price for encouraging excuses to maintain us in our comfort zones to override the learning of the necessity humanity has to meet challenges and adapt.

I am not saying relative mental health should be ignored or its causes and effects underestimated, but taking the trials of everyday life as 'traumatic' is a bit like calling a strong wind a hurricane. Looking at dictionaries of psychology, 'trauma' is generally seen to be a disturbing experience of a substantive nature that results in significant fear, helplessness, dissociation, confusion, or other disruptive feelings, intense enough to have a long-lasting negative effect on a person's attitudes, behaviour, and/or other aspects of functioning. Traumatic events include those caused by human behaviour – for example rape, war, industrial accidents – as well as by nature, earthquakes for instance, and often challenge an individual's view of the world as a just, safe, and predictable place.

It doesn't take too much to see the dangers of blatantly convincing others that the vicissitudes of human existence are likely 'traumatising' and as such unquestionably and invariably bound to hobble us. The well-worn adage 'what fails to kill you, will likely make you stronger' might not always be true, but human beings do tend to

On 8 October 1958, Bobby rounded off his England Youth career in Chamartin, Madrid, at one of the great palaces of football, the Bernabéu, in front of the biggest crowd he had run out to up to that point. The glorious 2-4 victory was a fitting farewell to this first stage in his journey as an international.

Malcolm Allison – Rebel without applause.

Bobby Moore's sixth of his record 17 outings for the England Youth side.

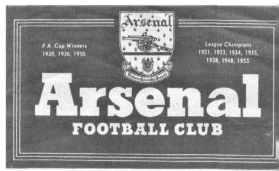

'Leyton Silver Band' – trail-blazing pre-match and half-time entertainment.

Robert with the London-wide under-11s Crisp Shield; his side was to take the trophy two years running.

Young Alf – Defending Tottenham.

Young Bobby.

9 May 1951 – Wembley – England's Harrold Hassall takes to the air. In response Argentina's goalkeeper, Miguel Ángel Rugilo, breaks into the Can-Can.

9 May 1951 – Wembley. Argentina's goalkeeper Rugilo is beaten by Mortensen.

ENGLAND v. ARGENTINA
Rugilo, Argentine goalkeeper, vainly tries to save, as Mortensen scores England's first goal

'Nippies' – Lyons Corner House.

Denis Compton – Test Cricketer and league title in 1948 and the FA Cup (1950) winner with Arsenal

...obby set up a sportswear shop in 1961. Many older fans will remember that it was situated almost ...posite the Boleyn Ground in Green Street.

John 'Charlo' Charles –
England's first black player.

London Blitz – St Peters Hospital after
the 'All Clear'.

bby Moore was born at the very height of the London Blitz, but like his family and the people he grew with, he developed a predictable desire to create order from chaos.

Bobby Moore's first England game: The match was the first meeting of England and Argentina; the South Americans were only the second country, after Scotland, to play England at Wembley.

Peter Brabrook – one of the many talented young players recruited by Chelsea 'Super Scout' Jimmy 'Rolling Stone' Thompson. Peter was to say that he '…could never seem to get passed Bobby'. Brabrook spent six years at Stamford Bridge before he was brought back to East London by Ron Greenwood in 1962.

The throw-in is perhaps the most neglected facet of football, but it is the most common of game interruptions, just pipping free kicks. Thus getting the best from throw-ins is a good asset in any game. Malcolm Allision saw this required upper body strength so that the torso could be stretched like a crossbow, with additional momentum coming from the arms. Today, the quality of a throw-in is almost always judged by distance, but Allison was more interested in accuracy and fast movement post-throw. You can see from this image how Moore maximised accuracy with a very square and rooted stance, much like an archer. Together with his strong upper body, this facilitated not only a good length of throw, but more precision than most of the throws we see in today's game

At the start of the 1962/63 season Greenwood sold Phil Woosnam to Aston Villa and made Moore captain, he was to say: 'I made him captain because he was such a natural leader and had everyone's respect... He was desperate to succeed and was a good captain because he didn't ask anybody to do anything he couldn't do.'

On 2 October 1957 Bobby was chosen for his first England Youth game. It to place at Olympisch Stadion, Amsterdam (since 2018 known as the 'Johan Cru Arena'), which was then used by the great AFC Ajax club for international gam (as it was up to 1996). Note the 'Marathon Tower'; it has four balconies, whi were used during the 1928 Olympic Games by horn blowe

Amsterdam, Stadion met Marathontoren.

...en Brown and Noel Cantwell.

West Ham 1955/56 – Malcolm Allison (front row, far right), Noel Cantwell and Frank O'Farrell (end of ...ack row, left to right).

Andy Malcolm.

When kids went to football on their own.

...d Fenton.

Ron Greenwood – genius.

...arking Power Station circa 1940 – where 'Big Bob', Bobby's dad, worked.

Bobby and Budgie – symmetry and poetry.

Charlie Paynter took the cake.

Phil Woosnam – an ambitious man.

'Please wear your mask' (World War Two style).

Len Cearns – The last 'Lord of the Manor'.

hnny Byrne – the Palace years.

Meet the Champion!

You'll be thrilled by its fighting-fit power and all-round ability—by those extra qualities that are the mark of a champion! First for style, the Zephyr is clean, crisp—flawless from graceful grille to vast luggage boot ... six-cylinders smooth and silent in action, effortlessly controlled with a gentle touch of foot or fingertip ... supremely comfortable and spacious, modestly priced, always ably seconded by famous Ford Service ... no wonder the Zephyr is a world-favourite! You can test-drive a Zephyr *now*—with, if you wish, overdrive or miraculous fully automatic transmission. Just ask your Ford Dealer!

ZEPHYR *£610 plus £306.7.0 P.T.=£916.7.0 (Zephyr Overdrive £980.2.0, Zephyr Automatic £1,088.17.0, both prices including P.T.)*

Bobby's first wheels.

change and develop more via need than choice, more in response to crisis than by way of the plodding routine of a trouble-free stasis.

My role as a youth worker has always been to 'accompany' young people as they walk their path, and celebrate their recognition, honing and use of their own resources. The more they discover their powers of accommodation and adaption, as they meet and deal with the challenges of life, the better they become at finding their way in the world and ultimately creating a world for themselves. This is an 'asset' approach – seeing humans as having resources and capacities, rather than assuming 'sickness' or 'weakness' and, as a consequence, branding kids as more or less 'vulnerable'. This starting point of seeing people from the perspective of their 'assets' doesn't discount supporting them at times, but it was never within the scope of my ambitions to pathologise or 'treat' them. Sadly, I have watched appreciable aspects of my profession contorted into the practice amateur psychiatry, with practitioners busily, often spuriously, diagnosing other people's children, usually without their or their parents' awareness, let alone permission – broadly a response premised on assumed 'deficit'.

Trials and triumphs

Robert had played in the district trials previously, but, with typical modesty, he hadn't given himself much of a chance of being picked. In the Leyton team he played at either inside-forward or wing-half. He didn't rate himself as the most skilful of players in the side, more the strong, hard-working toiler. He was to recall an encounter with Marylebone Schools, which concluded in a 19-0 win for his team. Robert scored eight and a friend of his, Tommy Long, notched up seven. At that time, most of the Leyton district games were played on Leyton Orient's ground at Brisbane Road and Tommy later signed for the O's.

Once he settled down in secondary school Robert began to lose some of his puppy fat, engaging in sport and, not long into his studies at Tom Hood, having eagerly taken up the opportunity to train at the Boleyn Ground, under the wing of Malcolm Allison.

Joan Wright, a teacher at Tom Hood during the time Robert was attending, remembered him as something of a 'heart throb' and a popular lad. The school, being a technical and commercial institution, offered programs in subjects such as bookkeeping and typing, woodwork and metalwork. It is much repeated that Robert got less than a handful of GCEs, in Technical Drawing, Geography, Woodwork and Art, but Joan was to assert that he got 'eight O-levels in one go.' I was not surprised to learn this. I could never see Bobby being glad to do the minimum in any aspect of this life. My guess is his self-organisation was a huge asset. My life in education and as a writer has taught me that task management is by far and away the greatest quality a scholar or author might command.

At the same time Robert was growing into an attractive, sports-oriented young man, with a growing reputation in football and cricket, representing the local schoolboy side in the summer sport. While most reports have it that he was 'sound rather than spectacular' as his skills developed, it looked more and more likely he might choose to follow a career in either game, so it seems probably his talents at this point have been underplayed. He was certainly making an impression more than an 'ordinary' performer might. His performance mattered to him in a way it didn't to many boys, myself included. I was deemed 'good enough' for trials in both football and cricket, but as a teenager my 'couldn't give a fuck' disposition was a major disincentive all round. I believe I knew this and can't say I have any regrets. Much the same pertained later. Being a strong kid, with decent awareness, I had a talent and advantages in the world of judo, but I guess it was all too easy. At the same time smoking, drinking and the futile pursuit of the opposite sex seemed much more appealing to my adolescent brain than hours in the dojo, doing the road and gym work with a bunch of sweaty, hairy-arsed geezers.

Moore became an exemplar to other kids with ambitions in sport who were maybe tempted to take that to mean they either weren't up to academic study, or just felt they could take their foot off the gas when it came to routine study and exams. For all this, Moore's Wednesday afternoon lessons included History and during that era England almost invariably played on Wednesday afternoons. So, when there was a game on that day Robert would get a friend to say he was sick and shoot home to catch the match.

However, the young Moore generally demonstrated that sporting ambition and academic success where not incompatible. He was keen on all types of drawing and, if his sporting ambitions had failed to have been realised, he would have likely either found employment in a technical drawing office as a draughtsman or else looked to the print.

As Moore approached his mid-teens, school had transformed from a place of humiliation and distress to a situation in which the young man could grow and experience some of the joys of what it is to be young. One of Robert's lasting memories of Tom Hood was afternoons that began with the boys going to Woodwork and the girls to Cookery. When the class came back together for the final lesson of the day there was pandemonium, as fairy cakes, baked by the girls, got thrown around the classroom while the teacher's attention was diverted elsewhere. We had much the same scenario, but lumps of timber from the Woodwork class, sometimes with the odd nail in, were also in the mix. Cries of 'yer could 'av someone's fucking eye out with that!', aping parental chastisement (stating the bleeding obvious), never failed to raise a laugh.

The desire and passion for football, together with the confidence young Moore gained from being chosen as one of the best of his peers, was a huge boost to his self-esteem. On this foundation he was able to build more resilience and capacity. He was made a school prefect and may even have made head boy if he had been on better terms with the deputy head, although this less-than-perfect relationship was an exception, as he seemed to get on well with practically everyone else at Tom Hood.

Cricket

Wielding a sophisticated bat, as well as being a fine fielder and able wicketkeeper, Robert had turned out for various school cricket teams before being selected for both London and Essex Schoolboys to apply willow to leather. He progressed to captaining the South of England under-15 XI, leading that side against the strong North of England XI, facing fellow tubby lad Colin Milburn, England Test batsman to be. Milburn was to aid with Moore's dismissal, taking the fateful catch. Robert remembered Milburn being the North's skipper, and winning the toss, 'We batted. I opened. I'd just reached double figures when I got an edge and "Ollie" [Milburn's nickname] caught me in the slips. He said, "On your way, Moore." I was sick. But half an hour later it rained. The match was abandoned. At least I got my innings.'

Later, they met again at a cricket coaching school in Twickenham, where the coach was celebrated England wicketkeeper Godfrey Evans, and struck up a lasting friendship until Milburn's all too early death, three years before Bobby's own passing. Milburn once told me about his relationship with Bobby, 'Cricket gave me and Bobby a connection. I knew right off he was shy, but a laugh or two breaks the ice. Cricket is different from football because you can do that a bit more on the field. You've got all day at least!

'People expect things of people in Bob's position. They expect they should act in a way that they imagine, and like to think they understand them. Bobby's fairly deep, careful and considerate with others. I suppose I'm a bit like that myself. You learn how to show what people want, to some extent anyway. For instance, I never knew him to talk a lot about football or cricket outside of the game – but that's all people think you talk about. If anything, you couldn't be blamed if you thought he was more interested in other sports.

'When you meet someone else that understands that, that you put on a bit of a front, so as not to disappoint or confuse people, you can be a little bit more yourself, you know the score and relax a bit. Maybe that's why Bobby might feel more at home with showbiz and sports personalities.

'I don't know if Bobby would have made county cricket. You'd needed to have seen him in more better-quality matches than he had as a youngster, and he'd have needed to have played consistently. But, yes, he had the potential, although I'd say he was made to do what he's done.

'If you know Bobby it's hard to do anything but like him.'

Bobby had a similar opinion of Milburn, 'You could always rely on Colin to be honest. He was also one of the nicest guys you could meet. He didn't like fielding much, but he placed himself brilliantly – at times he seemed to know what every batsman would do when facing any bowler, and so got to get himself under a lot of balls.'

From an early age Bobby was making his way to the Bat and Ball Ground in Gravesend to practice with his future fellow Hammer Eddie Presland, who was another fine cricketer. This involved catching the steam train from Barking to Tilbury and from there crossing the Thames via the ferry.

Presland and Moore, as schoolboy players together, came up against public school sides such as Winchester, Eton and Harrow. Bobby enjoyed taking the piss out of the young toffs, their accents and demeanour seeming almost cartoonish to the young east Londoners.

At 16 Moore was 12th man in a match between England under-20s and the Lancashire second XI at Manchester. He was to recall how most of his team-mates in that match were two or three years older than him. The Lancashire players were all county professionals. He remembered feeling 'like a small boy away from home for the first time'. He was not at all unhappy at not being obliged to actually play.

A little down the line, Essex were interested in Moore, as well as several other West Ham boys, Geoff Hurst and Martin Peters among them. The latter-day Eagles started to woo the deliberate batter and invited him to undertake trials. For a while Bobby had an idea that he might play both football and cricket professionally; the smooth and shiny Gunner, Denis Compton had been one of several others to do just that. In the mid-1950s Robert was likely a better cricketer than he was a footballer. At the time, physically speaking, the summer sport suited him much more than the 'beautiful game'.

In his early days the majority of Moore's fellow playing staff at West Ham were into cricket. Ted Fenton loved the game, and would recruit his footballers to turnout for his side, Clayhall. Robert had been at the Boleyn Ground for a week when he was called to the crease to play for a West Ham XI against Leyton Orient. Noel Cantwell, who represented Ireland at cricket, skippered the side. The new boy predictably wanted to impress.

With Cantwell coming in at number four and Moore at five, the apprentice got an edge from the first delivery he faced, at which the Irishman bid him 'Come on' only to be told by the kid 'No!'. Cantwell was run out. Robert was, predictably crushed with embarrassment.

The second innings saw Cantwell dismissed first ball. Moore made a respectable 20, although his overwhelming guilt caused him to endeavour to make his wicket more vulnerable. Bobby was to ask himself, years later, why seemingly insignificant incidents such as this experience, caused him such acute embarrassment as a teenager. It's not as if Cantwell held any grudges. He recalled the incident with good humour, 'I called Bobby on, but he left me high and dry! But to be honest, it was chancy and one or the other of us would probably have been run out anyway. I ribbed him thereafter about that at every opportunity, so I got my money's worth so to speak.'

It wasn't too long after this game that Robert met with Doug Insole, the England all-rounder and Essex captain at the time. He would ultimately go on to become chief selector for England. Insole told Moore that he showed promise as a cricketer and invited him to join the county ground staff. Doug attended the Monoux School, Walthamstow, a place I had some professional connections with in the last part of the 20th century. He lived most of his adult life at Chingford – the 'far east end'. He mentioned to me once that he thought Moore would have made the English Test team, and that the side would 'probably have been stronger for that'. He assessed Moore to have 'a strong stance, placing his feet well, an outstanding positional sense as well as good eye/hand coordination … but in the end, he made the right choice staying in football, although he probably should have moved on from West Ham after the World Cup'.

For a time, Robert was achieving somewhat headier heights playing cricket than he was in football, and likely first-class cricket then was a much more attractive option financially than playing for the mediocre, second-level football club that West Ham were in Moore's early days. He was tempted, holding on to the notion he might be able to handle two careers. However, he was to confess he didn't believe it to be in his nature to be the exceptionally adaptable lad who might shine at anything he turned his hand to. While there were examples of players who had divided their attentions betwixt bat and boot, he knew of others who had tried this tandem ride and fallen badly. Geoff Hurst was to see trying to play both sports had held back his initial development as a player.

Ultimately Bobby calculated that if all went well at West Ham, he would need to be on call nine months of the year; the commitment to one's county in cricket was about 15 weeks. The difficulty would be when the respective seasons overlapped. On top of all that, it boiled down simply to the fact that young Moore had a greater passion football than he had for cricket.

Robert did, on occasion, turn out for an Essex invitation team that existed in his playing era, composed of schoolboys and those already on the county staff. This was understood as representing the county and was thought of as an honour.

In later life Bobby played for a side set up by Frank Rist, an Essex coach, who had played for the county between 1934 and 1953 and also played at centre-half for Charlton Athletic. Frank often organised charity matches, which included Essex county players, such as England batter Keith Fletcher, along with the likes of Bobby and Geoff Hurst. Moore batted three or four and Rist rated him capable as a first-class cricketer. Rist was to reflect, 'As was the case on the soccer field, Bobby wasn't the fastest, but his anticipation more than compensated. That was a lot down to the coaching he got with Malcolm Allison but you are born with that kind of sense. You can build on what you've got, but you can't just plug it in.'

It is perhaps just as well Bobby was to devote himself to 'the game of winter'. When Hurst was considering playing both football and cricket, Ron Greenwood was quick to tell him he wouldn't keep him at Upton Park if he failed to focus totally on football. But Jim Standen, someone who knew Bobby both as a footballer and a cricketer, being West Ham's goalkeeper throughout their golden mid-1960s era and a county-level cricketer who at one time was on the verge of the touring England side, felt that while Moore was a useful opening bat he was not county standard, although that was likely related to him devoting most of his time to football in his early years.

Always someone else

As Robert broke into the under-14 and then under-15 district football teams, he found himself facing lads who were making connections with league clubs. Some of the professionals to be he met in those days included the likes Johnny Cartwright and Tony Scott, both of whom went on to play for West Ham, and Johnny Sanchez who joined Arsenal. Everyone appeared to be getting an opportunity to become a professional except the person he continued to see himself to be, 'Fatso Moore'.

Although no one knew it, Robert was understandably upset and certainly envious of those being snapped up by professional outfits. He wanted to be a footballer like seemingly most of the other young men he knew through the game, but whenever word had it that a club was coming in for a lad it was always someone else. He began to take this badly. It was more painful if a kid he knew well got the chance he so desperately desired.

While Moore was no longer the pudding he had been as a primary school kid, compared to most young teenagers in the game he still carried a bit of excess timber. He had come out of himself somewhat, but he continued to be comparatively shy. He was possessed of the overwhelming enthusiasm to learn about the sport he loved, but he saw himself to be understood as the kind of player often described as 'solid' rather than 'special'. He started to think that he would never catch the eye of the scouts.

From this distance in time such a feeling is just a bit puzzling. Moore had, for coming up to three years, been under the wing of the Hammers' club captain, training at Upton Park on Tuesday and Friday afternoons. He had impressed some of West Ham's best and most influential players. All the while, up to the end of his school career, he had a record of district representation. While he might not have been widely rated as an international star of the future, it would have been no less than expected that he might at least sign for a club outside of the elite setups, such as West Ham.

This is the point at which Bobby's move into football throws up several loose ends and contradictions that, if we are to have a clear view of his development, need a fair bit of analysis.

JACK THE LAD

For all his fears, Robert was being watched and assessed with regard to his capacity to join the production line to the professional football. He had been training with Malcolm Allison at Upton Park for several years, and while playing for the schoolboys in East Ham, then a local government district in the far south-west of Essex, at Flanders Field (which now boasts the Bobby Moore Pavilion), Jack Turner had been tasked to watch him in a competitive game.

A polite way of starting to talk about Jack, known to some of the stall-holding community of Queens Road and Rathbone markets as 'Tinpot Turner', might be to say he was a 'cryptic character' around postwar Upton Park, although my dad alleged that there was something of the 'wide boy' about him. This meant he inspired a frisson akin to the purveyors of the 'long-firm' school business ethic. I wouldn't dream of going so far as to say his intentions were infallibly 'rascally', but given Turner's opaque CV around and beyond the Boleyn Ground, coupled with the black holes in his backstory, it's perhaps unsurprising that he might provoke questions about his purpose, style and method, although in his pomp and around east London at that time he might be understood as a character not entirely without compare.

I have devoted much of this and another chapter to examining Turner's place and function around Upton Park as Bobby Moore was maturing at the club and for a time thereafter. I have done this firstly in order to look at his supposed part in 'discovering' Moore but also his presence, activity and relationships tells us a lot about West Ham as an institution at the time and Bobby's probable experience of the same.

'Tinpot Turner'

Now and then people, including former players, have told me that Moore did, from time to time, mix with a few 'dodgy/undesirable geezers'. I'm not going to say they were thinking of Jack Turner, but one or two might well have.

At mid-20th century Upton Park, the ground staff boys were requited to go to an office in the bowels of the Main Stand each Friday to collect their weekly wage. After their first week, on opening their initial pay packet, the lads discovered that after paying tax and National Insurance, they were £1 light of what they had expected to receive (a bit off ten per cent of their earnings). They were informed that the club was holding back £1 per week as 'savings'. No one could remember this being stipulated when they signed on, but there is no record of anyone complaining. Indeed a few playing staff, after signing professional forms, continued to add to this 'nest egg', to paraphrase *Father Ted*, 'resting in the club's account'. One or two used the accrued monies as the deposit for a house for instance.

I'm not sure how much, if any, interest was offered in connection with these 'savings', or if the club might have pulled a 'service' charge from any interest on the funds. There was no contract alluding to any of this that I've been made aware of (which doesn't mean that some type of documented agreement didn't exist). That aside, while there were potential benefits for the players, it all feels, detached from the situation by time, as my old mum might have it, 'a bit of a liberty', the process apparently being undertaken without consultation with or the permission of the players or their parents.

The person behind the players' savings arrangement was Jack Turner, under his very informal but oft-used title of 'property manager', while contradictorily never being an official employee of the club.

Solid and square in physique although perhaps not entirely in character, Turner, in his temperate grey suits, skinny ties and mirror polished shoes, might have been an impressive figure to young footballers and their families on first meeting. He was a man who knew how to make himself liked by players, being able to present himself as a reassuring figure, a font of seemingly sound advice and clam assurance.

Most mornings players queued at the door of Jack's office, looking for counsel. He gave the impression that he could be trusted to sort out mortgages, process tax returns, and throw in a generous portion of fatherly guidance on practically anything. No issue was too intimate or domestic for Jack's ear – he likely knew more about any individual young player than anyone else at the club. That said, given the absence of any kind of second opinion on any of his guidance, instruction or big brotherly wisdom, there wasn't much alternative to the matey oracle Jack cast himself as. He pretty much had the monopoly on 'official' player advice and guidance.

Often described as a 'scout' in accounts of the 'Flanders Field scenario' (see below) and repeatedly cited as the 'discoverer' of Moore, Turner appeared to have no single role at West Ham, but certainly 'scout' was not one that loomed large in what can be identified about his activity and connections with the club or in terms of his everyday doings at Upton Park.

Probably still one of the most thoroughly researched and well written books looking at West Ham is Charles Korr's *West Ham United*. Although necessarily filtered by the vestiges of the Upton Park feudal culture of the time, so 'old-guard' figures such as St Pier, Reg Pratt and long-term club servant Eddie Chapman are portrayed through a mist of sycophancy, which is not of Korr's doing. His analysis pulls aside some of the veils of myth, cronyism, legend, nepotism and paternalism that pertained in the structures and organisation of the club, that were by no means atypical in the footballing world of mid-20th century Britain.

At the time Korr was writing, Jack was out of favour at Upton Park. He was associated more with the 'less obvious' (not to say 'covert') side of Fenton's reign, indeed Korr refers to Turner as a 'shadowy' character; what one might have less generously or unkindly called in Fenton's time a 'spiv'.

Korr, diplomatically, also refers to Turner as one of several 'honorary' employees. He also writes that following Jack's time associated with the club he became 'even more mysterious'. According to Korr,

'No two observers share either the same opinion or even the same memory of what he did or what difference he made to West Ham. Turner was involved in scouting and dealing with professional players … Turner's time at West Ham coincided with two of the most significant administrative changes since 1945 – the elevation of Reg Pratt to the chairmanship and Ron Greenwood's appointment as manager. These events determined Turner's status at the club.'

Korr records a brief biography of Jack as related to him by the man himself,

'Turner's arrival on the scene was like a boyhood dream come true. He was born in 1914, and West Ham 'was my club as a child … If you cut your finger and your blood is claret and blue, that's me.' He grew up kicking a ball around the streets seven days a week, the only entertainment for him and other children. Young Turner didn't 'know anything about football', except, 'I enjoyed it. Football players were something special.'

Before Jack went to his first West Ham match in 1920, he was told by his father, 'Some of those men are cleverer with their feet than we are with our hands.' But they were more than clever, they were giants and heroes.' Because the players were locals, he knew where they lived and could see them on the streets.'

Jack would work closely with Reg Pratt almost 30 years later. He left school as a 15-year-old and went into property and insurance. Somehow avoiding conscription into the armed forces in 1939 as 25-year-old, in 1941 he turned down an offer of employment by Charlie Paynter, then the Hammers' manager, in the club offices. It seems the opportunities for money making were much healthier flogging insurance. Turner expressed regrets about that decision years later, feeling that had he accepted the position offered it could have led to something when peace finally broke out, the role of club secretary – which was nabbed by Eddie Chapman – being his ideal position.

Turner was a regular visitor to both Paynter and then Fenton when he took over the managerial reins at Upton Park. It was Ted who asked him to take on administrative duties for the club. An introduction to Reg Pratt followed. The chairman somehow saw Turner, who remember admitted to having no discernible footballing skills, as being potentially useful to the club and asked him to take up an 'honorary' position. You can perhaps see the 'courtly pretensions' of such a euphemism – what he was more likely and realistically being offered was casual or 'cash-in-hand' work.

Although Jack took no official wage packet or fee, he was happy to carry on his business while doing something, however enigmatic, within the structure of the West Ham organisation. Whatever it was, Jack was being given a 'captive audience', or 'exclusivity' to the player market for financial, housing and other personnel and personal services.

For all this, on taking up whatever his role was, Jack confessed to being mystified why the board failed to see football as business. This perspective is itself difficult to make much sense of because the board was entirely made up of businessmen, who were much more financially successful in their affairs than him; people who lived, ate, drunk, bathed, breathed and tangoed, first and foremost, business, and had always run the club according to that collective mentality, albeit in a fairly parochial, petty bourgeois manner.

Turner's view was that West Ham was a club that had several 'good houses and few good players … a middling club with little money or ambition. It had people with no vision and a lot of power.'

Jack correctly saw that the directors were aloof, effectively looking down on the club's playing staff and being 'almost 19th-century in its boss-worker relationships'. Jack's opinion in this respect was consistent with the body of the supporters, sections of the press, as well as many players around and before Turner's time.

Malcolm Allison, a players' player, and a persistently annoying rebel against the dictates of the board and management at the club, would have nothing to do with Jack, seeing him, probably accurately, as looking after no one but himself. In Malcolm's eyes Turner was Pratt's man, and vehemently advised other players to avoid him. Consequently, Turner had no affection for Allison, saying he took Big Mal's response 'as a compliment', and indicative of Allison's desire to dominate the club. There he got Allison totally wrong. What Malcolm wanted was to achieve something as close to footballing excellence as might be possible at West Ham, while doing whatever he could to challenge and undermine the club's exploitation of its playing staff. He had no interest at all in what the hierarchy did beyond those aims.

You can see that Turner being taken as a West Ham scout of any calibre is a bit of a stretch. That said, he probably did take something of a role in the procurement of players from time to time. Bluntly, the club needed someone who could make a sales pitch to younger players as the Hammers' patch had been repeatedly plundered of its talent by bigger clubs with more financial wiggle room in terms of offering families 'incentives' in exchange for their sons' services. Whatever payoff Turner got for this, it included the pick of clients for other 'services' he offered/peddled.

As far as can be seen, Jack made it part of his work, in the light of the club's inability or lack of desire to compete with the spending of bigger clubs, to frame the aggressive trawling of local players, propagating a high rate of recruitment with a matching degree of 'wastage' (keeping only the 'best' of the 'catch'). Jack's central selling point for kids to join the club was that they stood a better chance of playing at West Ham than they did at other clubs. Think about that, 'Likely you're not good enough for Chelsea, but you'll probably be good enough for us … you're not that great, but that's OK because neither are we!' You can understand why many of the best local lads, the likes of Terry Venables and Jimmy Greaves, who were lost to the Hammers, might have blanked Turner.

Flanders Field

For all this, the story goes that it was Turner's eyes at Flanders Field that first saw Bobby Moore's potential. However, a closer look at the situation might suggest Jack skulking around the marshland betwixt Upton Park and Barking was maybe more as an errand boy of sorts; he was supposedly there at the behest of Wally St Pier, the 'chief scout' at Upton Park. Unlike Baden Powell, however, Wally has traditionally been heralded as a kind of footballing emissary of the Hammers' postwar era.

The astute discovering of the talent that served as the means to take West Ham to Wembley glory twice in two seasons, and the unearthing of England's backbone of 1966, has traditionally been put down to St Pier, even though there was a network of formal and informal, ad hoc and official scouts that were on the lookout for the Hammers. Many of this extensive cadre offered their services 'voluntarily'. More than a few were also in the thrall of not only the Irons, but two, three and sometimes more clubs. In fact, the harvesting of football talent was a bit of a cottage industry across north-east London and west Essex, allegedly fired as much by competition for reputational 'Hawkeye' status as any chance clandestine pecuniary reward, although the potential for a drop of a 'saucy half-a-knicker' here and there was never far from local consciousness. Wally was sharp enough to tap into this 'jungle telegraph' of intelligence and eccentricity, having the wisdom to give ear to men who really did spend every spare hour patrolling the myriad touchlines of the adolescent game.

The mythology has it that Wally had followed a lead from West Ham manager Ted Fenton, who it is said was in turn responding to a recommendation from Tom Russell, a teacher at Tom Hood School, who was also involved as a part-time coach at Upton Park. It has been constantly reiterated that it was Russel who asked Bobby if he was prepared to go to Upton Park for coaching. Tom worked with Bill Robinson, taking charge of the junior players at Upton Park. Robinson had played for the club, making more than 100 appearances between 1949 and 1952. The under-18s teams that made the FA Youth Cup semi-final in 1954 and the final in 1957 were technically in his charge. Bill was promoted to assistant to Ted Fenton in 1957 and was also notionally responsible for coaching the first team, although Malcolm Allison alongside Noel Cantwell organised and led the training. Nevertheless, Robinson got a deal of credit when the Hammers were promoted to the First Division at the end of the 1957/58 season.

Robinson did however encourage the youngsters to be very competitive. He would present them with trophies at Mario's restaurant, in Cranbrook Road, Ilford. These were given for achievements like selection for England. At the time, the most popular order at Mario's was steak, egg and chips; not too many Italian eateries might boast that today.

There is no record of St Pier viewing Moore's game, although he might well have seen him working under Allison at Upton Park. Whatever, his oft-cited report pertaining to the teenager purportedly had it that the tubby blonde lad was,

'strong, full of endeavour and trying to do the right thing'.

I've never been sure about that turn of phrase. St Pier was born in 1904 in Beacontree Heath, Dagenham, not too long before my paternal grandparents, from an approximately similar background. I can't imagine Jim Belton or any of his peers using an expression like 'full of endeavour'. It feels more like the language of local newspapers of the time, or perhaps someone with a background like Eddie Chapman's, a faithful retainer to the West Ham board.

The folklore goes on to narrate how Turner watched the 15-year-old wing-half playing for Leyton Schools v East Ham in a 1955 cup tie. It was during one of those unforgiving, grey winter days that hung over the banks of the Thames of that period. On the exposed touchline, his gloved hands not feeling much warmer for being embedded in his overcoat pockets, Jack's minces, although moistened profusely by in the sharp wind that blew in from the river, made his assessment of the young man.

Turner had it,

'Looked fairly useful but wouldn't set the world alight, this boy certainly impressed me with his tenacity and industry.'

Now that don't feel much like a glowing assessment, does it? A sort of limited elaboration of St Pier's sparing compendious. A bit like 'tries hard, but no great shakes'.

The story continues that on Fenton's behest, Jack turned up again for the replay of the cup tie, the first match having concluded 3-3 (why – to check out twice reported 'okness'?). Although Robert hadn't shone in that first game, as reflected in Turner's cursory report, in the replay Jack's appraisal amounted to a suggestion that the lad might be worth continued oversight. However, that's not exactly a glittering evaluation either. It doesn't really add much to the first report. One might have said much the same thing about any player consistently chosen to represent their district! That aside, there was already 'continuing oversight' as Moore had been training at the West Ham ground with the club captain for the better part of three years. Might Jack, Robinson, St Pier, Fenton and all have possibly been unaware of that?

However, Jack's two wintery studies of Moore's apparent stoic ordinariness appeared to be the start of a lifelong association between the pair. In retrospect it feels like a bigger day for Jack than it might have been for Bobby; as Korr has it, should Turner be known at all, it is solely down to his association with Bobby Moore.

To say the success of this relationship had its ups and downs could be misleading. Whatever Bobby was, more than any other person he was responsible for West Ham being seen as something more than a relatively diminutive, less-than-fashionable side. Turner appears to have made sure he would get as much of the share of the resultant limelight as he could, being widely credited to have made the first report relating to Moore, although it was anything but shining.

The fact that Fenton got Jack to go back for another gander, and was later to ask others to evaluate Bobby, probably tells a story about the West Ham manager's faith in Turner's judgement about football quality, Jack being a person (to reiterate) who by his own admission lacked any hint of a playing background or credibility. That's like a hod carrier being asked to observe and assess the practice of a final year dental student.

The reality, according to Korr, is that the decision to sign Bobby was in part a response to the club's failure to recruit another youngster who chose to take up an offer from Arsenal. However, Allison's admiration for the young player, perhaps more than anything Turner or anyone else reckoned (which seems very little anyway) was what likely swung it for Bobby. That is certainly how Malcolm and Noel Cantwell told it.

It has to be said, however, Moore never contested the tale relating to Turner's involvement. Years on, perhaps he didn't see it as having too much relevance, and as a consequence went with the flow. Maybe his apparent compliance with the mythology was related to the ongoing business association with Turner. To his credit, Moore never spoke harshly of Jack, but he was never one for putting people down publicly – sleeping dogs and all that. But when Moore finally committed to West Ham it was Jack who did the paperwork, so straightforwardly he would have been the person to make the formal offer, the functionary who 'sold' the club to Moore's parents and got the player's signature.

Turner was a charmer though. He had perfected an approach to players that cleverly conflated business with personal relationship; the opening lesson of sales, 'engage the emotions' as they override logic. His activities gave him access to club property. West Ham owned a good number of houses in West Ham and Essex, which were offered to married players to rent on signing for the club. More broadly, his exclusive access to players gave Jack the wherewithal to gain oversight of their personal finances generally. He would make sure he started working on his 'clients' as soon as they joined as youth players, flogging insurance and savings plans.

Of course, players weren't forced to deal with Turner, but it was clear that Pratt and Fenton while not openly supporting and encouraging his activity, didn't discourage it either. As such, Turner's dealings with players became a sort of cultural norm of being part of the club. No one has ever suggested that management got any rake off from Turner's activity, but there has been no occasion to deny the same either. His activity can't be said to have been at all clandestine, but as Korr pointed out, his wheeling and dealing was certainly shrouded in ambiguity.

Finding Bobby

What are taken as the initial assessments of Moore as a young player have become part of the urban mythology that surround him and the club. Over the following decades there has been no end of claims, from a range of characters, about being the first to identify the talent of young Robert. As usual, everyone wants a shot at glory. If all the people who say that they were at the Sex Pistols' first gig had actually been there, it would have needed to have taken place at the Indianapolis Motor Speedway and not the St Martin's College of Art's packed audience of a few hundred. Much the same thing could be said to be true of Moore's 'discovery'.

The beginning of the 'trail' isn't that hard to find, and it doesn't start with St Pier, Turner or Fenton, who Malcolm Allison might have regarded closer to the Three Stooges than the Three Wise Men of footballing talent that as so often been insinuated by well-meaning students of the chronicles of the enigmatic Irons. In the early 1950s, Allison, West Ham's centre-half and captain, was Robert's footballing father. Later he would become one of Moore's closest personal friends. It was he who nurtured the Barking boy in the days when the lad's talent was budding and it was he who fought for him to be signed by West Ham.

Kids just didn't rock up to Upton Park and get automatically trained by professional players being paid relatively good money in overtime. Young players attended by invitation. Fenton, having asked Malcolm to start working with promising young local boys, plugged into a wide-ranging network that that resulted in the likes of Moore being invited to train at Upton Park on Tuesdays and Thursday. Sessions started at 6pm and lasted for two and a half hours. Sometimes the youngsters would still be involved as darkness fell.

The 30 boys involved were mostly recommended by local schools and clubs. This was part of Ted's effort to pull young talent into Upton Park and hone the best to West Ham's cause. Allison recalled how he had first worked with the 12-year-old Robert in this context: the better part of three years before Turner's first report. That was about 30 per cent of the young man's conscious life!

Even if one discounts such consideration, which is a bit of a reach, the handful of lines produced between Turner and St Pier combined are not convincing as the basis for taking Moore on at Upton Park. What worthwhile assessment might be made by watching one or two games a 15-year-old plays? Logic suggests the club would have been aware of the lad's progress under Allison for some time before the Flanders Field scenario; so his take on Moore was based on a whole lot more than the one or two games that Turner's mostly uneducated eye had taken in. Bobby also had the backing of Noel Cantwell's positive judgement, again established over years.

Another much touted story is that it was Tom Russell who first saw a drive and focus in the teenage Moore, while catching Leyton Boys under-15s games. This has also, over the years, gained traction. However, Russell was at Upton Park in the 1950s, when Moore had been training with Allison for years. So, it doesn't seem likely he just happened upon him as a teenager. At the same time, the young players invited to work under Allison were a select group of no more than 30 boys, out of the likely many thousands who might have wanted such an opportunity. This long-term embracing by the club says more than all the claims about Moore's supposedly almost instantaneous discovery.

While Russell was attached to Moore's school (by the time Ron Greenwood got to the club in 1961, according to Ron's biography, he had risen to be head of Tom Hood), the fact that he appears not to have known about the relatively long association the teenager he supposedly 'discovered' had with Allison – and so the club – probably makes Tom a doubtful candidate as the missing link who connected Moore to his childhood mentor at the Boleyn Ground. If Tom had recommended Bobby to West Ham as a 12-year-old, how could he be said to have discovered him years later?

Terry Wilkinson was a lightly built 22-year-old PE and Geography teacher at Tom Hood when Robert first rocked up there. He was also an enthusiastic footballer, good enough to have played for Brentford, and was later to become a respected member of the Sports Council. As such, he was well-placed, as a PE teacher with a respectable background in the game, to be the first to see Robert's potential not long after he had arrived at the school as an 11-year-old. In fact, Terry was to say it was obvious to him. He took a keen interest in Moore. Indeed, when West Ham wanted to sign Moore, his parents looked to Terry for counsel. The teacher advised them that they should go with West Ham, but to take a good look at the small print.

Unlike Jack Turner, Terry was a man with solid footballing credentials, who was in a situation to see Moore first hand and early on. Further, he was known and trusted by Doris and Big Bob. He knew Reg Revins, who spoke highly of Wilkinson's acumen with regard to nurturing young players. That Ernie Gregory recalled it was Moore's PE teacher who introduced Bobby to West Ham seems to confirm that it was Terry who created the initial link between the doughty young left-half and Allison. Apart from anything else, the role of PE teacher and coach is a natural connection with regard to the identification and referencing of young talent. At the same time, Allison and Cantwell were always going to listen to a fellow 'football man', certainly more than anything Turner had to say.

That said, Fenton would have wanted ongoing assessments of those his players were taking time over. At the same time, Ted failed to have complete faith in or an understanding of young Moore's ability or potential until his last months with the Irons. Thus, there was every reason, from Ted's point of view, to check and double check the boy. It wouldn't have been surprising if it might well have been within the ambit of Jack Turner's de facto roles to be sent on such errands. Although, being a bit of several things around the club, Jack was seemingly master of none, embracing some slightly contradictory functions like 'youth advisor', 'welfare officer' and 'Property Manager'. However, Fenton in his 1960 publication *At Home With the Hammers* has it that Turner

'does not normally watch players, yet here he was, producing out of the hat a lad who has all the makings of a star'.

But Moore wasn't produced 'out of the hat' and Jack's reports, from a man who had no credibility in football or reputation for 'finding' players, didn't tell anyone what wasn't already known about Moore: basically naming him as a 'willing horse'. Added to this, Fenton was to see Moore as anything but rising star before Bobby was in the last of his teenage years.

Another often-repeated story about Moore being adopted by West Ham has it that following a telephone call to Ted Fenton from Bobby's dad, it was the West Ham manager, without delay, who headed east to Waverley Gardens to get the necessary done. This version of events has it that Doris put a cup of tea in front of Ted while he explained that Bobby would get all the coaching required, plenty of games and be paid the basic apprentice wage. 'I'm certain you'll be all right,' he told Big Bob and Doris as their Robert signed the forms.

This might be taken as yet another example of the scramble to be seen as 'the' key figure in Moore being taken into the Upton Park fold. But what seems more probable is that Turner, given his 'suite' of roles, was likely to have been instructed, down the chain of command, to get the formalities done.

Fenton in *At Home With the Hammers* contradicts himself however when he confirms that St Pier, as adjutant to Robinson, was sent to make the approach to Moore to ask if he wanted to join the club ground staff. According to Ted it was Turner, following on from Fenton's decision, and the subsequent offer by St Pier, who undertook the official mechanics of the paperwork. This is the scenario confirmed by Moore himself more than once, and it feels appropriate to and in tune with two or three of Jack's actual and supposed duties.

It seems logical that the most likely person to have seen the initial glimmer of talent in Moore would have been Terry Wilkinson. At the same time, I find it hard to imagine South Park's Len Lilley might not have been active in promoting Moore with West Ham, and that there would have been no dialogue between Len and Terry about Bobby's potential. That would have been very usual. Like most things, there's nearly always more than one person involved in the identification of exceptional talent.

Revinsalia

Len, like many in the junior game, knew the fabled Irons envoi Reg Revins well; a man from a distinguished lineage of Hammers scouts, and probably the best known plier of that trade on the playing fields of east London in the early 1950s, Flanders Field and Barking FC's Vicarage Field included. The Revins name is hardly uttered in most histories of West Ham, maybe because above all he valued anonymity, seeing it as his 'ace in the hole'. Indeed, it has been suggested to me more than once that 'Revins' was a nom de plume, and I have heard him referred to by various names. He also had a bit of a reputation as a 'master of disguise', donning different hats, glasses, the occasional false moustache or wig. Humble to a fault, he shunned any kind of congratulation or publicity. He preferred to stay in the great shadow of the game.

An inspirational figure to later scouts, the likes of Arthur Lamb for instance, watching football in the parks and streets of the 'easterly smoke' was Reg's life, as it had been for his father and grandfather (both named Reg). For a long time it was thought he had no background in actually playing the game, but it seems his grandfather, although born and raised in Canning Town, had played the game for FC Tatran Prešov in Slovakia, his son and grandson also turned out for a series of amateur clubs. The last in the Revins line was offered professional forms for several top-line clubs, but chose instead to dedicate his life to the unearthing of talent, his and his forebears' true passion. This devotion had cost him marriage and, at times, his livelihood.

Hardly a day went by in Reg's existence, from his first steps, alongside his father and/or grandfather, when he wasn't watching football, be it matches, random kick-abouts or training. He was constantly preoccupied with seeking out the flair so often missed by lesser mortals. Reg and Allison were very different men. Revins, was almost a total loner, apart from a few close associates. He never swore, smoked and was strictly teetotal. He practically lived on pie and chips, his only vice was seemingly endless cups of highly sweetened tea – he would only drink Brooke Bond loose leaves, any other brand he saw as 'not being tea', and was known to walkout on anyone giving him a teabag. Nevertheless, his knowledge and dedication earned him the respect of anyone associated with football in east London.

There was a saying that knocked round the innards of Boleyn Ground from its first days as the home of the Hammers. This mantra persisted across the years up to the late 1950s, 'If Revins ain't seen you, you have not been seen at all.' It would thus be remiss not to expect the man they called 'the eyes' to have been involved in the Bobby Moore's adoption to the Upton Park cause.

Contortion

Jack Turner likely was a bit part-playing functionary in the process of actually signing Moore, but it was Allison who nursed the slightly more than average kid into one of the brightest hopes for the English game. Why the story of Moore's 'discovery' has been so contorted and maybe suppressed in such an unconvincing way is a matter of conjecture. Why Fenton gave Turner so much credit is anyone's guess. It might have been to play down Allison's role, there was no love lost between the two men, or it could have been Pratt and Ted felt the need to justify Jack's presence.

Why the role of Russell might have been emphasised is also a bit puzzling. He rose to be head of Tom Hood; Wilkinson was just a PE teacher, so Tom was seemingly the more ambitious man. But highlighting Russel adds to the obscuration of Allison's part in Moore's emergence. It is perhaps telling that Allison's role in building West Ham's over-achieving youth teams of the late 1950s, and the promotion side of 1958, was effectively all but hidden or underplayed, Fenton and Robinson being given the lion share of the credit for the same.

The Moore 'discovery' legend is full of contradictions, but mostly feels like the sort of thing that would be fed to supporters in the 1950s via match programmes and the local media; a tale of 'instant generation', rags to riches, a romantic narrative of a 'diamond in the rough', pulled literally 'out of the hat' by mystic insight, conjured out of the conventional practices of the thoroughly benign if elite 'founding fathers'. Such fairytales were favoured over the less starry-eyed history of application, dedication, endeavour, years of hard work, and the central place of a confounding and radical anti-establishment figure (such as Allison); the victory of the new and innovative over the old guard of tradition. Such adherence to naked reality though would have just underwritten Allison's assessment that the whole setup at West Ham was unimaginative and anachronistic, populated by ineffectual old duffers, clueless serial failures, talentless sycophants and over-blown egos. In the last analysis, as the star of the 1957 FA Youth Cup Final side, George Fenn, was to tell, while Fenton signed players it was often Malcolm who identified the ones required – and he wanted Moore at a point when others either didn't or just didn't care to argue with Allison.

Turner was later to say that Bobby Moore was not the type of player you could see just once and appreciate. In his favour, he did see him twice – at least – but he likely put his finger on something in relation to the supposed 'discovery' of the player. People are inclined to say what they last saw of a person is congruent with what they first saw – variations of 'you could always tell' abound in Moore's storied life. However, as a kid, Moore's authority on the field was not always totally apparent. Certainly, as a young man in the mid-1950s, teenage and maturity would have been considered strange bedfellows. Moore's predilection for little touches and forward forays premised on his spacial awareness, together with his inconspicuous instructions to team-mates, often made his play too subtle and nuanced to command immediate, glittering accolades. Such characteristics and qualities are hard to identify at first glance, and would not have had many exemplars before Bobby became England captain. Indeed, to fully understand the value of a player like Moore one needed to be something of a football connoisseur. His performance had to be seen 'in the round' and required an educated eye, by the likes Allison, Cantwell, Winterbottom, Greenwood and Ramsey, all of whom were themselves possessed of exceptional minds, attuned to the game.

Allison had no time for any of the figures portrayed as key in 'finding' Bobby. For him they were dinosaurs and hangers-on. He was a contrarian, in football terms a revolutionary even, one of the first voices of 'player power' in the game, definitely the first at Upton Park. As such, he was not the right 'shape' to be posited as part of the courtly mythology of the Hammers of that era. Hence Fenton's book marks the start of the stifling of his actually massive contribution – the very people Malcolm dismissed were 'bigged up' by Ted.

When Ron Greenwood took over from Fenton the board swiftly quashed his nomination of Allison to be brought back to the club as assistant manager. While that might not indubitably confirm Malcolm as 'persona non grata' status around the environs of Upton Park, it's a pretty smelly indicator.

The demise of Turner

For a time, Turner did have his own office at Upton Park, halfway along a corridor alongside others. The sign on the door said 'Property Manager'. Nobody was quite sure what that meant, except perhaps that Turner could be responsible for nothing or everything at West Ham United according to how the mood took him and the board. In Ted Fenton's time, the property manager found himself dealing with every problem which was thought – mostly by Ted – as either too trivial or too delicate to involve the team manager.

But titles emblazoned on Jack's office door seemed to change as regularly as the traffic lights at the top of Green Street. This reflected and confirmed his apparent 'chameleon persona'. However, appellations such as 'Property Manager' or 'Personnel Manager' didn't really pin him down. He certainly wasn't a scout as such. Over a period, he did have almost sole responsibility for property, while dealing with player finances, having access to and, as some (not necessarily me) might harshly have it perhaps, grooming players at every point in their career, even after their time at the Boleyn Ground was over. Ethically, and perhaps morally, this put him in an overly influential position with regard to human and financial resources, with none of the checks and balances via formal employee status.

One definite area of responsibility given over to Turner was the unenviable job of telling players to get out of properties following the termination of their contracts – in actuality this made him the club bailiff. He also did some of the administrative work that had previously been undertaken by the chairman and/or the manager.

Fenton had worked hard at the impossible, looking, simultaneously to be the boss and one of the lads (a bit like the conductor of an orchestra attempting to do that while playing the tuba). Notionally, Turner's manoeuvring allowed Ted to be more detached, particularly from many of financial considerations the players might have. To be fair, that wasn't such a bad idea. Later, Greenwood having to deal with player pay and their on-field responsibilities did much to hold the club back. This 'role confusion' was to be a constant frustration to him.

However, Jack elbowing his way in between manager and players was never going to have a place in Ron Greenwood's thinking. He and Turner failed to hit it off from the get-go; 'Jack-the-lad' likely too nearly fitting Ron's preconceptions about Cockney shysters, a sort of St Trinian's 'Flash Harry' to Greenwood's 'Keeping up Appearances' Hyacinth Bucket.

The offer to players of a house at a reasonable rent (a sort of equivalent to a tithe cottage arrangement in feudal agriculture) had always been an incentive to sign for West Ham. The subject of property was a regular item at board meetings, demonstrating the small, practically personalised, business ethos that pertained at Upton Park. The board, together with the club's estate agent, and Fenton, all had a history of being involved with the houses. The board chose not to simply delegate matters to the estate agent, as this would leave players totally exposed to their profit-making. However, perhaps the main aim of supplying housing was to consolidate the relationship between the club and its playing staff; it was part of the workings of patronage, but it was also an aspect of West Ham being thought of as a 'family club'. That said, dealing with housing issues was probably not the best use of Fenton's time. When Pratt became chairman in 1950 and brought in Jack Turner, he was to facilitate Turner's involvement in selling club houses to players. This meant that the club ditched its function as landlord.

This was a substantial break with the past, and a change in direction in terms of the club's attitude to the players. On the board's side the move was giving up a degree of control over the players, but it was a loss of an incentive for new players to sign for the club, and for others to stay at Upton Park.

Initially the new housing policy was not popular with the players. Few came from backgrounds that included a mortgage and most understood that their careers were anything but protracted or secure enough to realistically support decades long debt. If they weren't aware of such considerations, they were soon brought up to speed by the difficulty they had in finding a lender. Added to this, in the 1950s, most players would not have had the spare cash for a deposit on a house.

With all this in mind Turner set up a scheme that automatically transferred sums of money from the weekly wages of players to building societies, who in turn supplied the necessary mortgages. Jack followed this up by approaching insurance companies with a similar arrangement, thus transforming the club's aim to sell its houses into a species of annuity for the players. With regard to housing this turned the club into an entity partly concerned with property profiteering.

Turner showed his skill in weasel words by describing this process as 'politely compelling players to save' – as if it were about their welfare alone. Some players saw through this, others thought it immaterial. More experienced players, some of whom were home owners, were having no truck with a tangential representative of the club, and particularly the prospect of an insurance man (not the most beloved occupation of the working class of the time) orchestrating dips into their wage packets.

Jack was to tell of his relationship with Reg Pratt, 'We got very close … I would be at the ground three, four days a week … because I was a person he could talk to.' You might be forgiven for concluding it also seemed to be his own private gold mine. However, given all this, it is puzzling how Pratt, by the mid-1960s, dropped the axe on Jack pretty sharpish.

The arrival of the straight-laced Greenwood and his thoroughly, if painfully, straight bat, was the beginning of the end for 'Tinpot Turner'. Jack believed Ron was indeed his nemesis. He recalled how he and the new Hammers manager 'clashed immediately … Greenwood didn't want me there … I didn't blame him because he wanted to interfere with something he knew nothing about'. But what Greenwood did know about, perhaps more than any other Englishman before him, was football and Turner was clearly not lurking around Upton Park and its playing staff out of a passion for the game.

The tension between Greenwood and Turner, and Pratt's motivation to eventually be rid of Jack, was ignited by Turner's situation when it came to players establishing and renewing their contracts. Jack's loyalty to the club, with no employment ties, was trumped by his client/friendship relationship with players, most notably perhaps with its brightest rising star and the man the players were to grow to trust most at the club: Bobby Moore. In the adversarial game of wage negotiation, it was in Turner's interest to maximise player gains and so cost the club money, and it was Moore who took over Allison's role as the de facto player shop steward at Upton Park.

Ultimately, and most tellingly perhaps, Turner represented something less than the type of professional attitude Greenwood lived by and sought to cultivate. Jack was part of the antiquated club culture of informal patronage that Ron was never going to be able to tolerate.

Turner, likely overestimating his hand with Pratt, told the chairman he couldn't work with Greenwood, given that the situation had turned personal. It was an 'either he goes or I do' ultimatum. Ron, like Allison, was telling the playing staff to avoid Jack's seductive advances. Turner's eagerness to parachute, boots-first, into the personal, private and financial worlds of players was not the way Greenwood did things. A player asking him his opinion about football matters was one thing; what they might do about their finances would have been quite a different kettle of brass monkeys. There can be little doubt he would have either said it was nothing to do with him, or just gone into Socratic dialogue mode; answering any questions with a question. That said, his contempt for the likes of Turner, and any opinion he might have about football or footballers, would have been more than obvious – it would have stunk the place out.

At first Pratt asked Turner to hang in, but his position was not viable. His style and guile really backfired on him. In the words of one player of the time, 'He was exposed for the parasite he appeared to be.' His fickle friend Pratt reverted to the naked in tooth and claw businessman he was and concluded the cost/benefits of Turner warranted the order of the boot. Jack had long wanted an entrepreneurial attitude from the board and ultimately, he got it – slap!

Ultimately Turner was given the 'bum's rush', the cold shoulder, the elbow and a tea set while being shown the 'two-by-four' and its knocker by Reg Pratt. Turner, after his departure in 1966, continued to express his admiration for the former chairman, seeing him as the man who had been able to break the cultural mould fostered by Bill Cearns and his lad Len, together with the West Ham board, who for Jack had stymied the growth and success of the club – his view of Cearns was that he had 'ruled like iron and spent money like a man with no arms'.

Turner was to remark, 'For West Ham to buy me a silver tea service is a sign of how much I was doing, especially since the only thing the club bought was a wreath when you died.' This leaving gift, a bit short of 30 pieces of silver, was evidence of how his efforts were appreciated. A more jaundiced eye might see that confession differently, of course. He also had a good seat in the directors' box at Upton Park, as he boasted, 'Other people had to shift.'

Understandably Turner was pissed off and remained so for years. Of course, he would have been – both his social life and his golden egg-laying goose had been snatched from him, as his arse was kicked down Green Street, with his hi-ho silver teapot, after the club as good labelled him an anachronism, telling the world he no longer fitted into the modern football club that was West Ham United.

However, Jack would become, what might be labelled, Moore's 'business manager' or 'financial adviser' (or something). Maybe his role was closer to what would be called an 'agent' in later years (although that species of hirudinea was outlawed by the FA at that time).

It was really only after Moore played for England that Turner ingratiated himself fully with Bobby. Moore turned to Jack when he wanted to end an advertising agency contract. This resulted in Turner taking responsibility for other promotional concerns. Shrewdly, yet again he declined accepting any kind of employment role, he wanted to be more of a partner than a hired hand, so he formed Bobby Moore Ltd, making himself a director, which all but put Moore in the role as Jack's employee.

Turner worked with Moore to set up a sportswear shop in 1961 that many older fans will remember, situated close to opposite the Boleyn Ground, in 542 Green Street, a few doors away from the childhood home of the current West Ham owner David Gold. Jack had initially looked to get Lawrie Leslie to run it, but when the goalkeeper broke his leg and went out of the limelight, Turner lost interest in the 1962 Hammer of the Year. It was managed by a distinctively shiny-looking bloke called 'Squibbs', who, according to my dad, started life as a 'snow clearer' – which struck me as a nice, steady job. After his first marriage Bobby's mother-in-law, Betty, worked behind the counter. Bobby was sometimes around, but more as a 'promotional presence'. It did OK. although most of the rather limited stock range could be got much cheaper elsewhere. For a time, the shop offered a collect, wash and fold cleaning service for football team kits, advertised in the local press with an image of Bobby's head on one side. It was said that the shop at one point was making Bobby as much as he was earning from his football, but I'd have my doubts about that. Rowe Sports on Barking Road, just opposite the Boleyn pub, a two-minute walk from Moore's modest gaff, was cheaper and, in comparison was a veritable emporium, having a relatively huge range of goods. It was run by a nice guy with big glasses and a moustache, who was always up for a deal for a bulk buy or an 'exchange deal' for 'homeless stuff'. During Moore's last years with the club his gaff looked distinctly dowdy. Rowe Sports ceased trading around the time Bobby transferred to Fulham in 1974.

The shop premises was a converted terraced house. Jack had previously used the place as a warehouse for a football boots business he had some sort of involvement in. The running-joke, with no evidential basis, was they were all left ones and marked up 'Adidarse'. Turner, however, might not have been exactly the business guru some reports have indicated. From the time Moore got in deep with Jack, in terms of entrepreneurial and business ventures, the relationship can't be said overall to have been close to successful, which hardly provides Turner with glowing references. As Malcolm Allison had it 'Turner helped no one but himself.'

But we all help ourselves ultimately. The proposal of the selfless altruist is as fanciful as the streetwise saint (a banal inhabitant of my world of youth work).

Jack was just a man, like many, doing what he could to get by and rise above the disadvantage he, like many of us from the West Ham district, was born into. No one can be blamed for looking to make a quid where fair and rare opportunity shows itself and does no lasting harm to others. I don't believe Jack's advice to Moore was any worse than Bobby might have got elsewhere; these things are mostly a toss of a coin. Some years ago, the global website Freakonomics undertook a study of entrepreneurs. It found the most crucial factor in terms of business success was 'luck'. Certainly, Moore seemed more appreciative of Turner's influence and advice than otherwise, so I guess he was lucky – and if fortune favours the brave, it maybe won't be too bad to the cheeky.

A while ago I was invited to give a presentation to a group of students on a social geography programme. It seems in that sphere I am thought of as a 'social cartographer' (how about that!).

During the subsequent discussion one learner said she saw 'identity as a map of self, drawn in reference to other maps of self'. She explained that this means the map of self should be in a constant state of flux and revision. However, usually it's not, because this would be a source of existential anxiety. Thus our self maps ossify, trapping us in an 'unchanging map of self' – an illusion of who we and others are, premised on a landscape that has ceased to exist.

I told someone I worked with when he was a teenager about this. Now in his 50s, starting his brave battle against cancer, he said, 'Some people think too much.' I don't make him wrong, but this young geographer had a point. None of us are the person we look back on, and the pictures presented to us of people from the past are just impressions, the reality of them, who or what they actually were (Turner, Moore, St Pier, Fenton, Allison, my dad, you or me) is/was almost certainly different. Sometimes the reality was a diametrical opposite of the 'record' – things I've never really given biblical credit to – that kind of trust and error is a common trait so many amateur historians.

Turner was ultimately to admit he was anything but the best thing for Bobby. He told Charles Korr, 'Moore should have got away from me and been handled by someone like Mark McCormack[4],' which would certainly have been more financially lucrative for Bobby. But Jack had captured Moore's trust, which the cynical among us (not me) might see as effectively shanghaiing Bobby as Jack's cash cow. But Jack did his bit for West Ham, in his own way. With him it was a case of 'cometh the hour, cometh the man' (and 'endeth the hour, goeth the bloke'). He was the answer to a problem that threatened to cut off the very lifeblood of the Boleyn Ground. The slick Turner was pitted against a Puck-like nemesis from

4   The American sports agent, lawyer and author.

his own neck of the woods, in the mid-1950s, ensconced over in Romford, deep in the leafy heartlands of 'Hammerhood', Jimmy 'Rolling Stone' Thompson had to be thwarted, and to his lasting credit, 'Jack the Lad', fighting blatant temerity with guile and stealth, did just that – likely at that time, in that place, there was no better man for the job.

7

'THEN WEST HAM CALLED ME UP'

Just as it seemed to Robert that he had been passed over, he was asked to join the Hammers. Predictably he dashed home that night to tell his parents. It was August 1956 when Moore signed amateur forms for West Ham. He made his debut for West Ham Colts on 6 October.

Looking back at this part of his life, Moore understood himself to be fortunate. He saw West Ham as giving him a chance, by way of working hard, to make up for what he perceived as his deficiencies. He had an instinctive understanding of the truism in much of sport and life; that natural talent early on is often not enough. This was confirmed by his learning under the tutelage of Malcolm Allison. As he was to state, 'The schoolboy plodder never takes anything for granted, and is much more likely to listen carefully to all the advice he's given.'

Allison's greatest memory of Moore as a child was his persistent asking of questions, a rarity in most of us; we tend to ask fewer questions relative to the number statements we make – we live in world of 'know-it-alls'. The skipper of the early 1950s recollected,

'I was standing at the bus stop one day after training and he came up and said, "Mr Allison, can I sit next to you on the bus?" So, we are on the bus and he never stopped asking questions. He asked me what was the most important thing to do in football. I told him, "Knowing what you're going to do with the ball before you get it." He said, "That's wonderful," and wrote it down. He did that in every game he ever played around the world. He knew what he was going to do with the ball before he got it.'

At that time, Malcolm was lodging in Barkingside with Hammers striker Vic Keeble, so the shared bus ride and seminar would be a regular event.

Later Allison put his answer another way, 'Always ask yourself, "What would I do if the ball came to me now?"' If you think about it, this is a variation of the Scouts motto, 'Be Prepared'. Preparation will unquestionably trump planning as it relies as much on insight as it does foresight. Planning is really premised on hope, hence the old military adage, 'On the first day of the battle, forget the battle plan.' A plan is a comfort blanket, it gives us the idea that we can predict and so control the future. We really can't. One wrinkle in the best of plans would scupper them and the unpredictable is the only predictable thing in our universe. Moore's great ability was invariably knowing the answer the question Allison asked him to ask himself, and of course, the answer constantly changed second by second in every game.

In the dawn of his career Bobby thrived on the atmosphere of what he was to describe as a 'football school' at Upton Park. Critics in the early 1960s had it that the Hammers were too taken up with theory to win anything. However, for Moore, West Ham started thinking about football before most other clubs, at a time when game was changing dramatically, and that suited him.

The Boleyn Ground in the 1950s didn't really look like 'innovation ground zero' though. It was really a bit of a shithole. The North Bank – the Sir Trevor Brooking Stand to be – was open terracing with no cover. The terracing on the South Bank – what became the Bobby Moore Stand – was partly covered, but anyone standing at the front always got soaked in the winter rains.

The Main Stand – the future Dr. Martens Stand – looked a tad awkward as it only stretched along two-thirds the length of the pitch. It appeared that the builders had stopped building it when 70 per cent finished. Although there was a standing enclosure under the main stand that did stretch the whole way along the touchline. Later on, the North Bank was covered and the Main Stand extended, but apart from that the ground remained pretty much the same over the following few decades.

School's out forever

In the last months of his school life Robert was assigned to meet the careers officer. That rite of passage was still in place at the time I left school some 14 years later. I was working with my dad then, I had been from about the age of five, so going through the motions of pretending to identify a career trajectory was somewhere between a necessary chore and a bit of fun for me. I had no intention of doing anything else at that point in time (nothing else was going to pay me half as much to start with). But I had to show willing because my dad also wanted me to draw the dole when work slacked off.

The first person I saw told me there was a job as a lift attendant at the East Ham Co-op. I commented that it sounded 'like a job with its ups and downs'. I saw no sign that she had picked up on my rapier-like repartee. The next bloke I saw was a thoroughly decent chap, but had no idea how to deal with Cockney teenagers of my ilk. I told him I wanted to be an astronaut, which would have been a first for Burke Secondary Modern School (albeit West Ham owner David Gold had preceded me as a scholar at the same seat of dubious learning). Over several weeks, the guy from the Youth Employment Service got me all sorts of literature from NASA, while gently doing his best to persuade me that 'another role' in the aerospace industry might be a better idea. Alas, I told him. as he handed that last batch of this bumf over to me, that I'd changed my mind and had decided I wanted to be a shepherd. Again, that was a novel choice for a Plaistow lad. He sorted me out a training course in Cumbria, but by then I was offski, buccaneering round London Town with the old man. The YES bloke was a diamond, and maybe was more astute than I gave him credit for at the time; he walked with me for a bit, and that's sometimes just what kids need.

The young Moore was nicer than me and let the fella he saw know that he was going to be a footballer. Wisely they gave him the good advice to think about possible alternatives should this ambition not be realised, and he did half-consider other career paths. However, although advice is sometimes useful, hope is always glorious.

Like his study peers, Robert looked forward to the dance that would celebrate the end of their school careers, but it was cancelled because it was thought it would divert the leavers from their exams. So prefect Moore and the rest of his year went on strike. However, that week he had the job of delivering the teachers' lunches to the staff room. He was no 'blackleg' so he refused to fulfil this duty and as a result he was suspended from school. This was something of a rehearsal for his future in 'industrial relations'. Bobby was always a 'quiet militant'.

Ultimately the school was obliged to get back in touch with its erstwhile waiter as he had won a new school prize, the Sportsman's Cup. So, five days after Robert departed Tom Hood, on 24 July 1957 he was back to accept this award. Previously such plaudits had been reserved for learners who had served the institution's interest best in terms of academic achievement, accomplishment in the arts and so on. Robert was touched, and he showed his emotion; he was visibly moved at the end of his five years at Tom Hood. His teachers recognised that the young man was more than capable of handling a sixth year and do well at A-levels. However, Bobby's education was destined to take another route.

In 1957 no one could have imagined where the path Bobby had chosen might lead, even though a few months earlier, in April 1957, he had been with the West Ham Colts playing in an international youth tournament in Dortmund, West Germany. His travelling companions included Harry Cripps, Brian Goymer, Roy Walker, Bert Howe, John Lyall, Andy Smillie, George Fenn, Terry McDonald, Colin Norcott and Charlie Rowlands. The other teams involved were Vitesse Arnhem (Netherlands) Start Chorzów (Poland) Malmö (Sweden) and Borussia Dortmund, Sportverein 08, TuS Eving-Lindenhorst and VfB Alemannia (West Germany). This was a massive adventure for east London kids at the time.

Thinking of the time when the 1950s started to disappear over the horizon, Wally St Pier, albeit very retrospectively, named Moore as the greatest find of West Ham's scouting setup, but it is doubtful if he might have begun to conceive of the heights that the Barking boy would scale. Peter Brabrook, Moore's long-time Irons team-mate and a fine player in his own right, once remarked to have been proud to have played in the same side as Bobby, naming him as the best player he had worked with and, alongside Pelé and George Best, the greatest player he had ever seen. For Peter,

'Bobby's temperament throughout his career was outstanding and his ability was unquestionable. He was a model of consistency, who never had a bad game; he either had brilliant games or good ones. He was such a good reader of the game and a great passer, but he always played the ball so simple and he was a credit to English football.'

As a Chelsea player, before he made a move to Upton Park, Brabrook confessed to finding Moore a very difficult opponent, 'When we played West Ham, I always roasted Noel Cantwell, the left-back, who was probably the best left-back in the country. But I could never seem to get passed Bobby. He was nowhere near as quick as Noel or me, but he never let you get in a position to beat him – he led you into a trap and caught you by the byline or the corner flag.'

Bobby not so much played as thought football – for Moore, while others were applying mere physicality and fighting, he was using his mind, thinking about the whole game, and in the process, by predicting and anticipating, as Brabrook described, controlling the minds and so the actions of others.

Your left foot

Ambidexterity enhances control, enhanced control enhances confidence and creativity. The more you can control you, the less others are able to control you, the more you are able to control others.

Jeff Powell, in 1997's *Bobby Moore: The Life and Times of a Sporting Hero*, wrote of Moore, 'Knowing his left foot to be comparatively weak, he spent countless hours perfecting a curved pass with the outside of the right foot to achieve the same effect as a pass with his left. Knowing that he lacked a sharp change of pace, he painstakingly programmed into his make-up a positional sense which made it impossible for opponents to exploit that flaw … That intense concentration, that search for perfection, was just one of the investments which matured Moore into the best defender in world football.'

However, one of the first things Malcolm Allison worked on with kids was the use of both feet. Moore's temperament was not unlike that of Trevor Brooking, another West Ham product who went on to become an England international. Apart from wearing claret and blue most of their professional lives, the two have other things in common; both were slow runners, both hardly headed the ball and both taught themselves to be two-footed players. To quote Allison,

'Why would anyone think that a footballer is going to be anything but disadvantaged by being unable to use half on their "foot arsenal"?'

Moore was not the same as Brooking in that Trevor could use both feet equally well, but he wasn't wholly 'one-sided' – his left foot could work.

We are all born more or less ambidextrous, that is with a greater or lesser potential to use both hands and/or feet equally dextrously. Historically it was believed, and some continue to believe, that learning to use both hands or feet can make the brain work more astutely and swiftly. It has been claimed that training children to use their non-dominant hands might improve educational results.

By the age of four most of us have a propensity for using our left or right hand, and usually the matching foot more than the other. Almost invariably this doesn't change for rest of our lives. The vast majority of us are right-handed, but a very small group – less than one in 100 of us, are ambidextrous.

As far as we know, whether you are left-handed or right-handed is, at least in part, genetically decided. This is true of all other mammals, although science has no answer to the question why we are predominantly right-handed.

Right handedness is related to the left hemisphere of the brain, which predominantly controls the right side of the body; the left side of the body being mainly controlled by right hemisphere. The left side of the brain, in most of us, houses the brain's language centres, and so is believed to be dominant in relation to the right hemisphere.

At the end of the 19th century a movement emerged that believed the brain's hemispheres to be distinct and independent, and that because the majority of people being right-handed were underusing half of their brains. Effectively this suggests that humanity was wasting something close to half its potential to learn. This school of thought had it that each hand might be totally autonomous of the other in any task. This went as far as postulating that while one hand might be writing a letter, the other could be playing the piano, and that an ambidextrous population would in effect mean that people would have two-brains.

This thinking was based on early scientific observations, but it was never taken seriously. For all this, a body of thinking today continues to argue that learning to use the non-dominant hand (and/or foot) can improve overall brain function. This idea is based on notion of neuroplasticity, a term that refers to how the functional areas of the brain can change in response to experience. This capacity can be seen to kick-in when an area of the brain is injured. Not unusually another part of the brain compensates for areas disabled by disease of physical damage, to a greater or lesser extent taking over the functioning that has been incapacitated.

Simple logic might have it as the non-dominant hand, being linked to the non-dominant, less-exercised side of the brain, when the non-dominant hand is used more (activation is increased) both hemispheres are stimulated (instead of mostly just the one – as you are using both hands), which might result in people thinking differently, facilitating greater creativity and so on.

This proposal falls down somewhat as we know that all activities, even those that engage brain areas in a specific brain hemisphere, usually involve the synchronised activity of both hemispheres. However, it has become generally acknowledged in science and medicine that brain function and structure can be changed, sometimes dramatically by new experiences and focused training; right-handed people can be trained to use their left hand.

Although there have been a range of different positions, it has not been established that one might be advantaged educationally or intellectually by being or becoming ambidextrous. The focus has, for the most part, been on apparent brain development and/or activity or skill acquisition, perhaps suggesting positive or negative learning outcomes. There has however been relatively very little research about the impact of being trained or coached to be ambidextrous in terms of the development of attitudes, flexible thinking, imagination and so on – the potential outcomes of having to think hard about the way the body works and recognising its strengths and weaknesses.

For example, having perfected the use both hands to play the piano, you and your audience will hear you playing the piano better. Likewise, if you can use both your feet to equal effect in football or dancing (for instance), you are bound to see how this makes you better equipped than the one-footed player, or dancer. A two-handed snooker player is at an advantage. This, almost unavoidably, results not only in improved performance, but in greater self-confidence generally. So, there is not only a physical but also psychological development and enhancement, including perhaps even positive emotional impacts. If one has control over not just one but both sides of your body, it's predictable that your creative and so imaginative powers, with regard to innovation, strategy or whatever it is one is trying to achieve, will be (at least) doubled. Here we are talking about capacities and qualities of mind.

Both the focus required to acquire use of both feet and the potential for greater creativity and better/more successful outcomes will call on the individual concerned to use their reasoning, and so their 'higher brain' functions. This will enhance the chances of making better judgements (we use our higher brain to formulate judgement) both in terms of tactics and strategy, but also with regard to actions taken under duress and stress – the means to control one's temper and use reason.

By far and away, studies concerning themselves with the development of left-handedness have concentrated on potential and actual brain activity, but it has pretty much neglected looking at the impact on these aspects of mind.

All those who break into elite sport at the top echelons have learned 'control'. It was Ron Greenwood who told me that one of the few things he disagreed with Alf Ramsey about was he, unlike Alf, felt that in football the idea of 'controlled aggression' was inappropriate. Greenwood saw the phrase as pretty much a contradiction in terms, sending players along a very thin line. For him cold, rational control was undermined the more aggression is involved. Aggression too easily heats up and degenerates into violence and that means a loss of control.

An example was the 1966 World Cup quarter-final between Argentina and England. Bobby Moore held his side together in the face of naked violence (the predictable progeny of aggression); at the epicentre of the storm, he remained calm, as the South Americans expressed their fear and feeling of inferiority facing Moore, Bobby Charlton and co, acting, as Ramsey aptly put it, 'like animals'; almost a perfect definition of the lower brain functioning dominating thought, limiting action to 'fight or flight'. The basis of England's slim victory in that tie was control as their opposition went about defeating themselves. Bobby Moore exemplified that necessary discipline. Where did that start? Well, in part via thinking about controlling his body for so many years, but also, as a five-year-old, folding his fucking socks!

In the very last analysis, for the most part, football is not a cause for flight or fight, it isn't a do-or-die struggle for survival. Despite romantic and popular culture that might have us think otherwise, the best players have adopted the sort of attitude fostered by Moore. They have been controlled and so can be in control, Bobby Charlton, Pelé, Beckenbauer and so on. Yes, you can cite the likes of George Best and others, but such incendiary players do not, in the main, last overly long or reach the same heights of consistent performance and achievement over time that the more controlled players accomplish.

Football is a game played by humans and thus best played thoughtfully. Enter the fray as an animal, led by the 'lower', most ancient part of your brain, the remnants of reptilian forebears, and you are not in control. As such you will be controlled by those you face who have learned to control themselves, actually being 'more human'. You can't control them because you can't even control yourself. Thus, you simply will not be able to play – you will just fight or run away; either way, you lose. It seems trite, but personal control starts with control of the body by the mind – control of the mind cannot be attained while one lacks of control of the body.

This is more about control of relative physical resources than relative physical ability. Paralympians need to exert bodily control, perhaps sometimes to a greater extent than those crudely seen as not 'disabled' – pleasingly paradoxically (for me anyway) many of those labelled as 'disabled' are far more able to control their physical capacities than the vast majority of the so called 'able-bodied'. You try drawing an Olympic bow with your left leg!

'Fenton's Fawns'

No one concerned with Moore's development as a 'thinking footballer', the cultivation of a 'footballing mind' that produced a player of intelligence, found it hard to talk him into training at Upton Park and come under the umbrella of West Ham's then new youth policy, which was almost entirely financially driven.

West Ham simply did not have the means to buy expensive contracts or provide the sizeable under-the-table 'gifts' (cars, fridges, gold sovereigns) that it took to get the big stars of the game to come to a club in those halcyon days of the cheeky backhander and the bon vivant bung. Hammers had to be 'made', like the ships built by Thames Iron Works – they were wrought out of raw iron!

At the start of the 1950s it was becoming obvious to Ted Fenton that West Ham were having local talent snatched from under the club's claret and blue conk. Schoolboy players from the east London and west Essex heartlands of the Irons support were being lured to other clubs, in particular Chelsea, where manager Ted Drake had instigated his 'Drake's Ducklings' youth policy, following on from the likes of Manchester United (the nascent 'Busby Babes').

Protégées, like future England internationals Ken Shellito, Peter Brabrook, Terry Venables and Jimmy Greaves, were being sucked out of the bloodstream of West Ham. These kids had been weaned on the streets, playgrounds, bomb sites and playing fields of the Hammers hinterlands.

At that time, and up to when I was a kid, the top football clubs, especially in London, flooded east London with scouts. They were at school, Sunday morning and youth club games. Sometimes there were little troops of this fraternity lining the touchlines of every rough pitch you played on. Men from Tottenham Hotspur, Leyton Orient, Chelsea, Arsenal as well as the likes of Manchester United, all seemed to know one another and apparently did all they could to send each other on wild goose chases. I was useless, but big for my age, so with biology on my side, but alas not god-given talent, I found myself invited to trial with Orient. On my inevitable rejection at Brisbane Road a QPR scout asked me to give the Hoops the benefit of viewing my lack of skill – I did and lo and behold, experienced the same inevitable outcome, being told after a massive punch-up on the pitch to 'give boxing a shot'. But I had already tried that and having chased my opponent out of the ring with a stool (the bastard hurt me!) was effectively book, bell and candled from the 'noble art'.

Perhaps the 'vampire general' of docklands and east Thameside football talent heist was the somewhat peculiar if lively Jimmy 'Rolling Stone' Thompson. This former stevedore was predominantly a scout for Chelsea, but also Southampton and others. His list of credits includes discovering Jimmy Greaves, Barry Bridges and Terry Venables.

Unlike some of his Irons counterparts, Thompson, who himself was born and raised in West Ham, had an impressive background in football. He started out as an amateur with Charlton and Wimbledon. On his debut for the Dons, an FA Cup replay against Redhill during the Dons' first Isthmian League season, he scored five goals, but he only played in four FA Cup ties (scoring two further goals) and one league match as he was, at the same time, turning out for Charlton as an amateur. Described as a 'popular player' and 'a steady fellow', Jimmy was selected for a Southern League representative XI, and scored twice in a 3-0 victory over the Central League.

Jimmy went on to play for Millwall, Coventry City, Clapton Orient, Luton Town, Chelsea, Norwich City, Sunderland, Fulham and Hull City. He then moved into non-league football with Tunbridge Wells Rangers and Peterborough United, before signing for Tranmere Rovers, Sittingbourne and Aldershot. In his career, he played more than 150 professional games, scoring around 100 goals. Thompson wore the colours of Norwich for 30 of those appearances, putting 17 of his goals away for the Canaries. After his playing days Thompson managed Dartford for a while.

He came into the game as a winger, but was converted to a centre-forward upon joining Chelsea for the 1927/28 season. He scored on his debut at Reading, and was top scorer for the campaign with 25 goals, helping the west Londoners to finish third in the Second Division, just missing out on promotion to the top flight. He would play out of Stamford Bridge for one more season, a relatively disappointing crusade in which Chelsea finished ninth, though Thompson was again the top scorer, this time jointly with both George Biswell and Andy Wilson, all three achieving the more modest total of nine goals apiece.

Thompson, rarely spotted out not sporting his dark green bowler hat, was a throwback, even in the mid-20th century. An ebullient, flamboyant character, having been in hot water a few times for poaching young players, Jimmy used an assortment of pseudonyms: Don Donnell, Hughey Strop and Mr Pope among others. He pulled down a living from scouting for kids, but he also plied the dodgy service of placing bets for jockeys and racehorse trainers for whom, then as now, the whiff of the bookies was distinctly off limits. He had an abiding interest in the gee-gees, almost poetically, at the age of 86, he dropped dead at Epson races in 1984, wearing the beloved bowler that went with him to eternity.

When it came to signing kids, Thompson had a penchant for refusing to take no for an answer, persistently parking up his rose-red Sunbeam Talbot outside a prospect's house, seeking to win player and parents over. Thompson never learned to drive; his daughter chauffeured him about. She also kept tabs on the gossip in the wider scouting fraternity, such as how many times particular individuals had watched which teams or players. You can see why Jimmy and the likes of Reg Revins were careful about covering their tracks; leads were gold dust.

Ever the lovable cheeky chappie, once entry was affected Jimmy would turn to the boy's mum and cheerily instruct, 'Put the kettle on, ma, and we'll have a cup of tea.' Oddly to contemporary sensibilities, this assumption of domestic familiarity was taken as charming and not unusually won people over. His patter included asking lads if they'd 'go up town' with him and his daughter for a chat. Going 'up west' was an offer few boys then would refuse, and afternoon tea at the Strand Palace Hotel was always going to be impressive. None of the youngsters he took there had ever been to such a posh-nosh joint, and so they were dazzled by the place and all the well-to-do types who populated such a grand venue. Having won the son over, Thompson would then make for the kid's home and turn his attentions to the parents.

Jimmy adopted a way of speaking out of the side of his mouth, as if he was imparting secret information a sort of 'between you and me' vibe, telling the boys and their parents that the lad was 'a genius' or 'a rare talent', so Chelsea were very keen to sign him and that parents and child should be as keen for the youngster to join the Stamford Bridge cause.

Before he shot off, Jimmy would fish a spanking new pair of football boots from the boot of the Talbot, and place them in the hands of the drooling kid, saying, 'Tools of your new trade.'

Two or three days later, Thompson would be back to say everything had been sorted and the lad, a fortnight hence, needed, at nine o'clock on a Monday morning, to be at Liverpool Street, underneath the big clock.

On his way to the station the boy was understandably thinking he was a 'special find', but on getting to Liverpool Street he found he had company under the clock, being confronted with half a dozen or so other kids already waiting, all having also believed they had been the 'discovery of the century'. They would all recognise each other as the best players they had either that far played with or against.

After a while Thompson would turn up, count the heads, give everyone a Polo mint and a tube ticket to Fulham Broadway. Then it was on the underground, bound for Stamford Bridge. When they got to the ground the dazed little group followed Jimmy, Pied Piper-like, to the manager's office where Ted Drake was waiting for them.

'Here they are,' Jimmy would proudly proclaim, 'your future Drake's Ducklings.' That to be famous label had originally been the fruit of Thompson's gift for framing a catchy strapline.

One by one, the kids were summoned by Jimmy to do the necessary before he ushered them through another door into a billiards room, unseen by their peers still waiting to be processed. More than a few lads remembered the experience as at least stressful and a bit intimidating

Drake gave pretty much the same short spiel to each boy – a few personal comments and a rundown of the demands of the ground staff boys' job. He told them in turn, 'I expect you to be a distinguished player in the years ahead.'

Passing the paperwork to John Battersby, the club secretary at the Bridge (one of the lads' regular errands was to run over the road from the Bridge to Charlie's and get 20 Senior Service for JB). Thereafter Jimmy wished his latest consignment of football fodder 'the very best of luck' before, redolent of the Scarlet Pimpernel, striding off to get the gelt for his labours. The boys would rarely see him again.

Although Thompson was likely one of the best of his ilk, his methods were not untypical. I have covered the same at length to demonstrate what Ted Fenton was up against and why he likely turned to the similar talents of Jack Turner, although Jack had a different sort of charm, probably smoother and more businesslike than Thompson. Ted, tired of being fucked over by 'Two-Timing' Thompson, created a schoolboy scouting strategy, for a very short time nicknamed 'Fenton's Fawns' (don't quite work, does it?). The figurehead of this project was Wally St Pier, who had been in the job since the late 1920s. A pre-war West Ham player of small repute, Wal was out of his league against Thompson, being a sort of Captain Pugwash to Chelsea's Blue Pirate. Turner would prove a better foil for the likes of Thompson. In fact, Jack was a far classier operator – theirs was an engagement fought at distance and by proxy. Turner brought his wheeling and dealing against Thompsons's ducking and diving and prevailed, not only over Jimmy, but also the pretenders to his buccaneering ascendency, those carrying the colours of Tottenham, Arsenal and others.

Jack might not have actually found the talent, the likes of Revins were much better set than him for that task, but Turner did what St Pier and Fenton had serially failed to do – he closed the deal.

Looking back, Bobby spoke about his situation at the time,

'All my mates had gone off for trials with clubs around London, but nobody seemed to want me. I thought I'd missed out … then West Ham called me up for a trial.'

As Bobby told it, if West Ham hadn't come in for him, he'd probably have looked outside of football for work, and at that time it wasn't too hard to come by. Young people in the east London and west Essex district were moving into the postwar recovery economy. The tripartite education system had been designed to feed industry with appropriately skilled fodder. Bobby, having been a pretty decent scholar at school, would likely have done better for himself initially, in monetary terms, if he had been obliged to give up his dreams of football.

Apprentice

When Bobby told his parents that he wanted to leave school and join the West Ham ground staff, Doris and Big Bob, put an evening aside at the Moore family home to discuss the move with their son. It didn't take long to agree what Bobby should do.

The 13th player and last lad to be taken on as ground staff, the teenager considered himself to be nothing out of the ordinary in playing terms. Most people seemed to share that assessment and as such he felt lucky to be taken in by West Ham. Unlike all of his fellow apprentices, Moore hadn't won more than very local representative honours in football – neither London or Essex had at that point sought his services; he had not even been asked to trial for England Schoolboys when everyone else around him had at least been invited.

Naturally, during his initial weeks at the Boleyn Ground, Bobby felt very much the new boy he was. The other apprentices were the same age as him, but they all had left school a year earlier and so were acclimatised to the routine. This, together with his feelings of having inferior physical ability and skill, caused him, as was typical of him, to retreat inwards, which led to him becoming known as he had been before in his life, 'the quiet one', and a modest listener.

However, Moore's application to training and watching his diet was beginning to transform the fat kid into the 6ft, 12.5st (1.8m, 79kg) man he would be for most of his playing career, although his debut for the first team still seemed a long way off. Fenton was not inclined to take a chance on him at that stage, but he couldn't be kept out of the A team, playing at centre-half.

During an encounter with the Crystal Palace A side, the centre-forward he was marking had a bit of a name; his ball control being thought of as outstanding. Moore chose to play this bloke close, getting in his way from the first whistle. Bobby did all he could to deny the striker a sniff of the ball, which caused his opponent to complain bitterly.

Just before the break, Moore tackled the forward, robbing him of the ball. Right on the whistle his angry adversary dashed at Bobby to land a hard kick on an ankle. That was his first 'how'd yer do' to a future good friend, Hammers and England team-mate Johnny Byrne. They would continue to banter about that incident for the rest of their too short lives.

As Bobby's reputation was growing, Wally St Pier was to tell how when he first came to the club's attention the central concern and doubt about him was in connection with his weight. The chief scout saw this as the principal reason why Moore was overlooked for top schoolboy representative honours. For Wally, the weight issue had made Fenton hesitant about signing him at all. Contrary to Malcolm Allison's recollection, St Pier had it that it was he who convinced the West Ham manager to commit to Moore as his weight was puppy fat. The scouting tsar claimed that the club's training demands caused Moore to shed the excess weight swiftly, building 'a perfect physique'.

St Pier was to name Bobby as a disciplined, determined and polite young man. Well into Moore's England career at under-23 level, 'psychic Wal' talked of his confidence that the captain of the nation's rising stars had a great future, having an 'old head on young shoulders' and a capacity to listen. He must have polished his crystal ball up for that bombshell of a prediction!

For Wally, too many youngsters appeared to believe 'they know it all, but Bobby was always anxious to learn from his elders'. While Wally was recognised as a nice old guy, there is no record of Moore learning much from him. But Bobby was swift to find out who he was able to learn the most from and politely put aside those whose opinion might be stuck in some inane vision resonant of 'jumpers for goalposts'.

For all the mythology built on Chinese whispers and journalists being fed through the institutional channels of the club, when information about players was sought, no one but Allison had been too keen to offer Bobby an apprenticeship. It was only Big Mal's insistence that got the teenage Moore the ground staff job. Today such a position might be called an 'internship' if interns ever found themselves at the top of wobbling ladders cleaning windows, shovelling coke into a complaining boiler, or clinging on to floodlight girders (gallon pot of paint in one hand, ancient, balding brush in the other).

These kinds of duties probably came as a bit of shock to at least some of the boys. The only warning sign they got was the instruction to bring old clothes and a pair of working boots with them on their first day at Upton Park

One of the first jobs at the end of the season was to dig up the whole pitch from one goal to the other, although the penalty areas were left to the care of the groundsman alone. Digging up what was a bastard of pitch in the heat of summer, and laying fresh topsoil in the pissing rain, probably brought some of the more starry-eyed recruits down to earth (literally). The pitch, especially in the late 1950s, was in constant need of labour. The drainage was terrible – the ball sometimes sank into the sodden mire as it waited to be centred from a corner kick – so three or four lads spent up to four or five hours daily pulling the heavy roller around the wreck of mud, sand and patchy grass, just to give it the semblance of a level playing field. The boys were also tasked with sowing the seeds on the Upton Park turf and painting it – the lines that marked out the pitch had to be pretty much redone most days.

Along with the rest of the stadium, the old Chicken Run had to be swept. In the first part of the 1950s this was a shaky wooden structure, a standing enclosure, and had been around since the ground was first built in the early 1900s (it was replaced by the East Stand, but the supporters continued to refer to it by its traditional moniker). The lads almost invariably found a lot of coins wedged between the wooden steps, change out of their pockets dropped by the punters (more than a few being well lubricated before and during games). Probably more came by way of a peanut seller, George Larkin. He'd take money for his nuts and the return the change by slinging it at his customers. Overall, the general haul of stray coinage could amount to quite few bob most weeks.

It is amazing there was never a serious fire on the Chicken Run. There were thousands of cigarette butts all over the place; often the stand was carpeted with them. The whole structure was a fire hazard. I can only think that the rats' piss must have saved a conflagration – the bowels of the stand were running alive with vermin.

Anything that required slog and tedious labour was the ambit of the apprentice, including painting and cleaning the toilets, which involved retrieving rifled wallets, slung down the khazis by pickpockets (a relatively popular pass time at the Boleyn Ground in the 1950s, especially during evening games). After the first floodlit matches at Upton Park the apprentices might find as many as four dozen wallets in the lavs. Such was the stink from the bogs the lads were obliged to paint and clean the jolly old splash back holding their breath – so it was 'deep breath, dart in, bish, bash, bosh, dart out, recover breath' and then start again until the job was finished.

The Hammers' training ground at Grange Farm[5] wasn't too much of a journey into Essex from 43 Waverley Gardens, but the ground staff apprentices would spend the baulk of their time at the Boleyn Ground. An early start on Monday saw the apprentices cleaning out the stands, which involved scrubbing, washing out and painting. All the terraces had to be swept. Thereafter the professionals' boots and kit needed to be prepared, ready for when they turned up for training. Dressing rooms were required to be better than clean and tidy; spotless in fact. Showers, taps and baths were required to be pristine. Jobs abounded underneath the stands, including stencilling A block, B block etc.

The afternoon began with clearing away everyone's kit, followed by more terrace sweeping. There were also often more maintenance jobs to be done around the stadium. The likes of myself were always endeavouring to find ways to gain no-paying entry to Upton Park. The collective efforts to go over, under, around and through the ground's barriers, walls and fences incurred quite a bit of collateral damage that required ongoing repair, reinforcement and patching up.

When the chores were done, the youngsters were allowed to train on the car park by the Main Stand of Upton Park. If that was busy, an area of scrub land next to the Boleyn Castle would serve as a training pitch. Much the same practice was followed down the road in Custom House at West Ham Stadium – the young speedway riders practiced their runs and turns on the forecourt of that huge edifice that could hold twice the number of spectators that might be rammed into the Boleyn Ground. I went for trials there once as a young teenager, well short of the stipulated age to be offered training. After a few runs round Ken McKinlay, the somewhat dour Scottish team captain who organised the training, was to advise me to stay well away from all forms of motorised, two-wheeled transport to protect myself and the public in general and 'try drugs, rather than uncontrolled fucking throttle, to escape yer personal demons'. I both took and ignored his advice of the next few years.

Back at Upton Park, on Fridays, Moore and his fellow apprentices would stagger out on to Green Street at 6pm in the full knowledge that they would need to be on the move again the next day at 9am if they were to make the 11am kick-off for the game they had been selected to play in.

It took the ground staff boys about a month to do all the jobs around Upton Park at the end of the season. After that, they started full-time training, although they continued to be requited to get the training kit laid out for the entire professional playing staff and, afterwards, pack it all away. The kit needed to delivered to the

---

5 West Ham moved their training ground from Grange Farm, Chigwell, to Chadwell Heath, a converted cricket ground in Barking and Dagenham in the early 1960s

women who worked in the Upton Park laundry, to be washed and dried in time for training the following day.

There was a pretty strict hierarchy among the playing staff when Bobby got to the club. Ground staff boys weren't allowed in the first team dressing room before knocking on the door. They were required to wait until they were asked to 'come in'. The lads were each 'given' four first-team players to look after throughout the season, to act as a sort of butler or valet to their group. Apart from the responsibility for kit, the professionals' boots had to be cleaned and prepared to individual tastes each day and also in readiness for Saturday games. Allison made sure Moore was allocated to him, Cantwell, John Bond and Dave Sexton, all members of the 'Academy'.

This practice helped build relationships between the kids and the first-team players. Sometimes the professionals would give 'their boy' a gift at the end of the season as a way of saying thank you. In his first season Bobby got a pair of Adidas Nylon football boots and a copy of Charles Buchan's *A Lifetime in Football*. Perhaps tellingly, he still had the latter long after the former. Most of the professionals were generous to 'their lads' but if something was forgotten or messed up, most could hand out a healthy bollocking.

Ground staff boys were also obliged to attend first-team matches at the Boleyn Ground unless they were prevented from doing so, say by needing to travel back from a Colts game, which were mostly played on Saturday mornings. Being at first-team matches was seen part of the lads' football education, but it was also their job to clear up the dressing rooms, washing the baths etc after everyone had gone.

When Moore broke into the first team, he could have got away with all the apprentice jobs, training with the senior players at Grange Farm, over on the Essex side of the border with east London, but he still turned up for a shift. This won him a deal of affection and respect.

Ultimately, it all seemed worth it to Bobby when Essex's over-15s, in desperate need for a centre-forward, called him up. Moore remembered that game and how he had persistently, but ineffectually, lurched up the middle of the park, until the moment when the Essex goalkeeper punted a clearance straight into the opposing keeper's arms. At that point Bobby saw his opportunity and rammed the bewildered custodian into his own net, ball and all.

In those days, VAR was only a fevered wet dream of a business and economics undergraduate at the University of Lausanne, Josef 'shorter an' fatter' Blatter. This was a time when the attitude of the English game was predicated pretty much on an ethic of, 'all's fair in love, war and football'. The referee saw Bobby's 'barge' as a 'hard but fair' tactic. However, for Moore, the episode was recognised as ridiculous, a perception he believed was shared by his young team-mates, who he saw as having superior gifts and talents than his when it came to the requirements of better-quality football. For Moore, his performance just seemed to confirm in his mind that his team-mates were better than him

On the plus side, that moment marked a point when Bobby started to become conscious that one of his main resources was the will to succeed. Experience and history show that the resolve he marshalled was hardly surpassed in his generation.

During his first year on the ground staff Bobby saw next to nothing of either St Pier or Turner and not much of Fenton, so it would be hard to see how their initial estimation of him, not being any more than OK, might have altered. Moore was however continuously supported by the club captain Allison and later by another footballing genius, Noel Cantwell. The thoughtful Irishman was nicknamed 'Sausage' by his Cockney team-mates, so entering Cantwell into the realm of rhyming slang ('sausage roll' – Noel). Cantwell had high standards and was more wary about the likes of Moore than his friend Malcolm. He had seen enough boys, who were more able than Bobby in their childhood environments, look less than ordinary when thrown in with other young players who had shone in their contexts; the behemoth in the land of the height challenged isn't so impressive in the abode of giants. To confirm this one only has to look at the number of England youth players who improve enough to make it in the professional ranks, let alone maintain the qualities to play for their nation.

The wind of change

Bobby came to the Boleyn Ground during the same era as Geoff Hurst and Martin Peters. Cantwell had worked with Terry Venables at West Ham before the club lost him to the Blues. For Cantwell, kids from areas like Dagenham and Barking should have been grabbed by the Hammers; it was a no-brainer and for him that was a big part of the reason why Moore needed to be given a chance.

Fenton, who had played for the club from boyhood, understood that it needed to take advantage of youth. It was never going to compete on the transfer market at that stage, with the likes of the London First Division clubs Arsenal, Tottenham, Chelsea and Charlton. West Ham were Second Division in more ways than the obvious – Fulham and Leyton Orient were the closest local rivals to the Hammers in the second tier at that point. If West Ham were going to break away from clubs of that ilk and look to compete with the big boys, they had to find a 'talent conduit'. It was Allison, who had joined the Hammers from Charlton in 1951, who was the force of nature behind the policy that would ultimately lead to the eventual breakthrough.

While the received wisdom and urban myth gives much of the credit to old stalwarts of the club like St Pier, Allison, who was the nemesis of the traditions that Wally personified, was not only to drag West Ham into the 20th century but, over much of the second half of the century, he, and a handful of other revolutionaries, pulled the whole of English football out of its feudal slough. His influence, approach and philosophy could be felt in every corner of the game. For him, Fenton and, as time went on, even the likes of Alf Ramsey and Ron Greenwood, were archaic figures. On the other hand, Ted appeared to see Malcolm was an enigma and a bit scary.

Allison was intelligent, aggressive and dynamic, impatient and demanding. He wanted any side he was part of, as well as the game in general, to learn so it could kick on. The basics of his thinking were laid on the foundation of coaching courses run by Walter Winterbottom at Lilleshall. On his return to Upton Park with books and notes on different training methods and playing strategies, he'd pass on what he had learned, advising coaching staff, wanting the team to try new things. Like Winterbottom, Allison was student of the world game, and was excited about what other coaches all over the planet were doing. For him, Winterbottom was a masterful teacher, with an amazing understanding of the footballing mind.

Before Allison, West Ham were something of a hand-to-mouth club, pretty much OK at Upton Park, but outside east London they travelled as well as brie in a heatwave. The club was an institution, set in its ways, if not wholly complacent, certainly content with life in the second tier of English football. Upton Park had a sort tradition, but no type of ambition and the likes of St Pier, Fenton and Robinson for Allison epitomised the situation. Like Charlie Paynter, Fenton's predecessor and mentor, none of the aforementioned should be portrayed or taken as 'bad' people. Indeed, many if not most players remembered them all with affection – they were, for the most part, a nice bunch. Allison could be called a lot of things, 'nice' wasn't one of them.

The Boleyn Ground had been a sort of ghetto of pleasant, affable people, pleased to amble along within a regime of patronage and a species of vassalage, premised on master/servant relationships. Paynter, and others webbed up the culture he was part of, took a pride in knowing their place, relative to the board. The owners and directors were met with ingratiating sycophancy by their faithful retainers, who seemed to be grateful more than anything else. Let's face it, it beat actual work, like stoking in the gas works or shifts at Barking power station.

At West Ham, and pretty much across football up to the mid-1950s, players were expected to feel much the same; glad to be the minions of the board's trusted overseers. The playing staff were treated much the same way as domestic servants might expect, not the skilled artisans they actually were. There were some amazing players at Upton Park, certainly between the wars, and immediately after, but they hardly ever saw a ball or Paynter other than on a Saturday, and rarely more than a glimpse of a board member.

Allison was tearing into this culture in football way before he got to the Boleyn Ground. I have called him previously 'a rebel without applause' because he has never received the credit he deserves for his contribution to the modernisation of the game, but make no mistake, he was the person who was going to excite and engage young men like Moore. He was the born leader of the Hammers throughout the 1950s, a creative destroyer, a passionate advocate of change.

The New York educationist Herbert R. Kohl wrote a seminal book, *I Won't Learn From You*. It makes the case that young people make decisions about what, when and how they learn and from whom. Well, Allison was someone kids liked, and more wanted to learn from, not because he was 'nice' but because he was exciting. He had been infused with the will, enthusiasm and means to teach by Winterbottom, the England manager who was also a gifted educationalist. This collective insight, alongside his magnetic, interesting, inventive, funny, demanding, electrifying, ambitious personality, made him a hurricane of fresh air in the musty atmosphere of 1950s football.

Greenwood and Ramsey, like all good teachers, learned from those they taught, and that was exemplified in their respective and similar relationship with Moore, but by association both of them learned from Allison (albeit from a safe distance). He was the seed of 1966 and thus all English football success from the 1960s, the reverberations of which continued well into the first part of the 21st century.

Throughout the 1950s, and into the early 1960s, Upton Park was a thinktank of footballing minds that would collectively make a huge mark on the game. No club of that era produced so many top-class managers for the next generation of the leadership of the game. Allison and Cantwell were the leading lights in a group of serious students of football, including John Bond, Frank O'Farrell, Jimmy Andrews and Dave Sexton. This was the first wave of the Upton Park football intelligentsia that was to continue for decades to come; the likes of Bobby Howe, Phil Woosnam and Clive Charles took the gospel to American, and you can see the spirt of the 'West Ham age of Enlightenment' in all the successful US soccer teams, first the women and then the men, right up to the 2020 Olympics.

The epoch started as all great movements and revolutions do, from small/modest beginnings of promising local lads being invited to train at the Boleyn Ground on Tuesdays and Thursdays, and it was Malcolm who Fenton asked to organise the coaching. A little later Cantwell was also part of this, looking after the likes of Moore and Hurst. At the time Noel's payment for this task amounted to £1 15s a week (£1.75). That was the standard wage as allowed by FA for players allocated to such tasks, and in truth it was a handy few extra quid over a season, equivalent to around £200 a month today.

The training took place beneath the main stand at Upton Park and, weather permitting, use of the narrow track around the parameter of the playing area. Making use of the confined areas of the Upton Park footprint in some ways replicated something of how the Scottish 'close game' developed historically. While football was always a working-class distraction north of the border, as in England, the public schools played a significant part on developing the conventions of the organised game in Scotland. Something peculiar to those Caledonian institutions was the habit young scholars had of playing informal, cut-down versions of the game along the cloisters that were typical of the architecture of particularly the church supported schools. This restricted playing space might be thought of as the kernel of the culture and skills demonstrated by the great Scottish 'dribblers', the doyens of which can be traced from the 19th-century 'Prince of Dribblers' James Weir, to Celtic's Jimmy Johnstone and beyond. Something of the same skills could be demonstrated by some of West Ham's greatest ball artists, the likes of Martin Peters and Trevor Brooking, but most of the young players who moved from the 1950s into the next few decades demonstrated a high level of close ball control, Bobby Moore perhaps more than most.

So, when you next find yourself trolling down Green Street E13, perhaps take pause where the Boleyn Ground once stood. Maybe take a second to say a quiet 'thank you' to the ground beneath the capitalistic sacrilege that is Upton Park Gardens.

However, now and then the kids gained permission to fly and use the pitch, which was a thrill for the youngsters. This was a bit of a break with convention, although Allison ultimately dispensed with the monotonous lap running practically altogether in organised training, devoting the time to ball work. This not only broke with the traditions at Upton Park, but the mainstream of British football, the paradigm being that players needed to be made 'hungry for the ball', so were, outside of Saturdays, deprived of it. George Isaacs, the groundsman, who was nominally in charge of the ground staff boys with regard to their tasks around the stadium, had apparently been in place since the Conquest. He invariably threw a wobbly when any incursion to the sacred pitch was made, regularly complaining bitterly to Fenton about these infringements (something almost unheard of then at the Boleyn Ground before the coming of Malcolm). George's proverbial apple cart got particularly upset if encroachments occurred on a Thursday because

Friday morning was the time he would need to begin preparations to make the pitch fit for the Saturday game.

Malcolm didn't care at all about that. George was just another part of the antiquated character of the anachronistic Upton Park culture as far as he was concerned. Isaacs later became the club's 'boot man' and apparently mellowed in mood. Many players of the era were to remember him fondly.

George had alopecia, although none of the kids knew what that was at the time. He hid his condition under a cap. No one ever saw George capless. One day, when the apprentices were painting the stand, as George was tootling along on his tractor cutting the grass, all of a sudden a shout went up from Roger Hugo (who was to make the professional ranks at West Ham), 'The fucking hat's off! It's off!' The other ground boys looked at the macabre sight of George's bald pate; it was an almost transparent white, so long had George's noggin been protected from nature's weathering, giving him the appearance of an alien. The life of a young football apprentice was not easy and the pay wasn't fantastic, but such moments provided momentary compensations and were remembered for lifetimes.

Allison's dismissal of George and whatever Fenton had to say about the youngsters using the pitch, or anything else, was who he was. Any expectation that he might make any apologies or show an ounce of deference was ridiculous. His attitude was totally outside of the experience of the likes of Isaacs, the football club and the wider game. As Malcolm once said to me,

'Watching people be thankful for their servitude turns my stomach. You're in this world to make it as you want it, not to do what others want. That don't mean you can't agree and that you always disagree with people. Course not! But if you don't value yourself, how can people value you, and if you can't value yourself, how can you value others?'

Allison understood that the boys he was given charge of were not going to make football doing laps around the narrow stadium cinder track. He was convinced the talent he was given to work with could be developed and whatever it took for him to achieve that development, that's what he was going to do.

In the light of Allison everyone looked a bit pale, and it begs questions about how a somewhat retiring kid like Moore grabbed Malcolm's attention and imagination. Cantwell recalled the young Moore as a quiet kid, unassuming and polite, but after he joined the ground staff, as time went on, he began to increasingly mix with the professionals, particularly Allison and Cantwell, taking being accepted into their company as something of an honour. Bobby did Malcolm the service of listening to him, thus defining Allison as the prophet and teacher he set out to be; that is why they clicked.

Bobby would become very much his own man. He was unique in the way he played and impacted others, but he was to carry the influence of Noel and Malcolm with him for the rest of his life and in many ways, chunks of his personality and attitude to football, it's coaching and management, reflected the views and responses of these two men, but particularly Allison.

8

BUILDING BOBBY

In December 2021, having scored for the second successive Premier League game, helping the Hammers to a 4-1 victory at Watford, Saïd Benrahma turned to West Ham's travelling supporters as they sang his name in a congratulatory and strident manner. The Algerian number 22 responded by applauding the Irons' faithful. He then took off his shirt and handed it to one particularly pleased, smiling fan in the front row – his mum.

Saïd was repeating the gesture he had made during the 3-2 home win over Liverpool the previous November. Smiling, he celebrated victory by cuddling his happy mother, warmly handing her his match shirt.

It was a touching conclusion to a good day and an exceptional year for Benrahma, but he demonstrated he understood what he owed to the woman who brought him into the world and looked after him.

Bobby Moore was also deeply influenced by his mother. This was perhaps most noticeable in his polite and well-mannered demeanour. Such qualities are mentioned by most people who knew him. These aspects of his personal standards and self-discipline were fundamental to him as a person, but perhaps more so as a sportsperson and leader. They were tangible markers of his integrity and dignity, the main struts of anything that might be called 'professionalism'.

An aim of this book is to explore how Moore became who he was; how might one 'make' or 'build' a Bobby Moore, and in terms of his behaviour, the adage 'manners maketh man' rings very true.

Mind your manners

Language use is a complex collection of behaviours that rely on a number of regions of the brain. When we read – like you are reading now – or write, and use language to think automatically about ourselves and our relationship to others, we mostly depend on our prefrontal cortex, the 'higher brain' that sits (as it suggests on the tin) tucked behind the front of your skull. This part of the brain also deals with customs, traditions, and social codes of practice such as manners. Being the highly rational region of the brain, it is what enables us to plan and so control our impulses.

There is a connection between 'low' prefrontal cortex activity and a higher inclination towards violence. Violent offenders have poorer levels of self-control than people who are nonviolent. The prefrontal cortex in murderers, for example, functions, on average, relatively poorly.

But it is also understood by giving somebody training in exercising self-control that activity may flex (so to speak) the prefrontal cortex and enhance that part of the brain. This suggests people who are, from an early age, asked to control their actions according to accepted codes of conduct (which include respect, politeness and so on) will be less inclined to lose self-control, the extreme example of which is violence.

It is logical that if you practice a set of behaviours that engage areas of your brain, which results in a kind of virtuous cycle, your behaviour will become more moral (more human and less animal). The more you repeat such behaviour, the more you engage in it, the more it becomes part of who you are and the cycle allows you to further strengthen this 'virtuous circuit'. It may also cause others to react in a similar way towards you. The reverse is probably true too; the more you act like a pig, the more people will react towards you as if you are a pig.

The 'civilisation theory' proposes that by practicing self-control through good manners, being polite, respecting others and so on, the groundwork is laid for a personal and cultural shift away from violence. Language, in the form of printed etiquette books and novels that portrayed what was and wasn't virtuous in a civilised society, was what helped our ancestors to think and act more rationally and so virtuously.

Today, television, the internet, movies and spectator sport etc can do much to maintain our virtuous circuit. But the same media can have, and some say has, the opposite impact. The more we are encouraged or manipulated to discard self-control, the less our prefrontal context will be stimulated and the more our ancient brain, the remnants of our reptilian past, such as the hypothalamus, dominate our activity. Very basically we are more and more limited to 'fight or flight' behaviours.

So, what we know of the activity and functions of the brain tells us if we consciously engage our brains in the virtuous cycle, and foster this in our children, as Doris did with her son, then we will live in a society wherein people are more able to control themselves, and act compassionately and civilly. Thus, they will operate in groups and teams more effectively – making those groups and teams more efficient/successful. This is evident in Moore's behaviour. His 'civil' manner caused those around him to mirror him.

Aggression, a lack of control, has much the same but opposite impact; it spreads around and between groups. The higher levels of violence go, the higher they can go and ultimately, we all destroy each other. On the field of play the referee, by their enforcement of codes of behaviour, plays a part in short circuiting violence.

The very act of pointing to a code of conduct engages the rational (higher brain) and dampens the dominance of the lower brain.

Bobby often advised players, when they felt themselves losing control, to 'count to ten'. This is good advice, even more so if you count down from ten, better still 100. Why? Because doing so forces you to engage your rational brain; you have to *think*, if only just a bit. Writing down bad experiences has the same but more powerful effect for obvious reasons. If you get dangerously angry, try doing arithmetical calculations in your head. You'll find it makes a positive difference, sometimes bringing you to a place where at you become conscious of the extent to which your angry and/or aggressive behaviour risks making you seem stupid or even dangerous by others. More practically, anger, aggression, and violence are the great flashing signs of a loss of control, meaning you are more likely, ultimately to be controlled and overcome; you have literally 'lost the plot'.

We know that writing and reading, especially reading stories and novels, can have the power to make us more empathetic toward people who are different from us. And most of the time, empathy leads toward peace and away from violence. You reading this 'story' about Bobby Moore will have this effect on you. No, no; no need to thank me.

Bobby was attentive to every insight and instruction (part of his politeness). He took every opportunity to ask questions and discuss the nature and strategy of football. His family home wasn't far from where Malcolm Allison was lodging while he was with the Hammers, thus they often shared a bus seat commuting back and forth to Upton Park.

Allison pulled Noel Cantwell and the other more thoughtful players into his orbit. He and Noel became good friends, who would ultimately form a triumvirate with Moore, after he joined the intellects in Cassettari's cafe on Barking Road, local to the ground, drinking tea – at 3d (1.5p) a cup – and scoffing inches-thick slices of bread and butter. These seminars became part of this group of players routine. They would train with the rest of the playing staff between 10am and 12.30pm and while most of the players went home, they and a clutch of others would make their way to the cafe. Thereafter they would go back for extra training.

However, on Fridays, on the eve of a game, the sessions would go on much longer, as strategies and tactics were elaborated and reviewed – pretty much regardless of anything the manager had instructed on envisaged. John Bond was also an original member of this 'school'. He seemed to many younger players to have encyclopaedic knowledge of opposition players and tactics: 'he will cross just beyond the near post'; 'watch him, he likes to come in hard behind you'; 'if they go one up, they'll just shut the shop'.

It was in Cassettari's that Allison began to build his vision of what would become a characteristic of the West Ham game; the near-post cross. It was also at Cassettari's that Malcolm introduced the young players to hot rice pudding mixed with ice cream (give it a bash, it's irrespirable).

The group was fuelled on interest and enthusiasm, but more broadly its appeal related to players talking control, on and off the field, of oneself and others. This is, in the last analysis, what drew the congregation – taking authority leads to the acquisition of power, power is addictive, and power, in order to be power, has to be taken; if you think you have been given power, well you've actually given up power, you just haven't recognised it. It's that sleight of hand that helps the powerful maintain power.

Cafe life wasn't all theory and debate. There is a story that a group of players were in Eddie's cafe (which was just over the road to the Boleyn Ground). The youth striker Mike Beesley, looking for a loan of a couple bob from his team-mates, succumbed to the condition of cramming a whole cheese roll in his gob and swallowing it. Again, give it a go, it ain't easy.

The third place

Praxis: the process by which a theory, lesson, or skill is enacted, embodied, or realised: the act of engaging, applying, exercising, realising, or practicing ideas.

As is well documented, the Cassettari's cafe 'thinktank' would be together for hours every weekday, debating and arguing about the game. West Ham provided the players with luncheon vouchers, all of which were exchanged in the cafe. Literally food for thought.

The group was never huge, but their debates could become rowdy and likely took up more time and space than they were collectively worth, depriving the owner, Phil Cassettari, of income from other potential customers. Loath just to boot them out, the group were given their own room upstairs, and although he was mostly quiet and a listener, this would become a legendary place of learning and education for Bobby: it was the 'Academy of Football' and it fed his passion. He began to learn the joy of watching theory develop and adapting that to the field of play, which in turn would provide more material for more theory development. This is known in education as 'Kolb's learning cycle'; the process of dialectical debate – an exchange of ideas, knowledge and perceptions that, in the merging, give rise to new knowledge, ideas and perceptions. This is the higher brain working in overdrive.

Bobby was rapacious in his search to build his understanding of football, but he also appreciated the worldly wisdom of these men that surrounded him. He felt honoured to be in their company and that they included him in their deliberations. He would excitedly tell his girlfriend Tina about the debates and conversations, and how he looked up them. She also appreciated how they embraced him, and she grew to share his admiration. Each of these men, in their own way, represented the type of man Bobby wanted to become.

Close to where I was born there's a barber's shop that had, for as long as I can remember, been a place where men come together, ostensibly to get a haircut. But the place was more a venue for interaction, often energetic debate, sometimes argument and not unusually laughter. It was an example of the 'third place'; in many contexts it is a traditional area for people to congregate, a situation apart from the world of employment or the domestic realm.

In what has been called 'community building', the 'third place' is thought to be the social surroundings separate from the two usual social environments (home the 'first' place, and the workplace the 'second' place).

As such cafes, clubs and parks can and are third places. Oldenburg (1989, 1991) has it that third places are significant for civil society, democracy, civic engagement, and establishing the feeling of a sense of place. For him third places are 'anchors' of community life; they facilitate and foster broader, more creative interaction.

It has been mooted that the following are the signifiers of a third place:

- Free or inexpensive
- Food and drink, while not essential, are important
- Highly accessible: proximate for many (walking distance)
- Involve regulars – those who habitually congregate there
- Welcoming and comfortable
- Friends both old and new should be found there

Cassettari's was a 'third place' for Cantwell, Allison, Moore and the others involved. I don't think anything like it exists in contemporary football. This is perhaps related to the modern game's relative lack of innovation, its predictability and a lack of creativity that pushes top clubs to be almost totally reliant on their financial muscle to 'import' talent, being mostly unable to create it to a sufficient extent.

The cafe on Barking Road was essentially an informal situation where ideas could be shared, honed, elaborated and added to by the actual practitioners of football – it wasn't just 'theorising', but a situation where theory might be related to practice; a circumstance wherein theory could be applied to practice, which in turn could give rise to more or better theory, which could be applied to practice and so on. This is something more than chatting, discourse or 'dialogue'. It is not as formal as a debate or a classroom, but it is a place for the exchange of views, review and elaboration. This is the dynamic that generates 'dialectic' – a situation wherein your idea and my idea can come together to make a new and probably 'better' idea. It was 'praxis' embracing the 'learning cycle'.

The heated, sometimes incendiary arguments (not 'rows' – ideas are the fuel of an argument, rows thrive on the lack of them) between the likes of Bond and Allison contrasted and complimented the quiet and protracted 'Celt' discussions shared by Cantwell, O'Farrell and Andrews. The deeply thoughtful cross-examinations concocted by Dave Sexton were impactful, as were the practical but intelligent challenges of Ken Brown.

While dozens of ex-Hammers from the 1950s and early 1960s have told me, in one way or another, that Malcolm was the greatest strategist West Ham ever had, Sexton would come to be recognised as one of best coaches to emerge from this group. A quiet man, Dave, along with Andy Malcolm, was the hardest player at Upton Park in the mid-to-late 1950s. A dapper dresser, he was a very much his own man. A tough and passionate character, he and Allison almost inevitably clashed. Sexton was named as the 'biggest guv'nor of them all' by George Fenn, with West Ham playing 'a very big part with his training methods, awareness and innovations', in particular the strategy of full-backs moving up as wingers, which was unheard of at that time.

The seed that motivated this 'seat of learning' was Malcolm understanding the worth of the argument; it was part of his focused endeavour to make himself a better player. In the words of the Black Panther leader Eldridge Cleaver, 'Too much agreement kills the chat.' An argument isn't exchange of knowledge, it is a test of knowledge and out of it comes the alteration of, and learning about action, and thus the 'getting of wisdom'.

Malcolm was the leader. His persona dominated Upton Park. Regularly, the teamsheets were pinned up on Fridays by Ted Fenton, naming the respective teams (the A side, reserves, first team etc). Allison, not unusually, would just tear them down and replace them with his selection. This all fed, inspired and educated Bobby and he loved every second. When the group decided to return to training after leaving the cafe, Bobby was always there. He was never late for training nor was he known to miss a session and he always turned up neatly turned out, kit impeccably clean.

Moore thrived in the atmosphere and vitality of learning, but why? Well, learning provides us with hope, because it offers us a means to be better at something we want to improve, or get things we might want. Without learning, in some description or form, it would be hard to see where hope might come from, apart from superstition, which really is a sign of a lack of genuine hope. But hope is one of the two main motivates for action (crisis, and the fear that comes from it, is the other). In that respect hope destroys inertia. It is the last thing to die.

Action is life, inertia is death. Out of action comes learning and so hope. This is the 'virtuous cycle' of living, to work towards what we hope for; to realise our dreams that fortune sometimes seem to be 'always hiding'. Young Bobby found delight in the Academy because he saw it as a means to live his dreams, not to allow them, like so many of us do, to 'fade and die'.

One has to doubt how much this sort of 'active learning' might be available to young footballers today, an experience of reflection and consideration that not only makes for better footballers, but likely more rounded individuals. I hear a lot about people being involved in learning, but when I ask what they see the differences to be between learning, education, knowledge, memorisation, awareness and wisdom, mostly they clearly just make guesses or simply claim they are the same thing – they are not – and to believe they are, while claiming to 'do' them is to not know what it is you are doing or talking about.

Reading people

Phil Cassettari junior took over the famous Cassettari's cafe from his parents, who had opened it as the Boleyn Cafe in 1941. Well after the original members of the West Ham Academy had moved on, the cafe had continued to serve the new generations of Hammers, including the likes of Rio Ferdinand, Jermain Defoe and Michael Carrick.

Phil junior, who sold up in 2004 and later ran a place in Museum Street, Colchester, was to tell a story about a time when he had just started secondary school. He had got into a fight with an older boy. Feeling a bit anxious about this, he decided to say he had a tummy upset to get off school. His mum decided the best thing to do was to take him to see the family GP, who consequently pronounced the lad fit.

Phil reluctantly made his way to school. He hadn't got too far when he heard someone shout, 'Oi, Phil! Shouldn't you be in school?' It was Bobby, coming out of his sports shop in Green Street. Phil replied, telling him he was on his way.

Bobby, probably sensing something was up, offered him a lift in his deep red Jag. This was 1970, a time when no one who lived around Upton Park had that kind of car, and Bobby ranked alongside the men of the stature of Pelé in the canon of footballing greats.

They got to Phil's school in time for the morning break, so dozens of kids were milling around. As Phil was to say, 'My street cred went through the roof and I was never bullied again!'

This is the Bobby Moore we rarely hear about. He had a sensitive side that could read people, and was capable of showing genuine and immense kindness. He had remembered the 'cafe kid's' name (like he remembered mine) and knowing just his presence would make a difference to the boy's day, he gave him a bit of that.

Bobby knew all the moves.

Metacognition (and stuff)

Something else I find myself regularly asking about is the type of learning people claim to be involved in. This is usually met with a blank look, although sometimes something clicks and folk start taking stabs about 'learning by doing', or parrot a floundering recital of some snippets of a vague recollection of a long-ago training session, using words like 'experiential', 'kinetic', 'informal' and (maybe best of all) 'dialogical' (chatting? gossip? chin wagging?).

This ignorance (harsh word, but that is what it is) is not always the 'fault' of the ignorant. We can only know what we know. But it is a testament to the poor quality of education and training in the field I have spent my life in.

'Active learning' occurs when a person takes control of their learning experience. Since understanding information is the key aspect of learning, it is important for learners to recognise what they understand and what they do not grasp. By doing so, they can monitor their own learning and become aware of areas of knowledge they have and those they lack, and so might usefully pursue. The approach Allison took at West Ham really did fit this agenda.

Active learning involves learners in an internal dialogue in which they verbalise understandings. This and other meta-cognitive (thinking about thinking) strategies needs to be picked up over time (formative learning) and by repetition (embedding understanding, knowledge and so on).

Studies within metacognition have demonstrated the value of active learning, claiming that what is learned is usually at a stronger, more influential level as a result. In addition, learners have more incentive to learn when they have control over, not only how they learn, but also what they learn, when and with whom.

Active learning is a key characteristic of 'person-centred' learning. Conversely, passive learning and direct instruction (didactics) are characteristics of 'teacher-centred' learning, or traditional education. Expecting footballers to become better at the game by being deprived of a football, for instance, is a very basic example of this, something that was pretty much the way of things at Upton Park prior to the Fenton/Allison years.

All learning is formalised in its process and function. You reading this is a formal process, and you learned to read by way of formal processes. To claim otherwise is not to know what you are doing, and anyone doing so after reading this has A) not understood it; or is, by logical definition B) an idiot.

Learning is an internal process; it happens in the brain. Education is an external structure (schools, curriculum, and so on). So, for Moore, the external structure was the Academy and that facilitated his learning that he put into practice, and in doing so, he learned from in his actions in the world as a player: Kolb in a nutshell (with a Nutella topping).

First mention

After he signed amateur forms at the start of the 1956/57 season, on 6 October 1956 Bobby's name appeared for the first time in programme notes. He was detailed as playing centre-half for the Colts against QPR, appearing alongside youngsters who were already signed up as professionals, the likes of Joe Kirkup, Harry Cripps, John Lyall, Andy Smillie and John Cartwright.

Fenton invited a local journalist to watch one of Bobby's first matches for the youth team. The reporter's assessment was that Moore was just an unimpressive fat kid. That wasn't too far off par for the course, not entirely confirming the earlier Turner report, but pretty much what Fenton might have already thought, and maybe why he asked the hack to look at Moore – he perhaps expected the scribbler, lickspittle-like, to parrot back what he understood Ted to think.

However, as Allison had predicted, Bobby would become taller and stronger as he departed his boyhood. As the transition advanced, so he began to stand out of the field of play. Even in the 'no quarter given nor expected' local derbies, Bobby remained focused and good-humoured, albeit as the fists and boots flew around him; he just continued to foil and fool his opponents. He saw openings with increasing ease and aplomb, constantly reading the game like an experienced field marshal, from a lofty vantage point, might view battle. Every effort to pressurise, intimidate or harass him bounced off him like table tennis balls might.

Moore was one of a new species in the game: a reasoning rearguard ranger. I had the good fortune to talk about Bobby with the superb sports journalist and writer, Hugh McIlvanney. He saw Moore's 'real self' as remote, although it was clear he liked to enjoy life. I agreed with him that as Bobby's career progressed West Ham was increasingly superseded as an influence on his trajectory. In response to some symptoms of this he had seen Ron Greenwood hold his head in his hands and declare, 'I've failed. I've failed.' For Hugh, 'Bobby saw defensive manoeuvre as just a means to set up an attack. Lacking a turn of speed meant he had to think more, he had to cultivate a quickness of mind and gain perceptive alacrity, to time his moves faster and more precisely than those who could accelerate their bodies faster than him, but in that rushing they left their brains behind them.'

Time after time I watched Moore play, it was confirmed that he had trained his mind not only to be slick, but like the best of chess players, to envisage and so anticipate what would happen three or four or more moves ahead. Before the ball came to him, he made himself know precisely where his team-mates and opponents were on the field. He had surveyed the pitch long before winning or receiving the ball. This is an uncommon talent in the best of adult professionals, but positively a phenomenon in a younger player.

This ability was something fostered by Malcolm Allison. He would get the youngsters he trained to stop in the middle of practice games, asking them to close their eyes. Then he'd quiz individual lads about the whereabouts of their team-mates and opponents on the pitch. As this got to be a regular and fun part of the training, the boys began to make a habit of developing this awareness of space and the presence of others. Allison soon began to notice how young Moore had a particularly sharp capacity for this task, showing an unusual precision and consciousness in his response to the test.

Much the same emphasis was encouraged by Noel Cantwell, who saw Moore as 'a searcher', asking questions, but making few comments himself. Once he asked how a footballer could play with and against the best while lacking pace. Cantwell was careful to think about his reply. He was to tell how Bobby was 'very serious about his football', so Noel looked to avoid saying 'the wrong thing' to the lad. Cantwell told how Bobby worked hard to give himself a better turn of speed simply by running more, but Noel knew, 'If you're slow, you're slow.' As a coach, I can see what he meant. I have come across kids that look as if they've got the physique to be fast, but the character of their muscle fibre (lacking that essential 'fast twitch') was just not going to produce a turn of speed. This is made more the case if, like Bobby, you're a bit bow-legged.

So the man who would play 36 times for the Republic of Ireland (scoring 14 goals) told the young man about how the great Fulham and England skipper, Johnny Haynes, was able to get an impression in his mind and envisage what might happen before he had the ball (confirming Allison's lessons). Many thought this was uncanny, that Haynes might have some sort of mystic gift of foresight. He 'found' space, or more 'made' it, as he knew where each player on the field was – principally the strikers. As such, when he had the ball, he could make a pass instantly. When the ball wasn't with him, he was able to get himself in a place where he knew it would come. Talking of Bobby, Cantwell was to relate,

'He spent hours talking to Malcolm and me about how he could improve. We told him to watch the top players and learn from them. He had been modelling himself on the great Duncan Edwards and then he switched to watching Johnny Haynes … studying how he dictated matches, not only by his passing, but also his positioning. Most of all he took heed of what both Malcolm and I always used to stress, "Ask yourself what you would do if you got the ball NOW!" This meant he was always a thought and a vital yard ahead of the opponents.'

Moore was to relate how Allison had told him that this very quality was something the magnificent Real Madrid player Alfredo Di Stéfano had habituated. It has been likened by some writers to radar, but that is to misunderstand this almost instinctual capacity that a few players have been able to hone by concentrated and protracted intellectual and sensual endeavour – so it's more like a 'psychological cartography' and the result of hard work, more than the latching on to a mere personal propensity. Bobby was to nurture and ultimately carry this heightened sensitivity, dynamic and shifting mind maps, with him from Upton Park to Wembley, the Maracanã to Hampden Park and across the footballing universe. Reflecting on this Moore had it that,

'Wherever I was, I would always know that maybe the left-back was free, the right-winger running, the inside-left dropping off his man into space for me. There's nothing complicated about vision. It's pictures in your mind and I will always be grateful to Malcolm for instilling that in me. I'll always be in his debt for that insight. It was like suddenly looking into the sunshine.'

Haynes exemplified this 'vision'; he was rarely obliged to pause, put his foot on ball or look, he just acted according to the picture of the whole situation in his head. He once told me, 'You don't get taught that, you just do it … you learn what works. It's anticipation. Like driving, you don't even think about it usually.' Perhaps he was right about that, for him, and maybe others, but Moore did learn it, although he very likely had a propensity. Many of us probably have something of that proclivity, although most, like myself, might have developed it as a side-effect of 'hyper-awareness' of the behaviour of others. This is sometimes the result of feeling consistently under threat as a child.

Noel told Bobby with regard to the Craven Cottage maestro, 'Milk turns quicker than John, but that doesn't matter.' Cantwell had also suggested Moore take the time to observe Haynes in action with this in mind. Bobby started to study Haynes, whose name became synonymous with exact passing. He noted how Johnny hardly ever failed to hit the right pass, at the right moment, with just the right weight on the ball. He was to say of the man,

'Once you got used to watching that perfection, you realised the rest of the secret. John was always available, always hungry for the ball, always wanting to play. He was the master. I loved watching the player and later I learned to love the man. The two go together. I could never feel that close to anyone I did not respect.'

All this was a world away from where Ted Fenton was at, over Wanstead Flats, telling players, 'When I blow the whistle, knock the ball forward.' But he wasn't on his own, it was just he missed out on the influences and mentors that Cantwell and Allison had.

You only had to watch Bobby marshal a football field to know he built this 'Haynes insight' into his own play. The influence of former West Bromwich Albion man Ray Barlow had long been evident in Moore's game, the economy of his performance. The presence of Edwards also infused Bobby's style and approach. All of this was melded with the artistry of Haynes.

While influence isn't all, it builds and clarifies life destinations, and gives the likes Malcolm Allison and Noel Cantwell a means to work with others so they might chart their own fate and the wider destiny of teams, groups, communities, professions and societies. It was typical of Moore that because he felt he lacked pace, he would turn that deficiency to his advantage on the pitch. For all the goodwill, help, guidance and advice he got, regardless of all the answers to his questions, he, and only he, on his own, did that. Only he could.

Karesansui, spatial empathy and Natalio Pescia

While other players were looking for the ball, Bobby was looking for space. He certainly wouldn't have been aware of any cultural leap he was making, but he was seeing the dynamics of the game like the Japanese see a 'Karesansui' or 'dry landscape' garden, sometimes called a 'Zen garden'. These often miniature, stylised landscapes primarily consist of carefully composed arrangements of rocks. Westerners viewing these gardens tend to look at the rocks and try to find meaning in their placement or shape. The traditional Japanese perception is focused on the spaces between the rocks and the shapes of these 'gaps' in an overall perspective of what is 'going on', rather than a partial and fragmented view of the environment. Thus, a seemingly fixed or stationary array of objects is, perceptually speaking, in a state of constant flux as the mind interacts with the environment (light, weather, mood and so on).

Taking this attitude, one can understand, according to one's perspective, where one is in relation to the Karesansui. One will see something different to someone viewing from another standpoint or angle. This is a search for 'harmony'; a merging of elements. If you grew up in the west it is unlikely to be that what you look for. You are more probably going to see the Karesansui as a collection of discreet objects, like a menagerie of 'things'; you will think of what you are seeing as 'heterogeneous elements' which will, at least in part, blind you to the 'homogenous whole'.

A similar idea to this in perceptual science is the idea of 'spatial empathy' – you could see this as what Allison was looking to develop in the young men he was working with in the 1950s, although I don't think for a moment that he ever, in his entire life, used the phrase. His coaching and motivation was almost entirely related to the pragmatics of the football field. Nevertheless, the gift he noted in the young Moore was akin to his spatial empathy; the awareness that an individual has of the proximity and the activities of people around them. It is closely related to the notion of personal space, the idea that individuals have a sense of self and others in relation to their immediate surroundings.

The degree to which different cultures exhibit spatial empathy differs dramatically. Typically, many of us living in developed, western countries consider unnecessary closeness to, or physical contact with strangers (on a train or in crowds for instance) to be distasteful. However, many Asian and Eurasian cultures do not show the same aversion. Some might say, although with only anecdotal evidence, that the British during the 1950s had quite a heightened sense of personal space, especially perhaps in working-class communities like those in east London. Maybe this was more observable with males or in respect of male groups, wherein someone getting 'too close' and worse, getting overly touchy, would not always be greeted positively and often more or less discouraged or repulsed.

Conditions and circumstance change our range of special empathy. Most of us experienced this during the Covid pandemic. 'Spatial security' became something our everyday consciousness grew sensitive to.

So, we have an innate capacity for spatial empathy, which can be more or less developed by experience and learning. There is a whole branch of child developmental science connected to this, but basically, we have two ways, or frames of reference, that make us aware of the world immediately around us: allocentric (object-object) and egocentric (subject-object).

Allocentric: The information on the position of an object is encoded according to the position of other objects. The position of an object is relative to the position of other objects.

That is, very basically, 'I know where George is by way of where others [people or things] are in relation to George. Fred is there, Freda is over here, that means George is between Fred and Freda.'

Egocentric: The information on the position of an object is encoded according to the body axes of the subject. The position of an object is relative to the position of the subject.

Again, straightforwardly, 'I know I am here because Fred is there.' Taken a bit further, 'Freda is close to me; Fred is further away from me.'

This all seems very simple (or using difficult concepts and words to express straightforward things) but that's because you have learned to take these considerations for granted. However, on average, children up to seven years of age are in the process of developing the ability to assess a point of view other than their own (how someone is seeing them); they kind of have a sense of where they are, but mapping this is not fully developed. It is only when the child reaches the stage of what is called 'concrete operations', between seven and 12 years of age, that the ability to 'decentralise' starts to fully kick in.

Watch five-year-olds playing football. No matter how much parents and coaches shout at and/or beg them, they follow the ball as a bunch, like iron filings attracted to a magnet. Of course, those with more advanced spatial empathy will begin to be able to do what the coach pleads with them to do. Yes, we can all develop in this respect, but the height of the development of this capacity has peaked by the time most of us reach puberty.

The basic understanding of 'stage development' of this sort is that at one point a child is unable to think in a certain way and then, at a later stage, there's kind of 'flick of a switch' and they suddenly are 'enabled'. This is to misunderstand brain and child development. Our spatial empathy for instance is developing from our earliest weeks as our brains start to be stimulated by those around us and the world. But there are optimal periods for building our various capacities and functions. However, if a child is provided with the motivation and stimulation prior to the optimum point, the scene can be set (so to speak) to maximise the impact of learning/development at the optimal stage. That stage might even be brought forward, although rarely dramatically.

Hence it would have been inefficient for Allison to have asked five-year-olds the type of questions relating to special awareness he asked Bobby at 13. But it is clear that Bobby arrived at Allison's training sessions ready and more able to successfully respond to such a task than others might have been. This was likely, at least in part, to have been a consequence of his park kick-arounds with his dad, as an infant intensely watching other kids play while waiting to get a game. But also, his journeys to school may well have added to his self-consciousness (being 'hyper-aware' of those around him) when he got to Tom Hood (among other considerations).

Within all this are the junctions between brain development, general experience, formal and informal learning, teaching, the development of mind and the getting of wisdom. At the same time, wider environmental factors will have an influence. For Bobby these included his early years being lived through war, the response to him as the 'fat kid', the stress of his isolation he felt initially at school. When in stressful situations children can become 'hyper-aware'; they adopt and habituate a heightened awareness of the actions and expressions of others, looking for clues to anticipate behaviour. Anticipation of behaviour around him was going to be a very strong suit in Moore's arsenal as a footballer.

For all this, spatial empathy is a valuable capacity for a slow, tubby lad, striving to contribute constructively to a football team. You can imagine Bobby needing to or being obliged to push himself in this respect. This is what human beings do and successful people inure, using apparent disadvantages as the means to build advantage or the leverage to shift disadvantage to advantage.

We learn most of the everyday things we do unconsciously, and we act them out, at best, on the fringes of consciousness; smiling, walking, even talking and driving for instance. Much of the way we see and act in the world is picked up from others. The young brain is designed to be impressionable, and self-conscious – this is how it makes us who we are and prepares us for later life. Bobby Moore, perhaps more than some, would have gleaned learning from the world around him and the people who populated that reality. He would have been doing that at Wembley in May 1951 and one of his 'informal' teachers was a master spatial empath: Natalio Pescia.

We know that areas of the brain are largely responsible for specific functions, and when stimulated by carrying out those functions, those areas develop – in some cases they actually get physically bigger. The reverse is also true. If we fail to stimulate areas of the brain responsible for particular functions, they become increasing inactive (there is less detectable electrical activity or 'neural synapses') and sometimes these areas literally shrink.

Thus, we get better or worse at particular tasks according to how much or how little the areas of the brain that control those tasks are stimulated by doing those tasks. You get better at playing the bagpipes the more you practice; if you don't practice, you aren't going to get better, or even retain what talent you might have. The more you use both sides of your body, the more you make yourself aware of the people and movement around you, the better you will be prepared for what happens in the space that surrounds you at any given point in time. Few of us cultivate this potential to any significant or outstanding degree. Bobby Moore did.

De Bruyne

The method Malcolm Allison taught the young Hammers has recently been rediscovered. It is something that the likes of Manchester City's Kevin De Bruyne has highly developed. Recent research shows this skill to be something that separates the best from the rest

De Bruyne routinely demonstrates astonishing vision in his play. This was exemplified in the Euro 2020 group game between Belgium and Denmark. His assist that pulled his side level was probably the most obvious instance. De Bruyne's first touch left two defenders on the ground. His second went to Thorgan Hazard, who was left with a simple tap-in goal. Few had seen the potential for that De Bruyne pass.

More than a few commentators were puzzled about how De Bruyne had noticed Hazard when the Manchester City man had looked to be completely focused on the ball. Yes, he might have had the old 'second sight' bestowed on children born on the last Friday in June by Drongen tulip pixies, or it could have been that he just blindly poked the ball and hoped for the best.

Geir Jordet, a professor at the Norwegian School of Sports Sciences, heard the conjecture, but he understood that De Bruyne had 'constructed' an ability that was being called 'scanning'. If you observe closely, watching his play before the pass to Hazard, you'll see that De Bruyne makes a barely noticeable head movement, a glance, for no more than a second, away from the ball. In this instant he is registering a sort of map in preparation to receive or distribute the ball. He does this all the time. This surveillance is something less than momentary, as it is no more than a check. He already knew where he was going to deliver the ball – that final review just confirmed the intention.

Since 1998 Jordet has become an authority on scanning. He was the first to make a serious study this skill. His main interest is the role of vision, perception and anticipation of high performing individuals. This field was pretty much unconsidered prior to him publishing his research a few years ago, although something similar has been practiced in Formula 1 racing for some time.

The better part of half a century after Allison was teaching the young Irons to develop their on-pitch vision and awareness, Jordet, together with a team of students in Holland, was looking at player cam footage, picking up on what Malcolm had been developing many decades previously (although Jordet knew and still likely knows nothing about Allison's approach).

Jordet and his crew monitored situations involving 118 Premier League players and compared the frequency of their scanning to amateur players in the Netherlands. They found that scanning differentiates players; those in the Premier League were significantly higher-performing scanners than their amateur counterparts. This might not have been too surprising, but the research also indicated that the highest performing Premier League footballers were superior/ more effective scanners than their less-well performing peers. The best two scanners were Frank Lampard and Steven Gerrard.

Lampard, son of West Ham legend Frank senior, presents an intriguing case because when he was told about the findings he said, like Johnny Haynes decades previously, that he was not consciously scanning. However, when he was pressed, he recalled that when he was a lad Frank senior would repeat an echo of Allison's advice to Bobby Moore, 'Pictures. Pictures. Pictures.' This was something in the Upton Park cultural DNA. Frank junior, even as a Chelsea and England player, was at core a Hammer. Romford boy Lamps, who could strike a ball almost as hard as his dad, one of England's finest in his era, was made at the Boleyn Ground. He might have worn the west London blue for the best part of his playing career, but his abilities were shot through with east London claret and had not a thing to do with the pouting Portuguese Portobello ponce he was to work for.[6]

Jordet found top-performing players told much the same story as Lampard. They discovered or acquired the requisite skills at an early age. In fact, the earlier a player grasped the importance of this broad awareness, the greater their advantage over their peers seemed to be.

An interview with Glenn Hoddle was typical in that he revealed that as a young player he had watched Jimmy Greaves and noticed Jim hardly looked at the ball. What he constantly did was look over his shoulder. Hoddle basically mimicked this and in doing so found it gave him an advantage. Watch him on YouTube, you'll see it. Like Lampard he had taken on building this mindfulness at a young age and it became a habit; like much of our perceptive capacities, it became part of who he was. As is the case in the acquisition of many skills, this ability became automatic after a while – he just did it; it was something he did without conscious thought; it grew to be instinctive.

However, scanning does not tell us everything. It's complex, but it provides us a vista into the visual awareness process that players like Moore, Haynes, Greaves, Lampard, Gerrard and Hoddle acquired. It is a clue about the extent to which players can be aware of their surroundings or immediate and probable physical context – a broad field of practical empathy.

---

6 I do wonder though, now as a manager, how Frank junior, not being conscious of this ability, so not knowing how he did it, might be in a position to hone the same capacity in his players.

At the time of writing, Phil Foden has striking scanning capacity for a player of his age. Other examples include Kylian Mbappé, Jude Bellingham and Erling Haaland. Jordet detected this feature in some of the finest young players in football: working out where they are in relation to others marks them out from the rest. Haaland and Mbappé are particularly impressive as it is relatively rare to see out and out attacking players scan to the extent they do. Jordet's research with Premier League professionals indicated that most of England's best strikers, in terms of their scanning ability, are way behind Haaland and Mbappé.

Scanning skill is not just a question of the incidence or regularity of scans. What is critical is the precise timing of scans. For Jordet, Cristiano Ronaldo has been among the very best practitioners of scanning. He demonstrates the nuance and detail that is involved in scanning, making it practically a scientific practice.

Jordet watched Ronaldo playing live in a Champions League tie in Copenhagen. He was struck by his timing – it was like he had an internal metronome keeping rhythm. A team-mate would deliver the ball to him and in a heartbeat, he would look away. This was almost invariably followed by him looking back at the next touch; someone else touched, he looked away – touch/look away, touch/look away.

Observing Ronaldo led Jordet to understand how intricate scanning is, and how difficult it had to be to train someone to do it to any appreciable extent (or really for someone to train themselves).

When you know about this, when you have observed it, you can see that the timing of top-quality scanning, by the likes of Ronaldo, gives them an advantage that is glaringly obvious.

Jordet became involved in football coach education and development in Norway. He continues a dialogue with coaches globally, but the passion on of scanning skill is a challenge. Teaching coaches how to integrate it into their work is even more exacting. Making a start at a young age gives an edge, but studies of training have shown adults performing at a high level can also become pretty good scanners comparatively swiftly.

Indications are that it isn't too much of an ask for players to, say, double their frequency of scanning, but it takes more time and effort to really take in and process the information one might pick up; it is not just looking but actually perceiving, processing and finally using the information to guide one's action. This suite of capacities, achieved to a high level, will be partly innate, and partly the result of thousands of hours of practice.

Jordet has, with others, worked on developing a virtual reality tool to help with developing scanning ability, called 'Be Your Best'. According to him, the whole array of abilities involved in scanning can be more easily extended in the controlled virtual reality environment. He argues that because this tool provides feedback on aspects of scanning, such as the frequency or timing, it can foster the appropriate cognitive and perceptive skills.

Of course, Malcolm Allison was asking kids to use their memories and imaginations. I find myself wondering how much this virtual training might take the place of, and/or blunt the perceptive capacities that Allison tasked young players to exercise and deploy. In his words, 'There's not only no such thing as a free lunch, the better the lunch, the more you're gonna have to pay for it!'

The use of the virtual environment could perhaps transform coaching, or maybe do away with it altogether, but this comparatively new appreciation (or perhaps it would be fairer to call it a rediscovery or a renascence) of the importance of scanning could also ignite dramatic changes in the way players are scouted in the future; they could be 'cyber tested'. But again, I think that's all bollocks. In the end you have to actually 'do' what it is you want to do. *Call of Duty* will not prepare you for actual warfare.

Jordet's primarily focus has thus far been on the side in possession, but he expects consideration to shift to the scanning – or lack of it – by players not in possession. Sweden's Emil Forsberg scored a goal against Poland at the 2020 Euros. This illustrated a characteristic instance of the defence failing to scan; not picking up information about Forsberg's position throughout the whole attack that ultimately led to the goal. That is not uncommon and as such is prime territory for Jordet's research.

The findings from the focus on 'out-of-possession' players could give some insight about why the best defenders are better than others. Jordet suspects that, more than we might realise, errors made at the highest level of football are more numerous as a consequence of inadequate scanning in the defensive phase of the game. While opponents have the ball all the time, players make mistakes. What he has yet to consider is what Allison taught Moore to think about – what you do when mistakes are made; how to turn a mistake into an advantage? Every mistake is also an opportunity. Mishaps and errors can't be avoided totally, but they can be used to learn how not to make mistakes and how to make opponents make mistakes. Mistakes constitute critical feedback – seeking to sift them out is a mistake.

Watching football, Jordet always looks out for scanners, but there is looking and there is *looking*. If he just watches games that include a side that he has an interest in, he is invested in that team. In such a situation he will do what everyone else does, he will watch the ball first and the general pattern of play as a secondary consideration. However, to see beyond that, one needs to focus on a player in advance of them picking up the ball. If you don't do that then you will to miss important facets of the results of scanning.

Peculiarly enough, even when I watch West Ham, a team I have a huge investment in, I break Jordet's rule. I tend to watch the ball less than I watch players. But try it yourself. Watch the YouTube recordings of De Bruyne's quick scan against Denmark, at first, looking at the whole attack, and then looking just at him. You are unlikely to detect him scanning more than once or twice, but switch to slow motion and you will see that he scanned five times. You have to make the leap from watching it as a regular spectator to watching it as a scanner yourself.

Observing scanning is almost as much of a skill as scanning is on the field of play, although I might have the advantage of having a hyper-aware childhood, one spent watching Bobby Moore and a lifetime of following the West Ham and Malcolm Allison's 'invisible heritage'.

Ground boy Bobby

Well into his late teenage years, Bobby was routinely in bed before 10pm. Doris would call him in usually before dusk, and when she woke him come morning, he would need no more than one call. Even when he did go out with his team-mates, he was so quiet it was easy to forget he was there. At 17 his habits in this respect had changed little.

Doris had a huge and positive influence on Bobby. He adored her as she adored him, but neither she nor Big Bob interfered in their son's footballing life, although they loyally watched him play. Unlike most footballing dads, Big Bob was never heard to raise his voice at a game, something that young Robert was to emulate on the field of play.

As a member of the ground staff Moore started work on £6 15s (25p short of £7). As he was to recognise, that wasn't too shabby for a lad just leaving school at that time. A weekly wage was the standard form of payment back then, and Mr Average, because it was most often a 'Mr' who was the best-paid in the average household, took home £9.25 (about £230 today). They paid 47.5 per cent basic income tax and worked an average of around 45 hours a week excluding overtime. The kids who were watching West Ham, some older than the lads on the ground staff, were pulling down a lot less. For example, a lorry driver's mate in the east London area might have been paid approximately £2 to £2.50 a week

The basic pay of an apprentice at Upton Park could be added to by bonuses, £1 or £2 for playing in the Football Combination for the reserve team, while being picked for away games meant an extra five shillings (25p) of 'tea money'. Moore was to tell how the younger players were able to grab snacks outside London for about half that amount, so around half a crown was pure 'bunce'.

Bobby would pass on '50 bob' (£2.50) to his mum as 'keep' and lay a bit by to cover fares. This would leave him something for going out on Saturday evening. So, Bobby's basic pay just about covered his outgoings, thus the chance of bonuses was welcome. There were times when the club could be persuaded to allow a lad to play three reserve and youth matches a week, as such there the potential existed to earn a bit more (including 15 bob – 75p – 'extras'). Young players might run out for more than 100 games over any one season. Later generations might likely have collapsed at the very thought of such efforts.

West Ham's payday was Friday. With cash in his sky, Bobby made a regular habit, along with Harry Cripps and Andy Smillie to make his way into the West End, have a hot chocolate in a swish little cafe near Piccadilly Circus – you could only get the 'real' stuff 'up West' – around Upton Park the best you might hope for was the powdered stuff that tasted like grainy liquid leather. They'd also take a gander at some clobber in Cecil Gee. As a 15-year-old in 1970, I bought a shirt from that place, paying the best part of £100, which was exorbitant amount at that time. It was a horrible bastard thing; I don't think I wore it more than five times before it became the most expensive workshirt outside the stock exchange.

Later, the players would get their whistles made by Phil Segal, the tailors at 277 Pigott Street, down by the Blackwall Tunnel. Phil did a lot of work with the celebs of the day, which included local gangsters. Tonic mohair was the choice of the smart lads in those days. Phil would also kit the players out with striped blazers, and starched shirts with collar studs. The nights out at the Tottenham Royal or Ilford Palais were a bit of a fashion parade for the young Irons. I had several TM suits. I liked blue best, but the green three-piece was a bit much though – I looked like the Green Hornet.

In those days it was common practice for young players to also play for amateur sides before turning professional. Moore turned out for Woodford Youth Club, who had a close association with Woodford Town FC, a club he would be president of for a while in later life.

The work of the junior ground staff was not romantic; it was hard and some might say demeaning, but for Moore this made him more resolved to break through to professional status and first-team recognition. Today, the expectations of youngsters coming into the modern game are little more than making the effort to hone their skills; they train and they play a few half days a week. Bobby was to question if an unintended result of this was something of a culture of anti-authority, which fuels a lack of what he might have seen as professional discipline.

The young players at the higher end of professional football now appear to have more of a sense of entitlement than a hunger for the game. As Moore was to reflect, as a young player, he and his peers lacked the luxury or even energy to question those that set themselves up as their betters, although that was another skill he would build beyond the capacity of his peers, often for not just his own but also their benefit.

It was during the 1957/58 term that Bobby made his initial Football Combination appearance, on 7 December 1957, versus Birmingham City reserves at the Boleyn Ground. He had experience in the second string and A (third) team while he was a member of the Colts XI that on 22 April 1958, at Upton Park, defeated Arsenal in the Southern Junior Floodlit Cup Final. The experience stood him in good stead when the Colts won an international youth tournament in Belgium, to round off the Hammers' promotion season with high hopes for the future. One game in that competition in Ghent was played on a surface that resembled soot. The whole team finished the match looking like chimney sweeps, except of course Bobby who, relative to the rest of the lads looked pretty much spick-and-span. That probably says a great deal about the young Moore.

9

ALLISON

The first game West Ham contested after Bobby Moore joined the ground staff at the Boleyn Ground was a home fixture. The Irons were playing host to Lincoln City. On 24 August 1957, in front of a crowd just short of 20,000, the match finished 2-2, Billy Dare and Malcolm Allison scoring for the Hammers. That season Lincoln would escape relegation by a single point, while West Ham would win promotion and the Second Division championship. It was fitting as Malcolm Allison had been in at the start of this success. More than any one man, it was his doing.

In the early 1950s, not long after he moved over the 'rivva' to east London (proper) from Charlton to West Ham, at Upton Park it was Allison who started organising extra training for the playing staff. When invited to take the lead coaching young players by Ted Fenton, in support of the manager's youth scheme, it was a natural progression for him.

Fenton had laid the ground for youth development prior to asking Malcolm to oversee the Tuesday and Thursday evening sessions for local boys, following the examples of the likes of Manchester United and Chelsea, but he made West Ham the first club outside the top division to put in place a cogent and committed youth policy. Almost from the beginning of Allison's tenure, leading what was the Irons' nascent 'Academy of football', Bobby Moore was involved.

Allison was to outline the start of his involvement and his backing for young Bobby,

'Ted Fenton asked me to train the youngsters. After a while, he called me in the office and asked me, "Who's our best young player?" I told him I thought Moore was the best. He was surprised and said, "What about George Fenn? Everyone in the country wants to sign him!" I said, "Well, the only one I'm interested in is Moore."'

For Allison, Fenton thought Fenn was a 'certainty to make a big name for himself', but for Malcolm the natural talent Fenn exuded was trumped by Bobby's avid pursuit for excellence. Allison argued,

'George was big and strong, a good runner, a good finisher. But I was convinced Bobby was a better player and I told Fenton that again. I said when George Fenn gets bigger he won't be so good.'

Fenn, who had shone in side that met Manchester United in the 1957 FA Youth Cup Final, was indeed a very good player, and that Hammers youth squad, a year ahead of Moore, sparkled with talent, including Terry McDonald, Clive Lewis, Roy Walker, Brian Goymer, Bert Howe, Charlie Rowlands, John Lyall, John Smith, Johnny Cartwright and Joe Kirkup.

While Alex Dawson, who was to be a leading light in the Preston side that met West Ham and Moore in the FA Cup Final of 1964, played out of his skin for United in that final of 1957, it was injury to Hammer John Smith at Old Trafford that was probably the main reason why West Ham's kids, the first rumblings of the 'Allison effect', ultimately fell at the last hurdle.

1957
West Ham's first FA Youth Cup Final: Baptism of fire

West Ham: Brian Goymer, Joe Kirkup, Albert Howe, Clive Lewis, Roy Walker, John Lyall, Charles Rowlands, John Smith, George Fenn, John Cartwright, Terry McDonald.
First leg (home) lost 3-2 – Scorers: Cartwright, Fenn
Second leg (away) lost 5-0 – 8-2 on aggregate

In 1957 the Irons made their first appearance in the FA Youth Cup Final and became the first southern club to achieve that distinction. They faced the holders, Manchester United.

The first leg took place at Upton Park and a crowd of 15,000 turned up to cheer on the claret and blue progeny that included full-back Joe Kirkup, who would help West Ham win the European Cup Winners' Cup in 1965. The future Hammers manager John Lyall, who would steer his club to FA Cup glory one day, was also in the line-up.

West Ham took the lead through Johnny Cartwright, who was destined to become a coach with the England setup, in the 22nd minute, but less than a quarter of an hour later Dawson kept up his remarkable record of scoring in every tie in the tournament by grabbing the equaliser.

Two goals in five minutes just after the break saw United take a firm grasp on the final, but just after the hour Hammers forward George Fenn pulled his side back into the game. However, despite a spirited performance West Ham were left with a lot to do at Old Trafford five days later.

A crowd of 23,000 cheered two goals apiece for Mike Pearson and Dawson, taking his total to 21 in ten games, and another from left-winger Reg Hunter that enabled United to retain the trophy.

Many years later, all of those young Irons were agreed that the team they were part of, the foundation of West Ham's most successful era, was principally Allison's creation, and that he was the architect of that shining decade.

Social whirl, posh nosh and romance

This was a time when the stars of football were accessible to rising talent, but Malcolm wanted to understand the kids at Upton Park in a way that went beyond seeing them for a few hours a week in training; he sought some insight into their character. Thus, much in the same way I might have done as a youth worker, he would take some of the lads with him to the dogs and on jaunts into London's West End, at venues such as the fashionable All Stars club. The young players were in awe of Allison and the exposure he gave them to the 'high life' caused them to idolise him all the more.

Fenton also tried to broaden the lads' prospects, sometimes taking groups of players to Hainault Golf Club for the afternoon. It was a municipal course at the time. They would hire a few clubs and play in tracksuits and their everyday shoes. Although this was novel for the kids, it had none of the excitement and exuberance of the experience of Allison's heady nightlife sojourns.

Malcolm had a taste for the better things in life. It was the start of the Swinging Sixties era, and he had become part of the 'scene', but it was all new to Bobby. He really was an 'innocent abroad'. At one point Allison had a thing with a fishmonger's daughter (let's face it, who hasn't?). Bobby and Tina were invited to a bit of shindig round the fishmonger's gaff, a rather grand place in Loughton, Essex, on New Year's Eve. During the course of the evening, by himself, Bobby scoffed a whole side of smoked salmon. Can you imagine the thirst that might have generated?

The UK had not ended wartime rationing until 1954, but the rest of the 1950s and the early 1960s was pretty much devoid of fine dining options. It was a time of bangers and mash, or boiled beef and carrots (if you were lucky). But Bobby liked his nosh and his courtship of Tina early on included visits to the Spaghetti House in Soho, which was considered quite classy. The first time they 'cenato Italiano' pasta was a stranger to both of them. Tina was amused to watch her perfectionist beau wresting with the spag while trying to look like it was second nature to him. They shared a bottle of chianti – the drink in the UK was usually nestled in in a straw basket, very chic.

One place Tina introduced Bobby to was Sheekey's fish restaurant in the West End, on St Martin's Court, close to the National Gallery. It's still around today, and has a history going back to 1896 when stallholder Josef Sheekey was given permission by Lord Salisbury to serve fish and shellfish in St Martin's Court, on the proviso that he supply meals to Salisbury's after-theatre supper parties. It was Tina's mum's favourite eatery and Tina had often dined there with her; they'd have steamed Dover sole with lobster sauce. The Beverly Sisters were regulars, the UK's answer to the Andrews Sisters – the Spice Girls of their day. Joy was married to England football captain Billy Wright. They and their family were the 'stars' of many a TV advert, in particular for Wrights Coal Tar Soap, which as a child always sounded like a contradiction in terms to me. Still, good to know Bill was blowing bubbles.

I suppose I was a bit younger than Bobby in his Spaghetti House period when I started taking girls to the first Pizza Express, on Wardour Street. I'd grab a cab in Plaistow and we'd go 'up west'. It never failed to impress, but sadly that's all it did.

Pretty soon the Spaghetti House was forgotten and deposed by places like the 21 Club. By the early 1960s Bobby and Tina were exploring the culinary horizons that most people would never know (and many wouldn't have wanted to). Melon, avocado, international cheeses and wines. They even broached the gastronomic boundaries of broccoli (which I always think of as 'sprouts lite'). Before Bobby met Tina, his mum mostly served only the third division vegetables, the solid back four of peas, carrots, cabbage and potatoes.

Win, draw or lose, we're on the booze

Doris, coming from a background of abstinence, could never accept that her Robert could put away a lager or eight. If he'd had too many, she'd say he was 'under the weather'.

A lot has been said and written about West Ham's 'drinking culture' and there is no doubt it was a phenomenon at Upton Park, as it was across football. It was remarkably enduring, continuing up to the 1990s. One hesitates to say it has been over-stated in relation to mid-century West Ham United, but it was not exactly ubiquitous at the club. Booze had been a periodical focus around Upton Park since West Ham's first manager, Syd King (see Belton 2006c, 2006d), but it wasn't a marked concern during Charlie Paynter's reign or most of Ted Fenton's era. In Moore's time it really only emerged when players began to have more of a disposable income, after the abolition of the minimum wage.

It has to be said that Malcolm Allison was very much central to the determined 'high-life' ethos. He once popped round to goalkeeper Noel Dwyer's place. Noel told his Mrs that they were just going to get a loaf of bread; she didn't see him again for two days. As any kind of issue excessive drinking all but disappeared at Upton Park by the time Bobby left the club after the Blackpool affair , but it was always something of a minority pursuit; the likes of John Lyall, Geoff Hurst and Martin Peters were never part of the core group of 'serious drinkers' that Moore became pretty central to not too long after Allison departed Upton Park. Perhaps an overly critical eye cast over Bobby's drinking habits, maybe particularly from the mid-1960s, might raise concerns.

Moore had tactics to disguise the extent of his proclivity for 'a drop of sauce'. For instance, avoiding loosening his tie and not leaving empty bottles to line up on a bar or table. 'Friday Phil', who run the players' bar, situated conveniently next to the gym at the Boleyn Ground during the 1950s, would sometimes be kept busy several hours after home games 'filling the trough' (as he had it). Phil had watched over many a hard-drinking east London bar, but confessed he had never met anyone who 'could sink as many as Mooro and look like he was just back from a stroll along the prom. Bobby was at the front of the queue almost from the time he signed professional forms. At Sulky's, a club the more determined drinkers customarily visited on returning from away games, Moore, although often turning up later than others, surpassed any of them in terms of his capacity to 'salute John Barleycorn'.

Drink seemed to flow in the very veins of the club for a decade and more. Even with the relatively straight-laced Ron Greenwood, after taking over as West Ham's manager, would serve behind the club bar after games, although I suspect this deterred many players from that venue. Exposing their appetite for the 'devil's milk' to Ron might not have been a good idea – perhaps that's why he took the role? Paddy, the Upton Park groundsman in the 1960s (who always made a point of being around as the players took the field for matches – he 'photo-bombed' many a press photo during that decade), kept a supply of whiskey under the fish tank in his little office, just by the players' tunnel, and he often shared a 'dram' or several with practically anyone who was passing.

We can of course point a 'holier than thou' finger at the vices of the past and of others, but in the last couple of decades of the 20th century I have been to enough professional football-related gigs to know it had no grounds for such sanctimony. *The Last Days of Sodom and Gomorrah* might have looked like a Teletubbies tea party in comparison, toilets with a merry yuletide dusting of 'snow' in middle of June being the least of it. I could tell stories that would likely land me and others in court or perhaps St George's Canal.

As in all organisations and groups of people, there were overlapping cultures at West Ham over the decades from the late 1950s to the early 1980s. Drinking was one and the Cassettari's 'Academy' was another, although the latter was not as long lived as the 'booze crew'. Phil Woosnam tried to continue 'tea and toast' seminars, but it was sometime between Allison's departure and Cantwell's move to Old Trafford that the forum, as the semi-formal institution, pretty much ceased to be in the 'cafe context'. However, both groups consisted of relatively small clutches of players. At the same time there were players who trained, travelled and played together and just went home thereafter, some perhaps dipping a toe in these and other groupings now and then.

After promotion there were at least three main friendship groups within the first team: the gamblers, the drinkers and the lads who went home to their wives and families. None were entirely mutually exclusive. Vic Keeble, for instance, neither drank nor smoked his whole life, but he liked a bet. By the mid-1960s Bobby's group included Ken Brown, John Bond, Peter Brabrook, Johnny Byrne and Eddie Bovington. The more 'homebird' lads included Geoff Hurst, Martin Peters, Jack Burkett, Ronnie Boyce, Johnny Sissons and Joe Kirkup.

Alcohol produces stimulating effects, but it is a depressant. It impacts your central nervous system, influencing the way your brain communicates with the nerves in your body. Alcohol thus can act as a sedative, helping the drinker to feel more at ease. This is a short-lived effect but it may temporarily enhance social confidence, so the appeal for relatively shy people, like the young Moore, might be obvious.

For all this, it is as well to hold in mind that true confidence is the child of a relative lack of confidence. Those we think of as coming into this world born confident are likely shallow narcissists or nascent sociopaths. All self-assurance is hewn out of the granite of self-doubt, else what is seen as 'natural confidence' is merely a pastiche behind which is hidden feelings of inferiority and ineptitude.

You don't repeatedly, maybe hundreds of times in a month, kick a ball at a bucket 60 yards away because you know you can do it. You go through that process because you start out doubting you are not going to hit that bucket many times in dozens of attempts. How you chip away at that doubt is by building the ability to hit the bucket. Over time, the more you hone your feel and skill the more you build the confidence you that can do this task; you turn the foundation of doubt into the means to produce increasing confidence, until hitting the bucket is no longer blind luck, an unexpected outcome, but a foregone conclusion – failure to hit the bucket becomes rectifiable error rather than par for the course.

Taking authority

Looking back, George Fenn had it that some of the younger players were a bit weak, seeing Allison as something of an idol, including himself in this group. However, George regretted staying out drinking, seeing it retrospectively as destroying himself. Almost certainly this was part of Allison's testing of the young men in his charge. It was Malcolm who told me, 'Even as a teenager, a player has to know when enough is enough. If they don't get that, then that is going to stop them.'

Fenn was once described by Ted Fenton as 'the most exciting prospect in the country', but ultimately, in 1959, he moved to Southern League Bedford Town. George was never less than complimentary about Malcolm (he and his wife Valerie named their daughter Allison after Malcolm). For Fenn, Bill Robinson, who was nominally in charge of that 1957 side, had no eye for talent. In fact, according to George, Robinson, had no clue how to cultivate youngsters, effectively destroying the future of too many budding players. Fenn saw this as the reason Malcolm was given the coaching rudder at Upton Park.

As George saw it, Allison effectively took control of the club and totally altered the way the younger players were trained. The mind-numbing laps of running around the pitch, much deployed by Robinson, were replaced by the use of pressure training, weights, and sprint coaching and ball work. Being not much of a sprinter himself, Allison recruited athletics coaches to do the job. George was to relate how Malcolm, inspired by continental sides, introduced shorter shorts, lighter boots and cut-down shirt sleeves. All of this was a mystery to and even a source of shock for the old hands at the Boleyn Ground.

Fenn's playing colleague and contemporary, Terry McDonald, confirmed George's perspective, that during Bill's coaching sessions the players hardly got sight of a ball. Unsurprisingly, Robinson and Allison didn't get on too well, but this was probably because Malcolm was essentially a disruptor, a breaker of the kind of traditions that Bill was a product of. According to Fenn, Allison was like something from the future, a decade ahead of his era. The boys of '57 agreed that the sophisticated play associated with the Hammers was instigated by Malcolm. They saw that the innovations and commitment were a product of Allison's passion for the football. Indeed, he appeared at times to value football as much as life itself.

Malcolm was never a prisoner of custom and practice; there was always more to learn, so more to change, stuff to throw out and things to introduce. You can't learn much by just repeating what has already been done a million times. You need to experiment and innovate. Today soon moves into what is past, tomorrow and future success will always demand adaptation and new ideas; tomorrow is always new. Allison was never going to warm to the likes of Robinson, those who followed credo and sanctified baseless habits – doing things because they are the things you do. You can see how Malcolm and Moore were kindred spirits; the lad who was keen to learn, practically salivating for knowledge, and the man who was looking to invent a new order of things.

For all Allison's philosophy and high footballing principles, it would be a mistake to make him out to be a saint. Much of his time he came over as an angry person, and he could be vindictive, even a bit of a bastard. Harry Hooper, one of the most unassuming and pleasant people I have met, was a high-quality winger. For much of the mid-1950s Harry was on the verge of the England team, quite a rarity for a player in the second tier of English football. During a training match, Allison decided to rough Harry up a bit. It has been said that Malcolm envied Harry's talent, but Hooper saw the incident as Allison demonstrating how he could be stopped by a determined defender. Hooper's best mate at the club, West Ham's first youth international and Irons hardman Andy Malcolm didn't see it that way and tore into Allison, grabbing him by the throat and warning him not to chance his arm with his pal again. The Hammers' skipper was a tough cookie, but he wisely steered clear of open violence; he could see no benefit in it, it being a waste of time and energy. A confrontation with 'Shadow'[7], however, would likely also be a waste of teeth and blood.

Sometimes, Ted Fenton and club secretary Eddie Chapman watched the younger players training, but for a time the manager had no idea about Allison's afternoon training with the senior players. The first he knew of it was when George Isaacs, the groundsman, complained about Allison using the pitch for ball work.

While he was puffing on his pipe in his office or back garden, Fenton's most energetic and intelligent player was applying and forming new ideas about the game. When Ted did finally find out what was going on there wasn't much he or his tweed jacket could do about it. Although he never ceased to be curious, albeit from a safe distance, Fenton's inquisitiveness was probably tinged with a generous portion of suspicion, maybe a touch of envy too, and perhaps a sprinkling of paranoia, the likes of which we all might endure when we are not sure of what exactly is going on in and around our own patch. Much the same situation pertained when Allison took over school boy coaching.

All this said, there is part of me that admires Fenton for standing back somewhat. He made this insatiable antagonist his captain and gave him his head, which demonstrates trust in the heretic's capacities and respect for his approach. I do believe Ted recognised what Allison brought to the table, and that it was something special, that in the last analysis he himself lacked but admired. The ability to grasp that and act on it, allowing a subordinate to *take* authority, is a

---

7   This was the nickname given to Andy Malcolm by his fellow players, as they felt more likely to get a kick from him than a kick of the ball.

mark of good management (expanding on the point made earlier in this book, giving someone authority is a contradiction in terms; like power, authority is either taken or else it isn't authority at all, it's merely a delegated responsibility or duty passed on by a higher authority).

It was not St Pier, Turner, Robinson or Fenton who had an eye for future talent – it was Allison who knew that the best players are made more than born, and the trick was literally to see, sense and focus on the ones who could 'make it'. As he told me, 'No one "found" Bobby Moore! Bobby Moore was "made"!'

By this I'm confident that Malcolm was pointing out how Moore crafted his own talent out of what aptitudes he had, as if out of stone, although Allison might have shown him some tools and helped him to learn how to use them. There's a lesson in that for us all perhaps?

As Bobby entered the last quarter of his teenage years it seemed as far as management were concerned that he was no better thought of than when he first joined the club, no matter what stories they told later, salivating for some crumbs of congratulation and a place in the aura of Bobby's glory. West Ham weren't in the front line of clubs kids wanted to join – Upton Park couldn't offer parents any of the 'incentives' that clubs like Chelsea could. These included TVs, fridges and even the odd three-piece suite. George Fenn, who was signed by the Irons in 1954, had been on the radar of Arsenal and Manchester United. His father, a professional boxer, was offered a turkey in exchange for his son's services by Spurs! However, George was a local lad who supported West Ham from his earliest years. For the cost of a few pennies, like many of us, he had watched the Irons from the Boleyn Ground's North Bank. Sadly, few had Fenn's fidelity; so many good young East End players literally went west. Fenn later said only Allison was responsible for keeping Moore at West Ham and thus in top-class football. Malcolm had a belief in the lad that others lacked. This contention is consistently confirmed as one analyses Moore's early biography.

In many ways Moore and George Fenn were the mirror images of each other. If there had been some way to merge them into one player you might have got the perfect personification of a footballer. In his 1975 book *Colours of My Life*, Allison provides a parable about talent and application,

'George Fenn never played seriously after drifting away from West Ham. It was a tragedy, as sad in its way as the early retirement of that other Georgie, Best. Fenn could have been just as big as Best. He had sensational speed, all sorts of trickery and a tremendous shot. But however hard you tried with him you had the sense that it was all futile. Deep down, perhaps it was the drudgery of training and the battle for constant fitness that put him off.'

Fenn has agreed with that assessment, and it was likely this lack of application, George seemingly wasting his talent, that appeared to frustrate Malcolm, and thus he seemed less than fond of the young centre-forward, although my impression when Allison talked about him it was more with regret than any breed of personal acrimony.

Like others, George was to remember how Moore returned to Upton Park in the afternoon for extra training after all the other lads had gone home. His appetite and commitment were as such extraordinary, and there is nothing that makes a good teacher a better one than an engaged and dedicated student. So, Bobby pulled the best out of his mentor and likely made him a better coach.

In the early 1950s the Hammers were obliged to undertake a bit of alchemy and look for 'hidden treasure'. Moore himself owned the reality that when he came to Upton Park he was slow over the ground, appeared allergic to heading a ball and seemed unable to tackle. Years on, he confessed he couldn't recall what he was thought to be good at. What people, other than Allison, saw was a lumbering left-half, perhaps with a role as a defensive midfielder. His main quality seemed to be determination that could maybe be used to bludgeon more artistic adversaries in much the same way he managed during his earliest days on the schoolboy playing fields.

What Moore had, and what Allison nurtured, what they literally grew together, was a highly active reality check mechanism. At school, Bobby did not spend his time dreaming, he worked hard. He did the practical work needed to realise his ambitions. Yes, there was a sort of half-hearted plan B, but he was doing the groundwork to get to the place he wanted to be, even he though, in his most realistic moments, he might have thought making a career in professional sport marked the limits of possibility.

After sharing bus rides and with Bobby, Malcolm got himself a car and so, by way of young Moore getting lifts home, the partnership continued to blossom. In 1950s east London, car ownership was a rarity. I recall in my street, an eight-minute walk from the Boleyn Ground (passing John Bond's front door) as a small boy, my father's Volkswagen camper was one of maybe three cars in the whole street. These were the days you could park almost directly outside the Old Bailey with no fear of traffic wardens. I know because I waited there for my dad, who, although not in the legal profession, spent a lot of time and dosh seemingly funding it (and that is yet another story).

Allison wasn't up for the Greenwood 'lecture-on-pitch' style, nor haunting the blackboard, as was sometimes Ron's wont. That level of formality really wasn't up Malcolm's alley, but he was prone to the odd soundbite: 'Even when you're not the captain, act as if you are'; 'Think big, be bigger'; 'Take control, or you will be controlled'.

Whenever Bobby expressed doubts about his ability Malcolm dismissed the notion, telling him he'd be better than the rest and to think otherwise was daft.

As far as Allison was concerned, all Bobby had to do was what Malcolm told him, and part of that was lay off judging himself and let Allison do that job.

Straightforward perhaps, but the process could be anything but comfortable at times. For instance, in a youth team encounter with Chelsea, Moore was deployed in defence, assigned to mark the brilliant Barry Bridges. He cancelled out the talented Chelsea youngster completely. The game finished goalless, so Bobby seemed to have cause to be pleased with himself. However, to his surprise, Allison was incandescent with rage, telling him in no uncertain terms, in his loud and intimidating fashion, that if Bobby ever performed that way again, he would give no more time to him. Malcolm's booming assessment was that Bobby had been lazy and thoughtless, restricting his play to a mere demolition job on the young Blues striker, shirking his responsibility to develop play from the back. As Bobby was to say, 'You haven't had a bollocking 'til you've been bollocked by Malcolm.'

Allison was peeved because each time the goalkeeper got the ball, Bobby darted up the pitch in search of Bridges, pursuing the forward's shadow. For Malcolm, Moore had failed to do what he had taught him. He had not dropped back, ready to collect the ball from the keeper or assist a team-mate.

It was experiences like this that caused Moore to recognised that if it had not been for Allison, he would not have made the professional ranks. In training Malcolm worked with Bobby day in and day out, emphasising playing out from the back until the practice became second nature.

The source of the young man's motivation to learn and develop his game was self-doubt, a lingering misgiving that his skill was limited, which is always actually the case at some point in anyone's career. Unlike the attitude of the young George Fenn for example, there was not a moment when the youthful Moore was able to convince himself that success was in any way a given.

In the current era, we tend to take such a lack of confidence in young people as something that we must make every attempt to rid them of, as if the achievement of an optimal point between lack of self-esteem and arrogance might be definable or reachable as a consistent standard or state of being. This, of course, is patent nonsense. Contrary to the popular belief that success is the child of confidence, it is anxiety that drives us to achieve; the fear of failure, and the need to compensate for, or craft our weaknesses into strengths. Such qualities are the consequences of the survival instinct. Moore's doubts about himself were the fuel that fired his steely commitment to training in a way that was second to none. The need to 'get confident' was the motivation to demonstrate extraordinary endeavour, to listen diligently, while concentrating intently on what he did, how he did it, when he did it, and what he was told about what he was and wasn't doing.

The narrative that one can be 'anything one wants to be' just by wanting it is a destructive lie. It gives rise to a false sense of entitlement that when thwarted provokes resentment. The expectation that one might work for what one wants is replaced by a fantasy that others need to work to give me what I want. Moore's engine was his self-doubts. He did not kick on in his development because he was in some way hypnotised to simply and mysteriously drop his doubts about his abilities, just somehow switching them off. Yes, Allison got Bobby to a place where his sense of inferiority could be rationalised and converted into assets, handing his misgivings over to his mentor to deal with, so that they might be interpreted and transformed or compensated for. But we don't continue to develop by thinking we have got to a place of perfection. Learning is facilitated by a knowledge of our own ignorance. Likewise, we only do things better by understanding that we are doing them not as well as we can or might want.

Being convinced of our capacities, and knowing the limits of the same, are products of endeavour, not merely 'change of heart' or 'attitude management'; notions that mean little really. The shy, nervous young Eric Clapton didn't become a guitar genius merely by thinking positively. Liz Diller didn't just rely on adopting the right frame of mind to become an award-winning architect. Wishes don't really work, despite the Noel Edmonds *Deal or No Deal* philosophy of 'positive thinking'.

Motivation has to have a wellspring of more than ethereal intentions; as the word suggests, a 'fuel' is required. For instance, Allison would require young players to lie on their backs and raise their feet about a foot from the ground, developing and testing core strength. Not only did Bobby still have his feet raised when everyone else's had succumbed to gravity, his feet hovered in the air until he was told to drop them. Later, Ernie Gregory would run the players through a similar exercise at the Grange Farm training ground, rewarding the person who kept their feet off the deck longest with a chocolate bar or drink – Bobby always got the prize. Soon he was easily the fittest of the apprentices – despite all that chocolate. Try this, and see if you can hold the position for a few minutes. Most of us will crumble after not very long, in part because we are not physically attuned to such an exercise, but also partly because we lack the motivation to do anything other than only go as far as the extent of our pain barrier – which is another expression for 'will'.

No matter when the training was, or when it concluded, Bobby stayed on for a least an extra hour. One just doesn't 'do' that, the drive to realise that type of application and resolve is generated; it is a quality of resilience that is the incubator to the development of talent. Any achievement is likely the result of our will to endure.

Noel Cantwell tended to be a little more subtle with young players, and people in general, than his forthright and often unfiltered team-mate and pal. He talked about 'game intelligence' and how this could compensate other deficiencies, for instance pace. Moore was able to understand how this related to Malcolm's credo – not just responding, making oneself purely reactive, but to be constantly thinking ahead, that is, being 'proactive'. This is proactivity trumping reactivity; making stuff happen rather than waiting for happenstance to impact on you. You can live your life like an ambulance on acid, but you will not be able to sustain any kind of standard other than relatively mediocre.

As today, however, most drooled for immediate results rather than acceded to the patience needed to harvest the fruits of the honed effort. Fenton's consistent doubts about Moore, in fairness, were shared with others. He just didn't see what Allison saw in the boy. Indeed, if you take a detached look at both St Pier's and Turner's original cursory assessments of the lad in his mid-teenage years, after he had been working with Malcolm for sometime, it is hard to see the reasoning why Moore might have been given a place at the Boleyn Ground, how he might have been selected for one of the relatively few available for apprenticeships. These pretty superficial and less than encouraging evaluations look more like attempts to question and/or temper the enthusiasm that Allison had for the young player.

George Fenn remembered, on getting back from a youth tour of Belgium and Germany, Ted Fenton telling the boys who among them he thought would make it. George told of how Ted let Moore know he had 'no chance', that he 'wasn't up to it'. Fenton had a similar opinion about Harry Cripps, the man who was to become a legend at Millwall's Den. On hearing the manager's judgement, the fabled 'iron man' of the Lions to be was reduced to tears.

However, by that time Moore had stopped taking much notice of Ted. That wasn't disrespect; Bobby certainly gave Fenton credit and appreciation for taking him on in the first place, it was just that Allison had persuaded him to keep focused on informed assessment rather than rough and ready opinions.

It could have been Ted's assessment of Moore and Cripps was meant to 'gee' them up, a sort of bluff to provoke an 'I'll show you' attitude. But another player of the 1957 generation, Terry McDonald, confirmed Fenton's likely authentic view, commenting that if Moore had been in the same group of players as himself and Fenn, probably England's greatest captain would have been let go – as Terry said, it was Allison who saw and insisted on his potential.

Play that posterior parietal cortex, white boy

The area of the brain responsible for planning movements and spatial empathy, the area of Bobby's brain Malcolm was stimulating, is known as the 'posterior parietal cortex' (PPC). It is an area of our 'higher brain' which also plays a major role in decision making, specifically deciding what images should be in the field of view.

It is worth here reiterating that our brains, throughout our young lives, are being shaped, or more accurately sculptured. We physically shed material from areas of the brain we don't use, while areas we call upon grow. Our brains morph to best fit what we ask of them in response to our environment and context. Allison and Moore collaborated in 'brain building', growing a footballing brain/ intellect; a *mind* attuned to the tasks of football. This is why Moore took every opportunity to discuss the game with Allison, Noel Cantwell, Ron Greenwood, and Alf Ramsey as well as his early England team-mates, Bobby Charlton, Jimmy Greaves, Jimmy Armfield and so on. When we have developed areas of our brain to a particular extent, we seem to want to continue the process, a sort of feeding of a hunger.

By the time Jack Turner supposedly got to Bobby it would have been too late for any this to happen to any appreciable extent. At 15, the vast work of brain architecture is close to complete, although if appropriate stimulation is available, development continues, even if at a comparatively modest rate. Turner, Robinson *et al* would have about as much impact on Moore as a teenager as Jacob Rees-Mogg had on the development of hip-hop.

Perhaps we can also see something of Moore's childhood development of his PPC in relation to decision-making; crucial for the telling pass or tackle of course, as well as judging where to be on the pitch, 'creating space' as it is sometimes misleadingly put, as it is more about reading and anticipating patterns and consequences of actual and potential movement than grafting out room.

However, decision-making is a response to our emotions; how we make or fail to make good/useful judgements is dominated by our temperament. Moore would never rise to any insult or intimidation; the irrational (non-rational, unjudged) response did not seem part of his emotional repertoire. His rejoinder when team-mates were sent off was a sort of low-level disapproval, tinged with disappointment; that of a caring father or older brother, expressed in a shrug, the rising of an eyebrow, a slight shake of the head. It said all over, 'What a shame, you let yourself down, mate,' or, 'Now, that was daft wasn't it; from here on in we've got to do your work for you.'

It's quite a jump for most of us to see that what feels at first not much more than enlightened coaching methods can lead to consequential improvements in character and civility, but that's the power of our brains. Your brain is you; change your brain, or more rationally, how it works, and you change. Of course, environmental considerations can change brain activity, so what the brain 'becomes' (who and what you turn out to be) is something of a two-way street in that respect. However, we are, to a large extent, a reflection of what we do and don't do.

The bigger picture is that Moore's approach to football developed the whole of his neocortex, the pink cauliflower inside his (and hopefully your) head – the higher, rational brain, that last part of the brain to evolve. Getting this in gear gives us the means to quieten our lower (flight or fight) brain; hook the rational brain, and so gaining the power to make better decisions, 'Where does nutting the bloke get me or anyone else?' for instance.

As he passed his mid-teenage years, Moore was knocking on the door of the West Ham first-team squad. The development of Moore's footballing brain was being consolidated under Cantwell and Allison; the slog of what passed for the club's conventional training programme could only have had tangential physical effects.

Tick for Ted

The position of Ted Fenton by the start of the 1960s was opaque. One of his new signings, goalkeeper Peter Shearing, recalled Ted briefing a first team meeting, going over tactics for an upcoming game. As was usual for Fenton, the strategy was man-to-man marking within a 4-4-2 formation. When Ted concluded he left the room, whereupon Noel Cantwell and Phil Woosnam took the floor, stating quite plainly that the team wasn't going to play the way Fenton had prescribed, but adopt the 4-2-4 system,

However, under Fenton's management West Ham had become one of the most forward-thinking and innovative clubs in the English game. The introduction of weight training for instance was pioneering, calling in Bill Watson to oversee the programme.

Watson had been discharged from the army in 1942 with what was described as 'the lowest medical category'. Consequently, he took up weightlifting, and began a regime of physical training to develop fitness. It was not long before he was winning championships, and in 1948, after claiming the British middleweight title, he was selected for that year's London Olympics. He finished a creditable eighth out of 24 starters.

In the 1950s, many notable sports teams introduced weightlifting into their training programmes, and Bill's expertise was called upon by the likes of Arsenal, Spurs, West Brom, and Wolves among others. He also helped the Essex and Warwickshire county cricket teams.

Some of the older, bigger-built players, Ken Brown or Noel Cantwell for instance, would often perform 30 squat jumps while holding two 15lb (just under 7kg) dumbbells; that called for a high level of stamina. This sort of exercise was good for some of the younger players, providing the means to gain bulk and strength. The players did a lot of strength work in the gym, sometimes working in pairs with a medicine ball. These were very heavy and while it was mostly OK for the bigger fellas, when they threw these weighty orbs at a youngster it could knock them completely over.

In later years, some of the then young men, such as Geoff Hurst, Martin Peters, Jack Burkett and Ron Boyce, all had trouble with lower back injuries. We now know until the end of the final major growth spurt in later teenage years that consistent and heavy use of weights isn't a great idea. Even afterwards, usually the heavier the weights used the more likely back injuries or 'early wear' might result. Even today, I watch young men working out and wince at their antics, attempting to 'out-man' each other, or just to impress an audience of strangers. I have often thought it'd be a great idea to take out shares in an osteopathy clinic – might compensate for all the money I've wasted on gym memberships over the years.

Like Allison, Fenton wanted to bring new ideas to the club. He introduced a trampoline into the gymnasium at Upton Park, his basic thinking that it would help develop leg muscles and balance. It was a notion way ahead of the times. For all this, relative to Malcolm having been a player with the club since boyhood, Ted wanted to be much more diplomatic with Upton Park's traditions and hierarchy in mind – keeping people sweet.

Under Fenton, it's unlikely that the West Ham playing staff had ever been better-conditioned or fitter, although, as with the weight training, there are always potential hazards in such ambitions. For a time, Ted encouraged some of the younger players to take supplements, passing them some 'little white powder' to add to their meals over a series of weeks. Rumour had it that this was a calcium powder which, supposedly, would work to fortify the young men. From the current period it doesn't sound too healthy and apparently it tasted disgusting. It might have been a theory Ted had picked up in the forces, but today we know that symptoms of a high calcium level include:

- Loss of appetite
- Nausea and vomiting

- Constipation and abdominal pain
- The need to drink more fluids and urinate more
- Tiredness, weakness, or muscle pain
- Confusion, disorientation, and difficulty thinking
- Headaches
- Depression

However, no one but Ted had any idea what his 'little white powder' was exactly; maybe he didn't, but perhaps it was fortunate there no drug tests in that time. Other sorts of 'white powder' have this issue today, of course.

Under Allison's influence and sometimes nagging, Ted ditched the baggy shorts and blanket-like shirts of the time and brought in tighter-fitting, short sleeved, V-necked shirts and 'abbreviated' shorts.

This said, Fenton never really got involved with a 'hands-on' approach in terms of coaching of the young players. Despite Bill Robinson's position, the training was routinely left to the likes of Malcolm Allison, Noel Cantwell and a bit later, John Bond. Fenton likely realised (giving him the benefit of the doubt) that he was lucky to have aspiring coaches and left them to do the job.

Cantwell seemed to be the 'go-to' person in terms of the pastoral care of the kids. He always seemed conscious of their concerns and was thus, more often than not, able to help them feel more at ease with their deficiencies, so enabling them to work on making aspects of their performance stronger. Many players benefited from his advice that typically started out with 'don't worry' and usually concluded with the guidance to be patient with themselves and trust in their own development.

But it was Ted who brought in a procedure of sending a report on the progress of each Colt player to their parents at the end of the year. This was both clever and caring. It really was the first step by any club to create a 'community involvement' in player development – and was the initial realisation of West Ham as a 'family club'. It did no harm at all to the commitment and focus of young players to make parents aware of their development (or lack of it) and as such recruited parents' encouragement to the West Ham cause.

Ted was quite strict with the younger players. During the war he had been an army PT instructor in Africa and Burma, and this was to some extent reflected in his managerial style during his early years in charge at Upton Park. Some of the kids were a bit frightened of him, especially the lads who were sent to his office following misdemeanours such as messing around during training. Harry Cripps was one such offender. Most of the times he spotted Bill Robinson from afar he'd holler, 'Did you get stuck in a jam, Bill?[8]' The veteran trainer would look round, but wasn't able to pick out the apprentice who had shouted the question. They all continued to labour away as if nothing at happened. It was thought it was groundsman George Issacs who had grassed on him.

Ted could be protracted and a tad ruthless when it came to the art of admonishment, sometimes reducing younger players to tears. However, much of this appears to have been front or bluster, as while many of the rank-and-file players respected Fenton and his authority, some for the rest of their lives, those such as Allison got close to bullying him at times, while Cantwell pretty much managed Ted.

Fenton most certainly cared about West Ham and showed admirable commitment and loyalty to the club, man and boy. The man deserves a deal of credit for signing Allison from Charlton Athletic in 1950 and making him club captain. It was perhaps his most astute act as manger to give Allison responsibility for coaching the young players, and turning a blind eye to what the traditions of the club would have seen as insolence. For many in Fenton's position it would have been instinctive to undermine Allison's relationship with the rest of the playing staff, but Ted never did that; he was the bigger man for it, although probably because, overall, the dynamic was positive. Fenton gave Allison something to crusade against, and Malcolm needed that type of motivation; all his life he sought to prove himself in an ongoing war with institutional authority.

Allison was a tall, dominating centre-half, and he went on to play over 250 league and cup games in the Upton Park cause. An ingenious tactician and consistent innovator, he was light years ahead of his era in terms of coaching and fitness training. An avid learner, as all skilled teachers are, he brought continental ideas to West Ham and English football more generally.

Although he adopted a disciplined approach, Malcolm made training interesting and fun, especially for the kids brought to the club as part of its youth scheme, inspiring the young men in his care to think about the game.

Moscow Dynamo, the Red Army's team, were an early inspiration for Allison. In the last part of the 1940s he watched them training while he was undertaking his national service in the army. This experience, together with the influence of the Hungarian team of the early 1950s, was the kernel of his philosophy of football.

The first non-British side to have beaten England on their own soil played a system that nullified the great English widemen, Stanley Matthews and Tom Finney. Most football in Britain before that seminal match against Puskás and co stuck with man-to-man marking all over the pitch. Within such a system the likes

---

of Moore would always be let down by lack of pace, the ball being lobbed down the centre for a nippy striker, who would leave the slow defender for dead.

Like Ron Greenwood, Allison wanted the game to be something akin to art; to be played with an aesthetic beauty that the physical side of the sport could compliment more than dominate as it had in England up to the 1960s. He also wanted his teams to be effective enough to win, and his emphasis, his drive in that respect, was where he departed from the 'Greenwood school'.

The eventual demise of the man-marking default freed defenders to roam and mark space, which favoured players like Moore, those with intelligence, technical ability, and strong powers of anticipation. Bobby had practically made himself for such a role, and was more prepared and so able for it than any other player in Britain

For whatever reason, Fenton allowed the likes of Allison and Cantwell their head. This was not something many managers would have done at that time and it is hard to see anything like it in the modern game. It opened the gate to innovation and experimentation. For instance, the Colts were among the first to start experimenting with the attacking full-back strategy, advancing the ball down the left flank, adding support to the strikers; they were among the first 'wing-backs' to be consciously nurtured for the role in the British game.

Traditionally full-backs had been very static, rarely venturing out of their own half, their task being purely defensive – covering any threats from the wings while marking the opposition's widemen. Roger Byrne, who was lost in the Munich air crash in 1958, and Nilton Santos, a member of Brazilian World Cup winning teams of 1958 and 1962, both played a part in totally transforming ideas about the role of the full-back. This was picked up and adapted by the youngsters at the Boleyn Ground. What they pioneered and tested in the adventures of youth football was refined for the first team's strategy. The Irons were lucky in this respect because they had John Bond and Noel Cantwell in their ranks, two full-backs who were attack-minded and able to make this transformation for their team.

John Cartwright, who went on to become an influential voice in English coaching, was to say that the only reason he, Bobby and many other players came to and stayed with West Ham was because of Malcolm Allison. However, in the context of the English game the Hammers were influential in changing its tactics and look. It should always be noted that Fenton, because of his attitude towards Allison, was instrumental in this development at Upton Park.

Ted, however, had little part in developing the play; that was almost entirely down to Allison, Bond and Cantwell, a trio of relatively young men, interested in, and excited about transforming the game into something more dynamic and beautiful. But Ted facilitated the revolution, and it should not be lost that a good manager doesn't so much make things happen as make space for others to manage and together the organisation makes things happen. It's a big person who knows when they are in the way, and a bigger one who has the integrity to clear the way for others.

10

ENGLAND'S YOUTH

In the final months of 1957 Bobby was playing for West Ham's Metropolitan League side, feeling increasingly optimistic about his future in the game. This sense had been bolstered when he received, just around a year after signing for the Hammers, an FA-headed letter, underwritten by Sir Stanley Rous's moniker. It was an invitation to play at centre-half for England's youth team. The opponents were to be the Dutch. The team would be travelling by air, which was a first for Bobby, indeed for the Moore family.

Bobby had failed to be selected for a schoolboy cap, so the call into the England youth side for the first time on 2 October 1957 was a huge boost for him.

Prior to that game, Malcolm Allison counselled that Bobby needed to 'be' the captain. The young man wasn't too comfortable with this – Barnsley's David Wright was the side's skipper, but Malcolm didn't mean that he should effectively usurp the captaincy. Allison told Bobby that what he was asking him to do was assert himself; to craft the game, influencing those around him, so as to dominate proceedings. In other words, *take* control of his environment to avoid, as much as possible, events controlling him. Control is a consequence of power and authority, and just as is the case with power and authority, no one *gives* you control. Control, to be control, is necessarily *taken*.

Sense of place

The friendly against a rated Dutch side was played at the Olympic Stadium in Amsterdam, which was then used by the great AFC Ajax club for many of their European games, as they did up to moving to their new stadium in 1996. Designed by architect Jan Wils, the structure remains one of the finest examples of the 'Amsterdamse School' of architecture. It was the biggest stage Bobby had played on to that date and an awesome sporting cathedral.

The design of the stadium won the gold medal in the architecture competition at the 1928 Olympics. It was the main stadium for those Games, which introduced the idea of the Olympic Flame. The flame burned for the first time in a tall tower, known as the Marathon Tower, adjacent to the stadium. At the top of the Marathon Tower there are four balconies, which were used during the Games by horn-blowers. Above these balconies, four speakers (made by the Philips company) were attached, from which results and messages were broadcast into the Olympic arena, a novelty at the time. The bowl on top that held the Olympic flame was known to Amsterdammers as 'the ashtray of KLM pilots'.

When completed, the stadium had a capacity of 31,600. In 1937 the capacity was increased to 64,000 by adding a second ring to the stadium. In 1987 the structure was listed as a national monument, a bit like Clive Myrie is to us today.

Lion cubs roar

After just five minutes of the match the home side were two goals up, but ultimately England won by the odd goal of five.

The England team had one or two famous names of the future in its ranks, including long-time Chelsea top scorer Barry Bridges. Looking back, Bridges was to remark that it felt like England played a lot of youth games, seemingly about once a fortnight. His Stamford Bridge team-mates pulled his leg, asking whether he played for the Blues or England. Bobby was to have much the same experience throughout his career.

Reflecting on the tension most players experienced prior to England youth games and the awe the side felt performing at the Olympic Stadium, Bridges had strong memories of Bobby's poise, calm demeanour and his ability to take those qualities into a game. He remembered how Moore seemed possessed of a controlled aura; he exuded unquestionable and apparently innate qualities as a leader on and off the park. For the young Chelsea man, Moore appeared unflappable, to such an extent that later he was to wonder if it was a means of hiding a level of insecurity. This was probably quite an insightful observation. For Bridges, 'Bob struck me as being a shy lad, to a degree you might take him to be less than sociable, but perhaps that was a plus, as it let him rise above some of the argy-bargy that can mess up a side's rhythm.'

As well as appreciating playing alongside Moore, Bridges relished the opportunities he had over the years of pitting his wits against him. Barry had it that Bobby 'gave you a chance to play' because his lack of pace was common knowledge. But Moore had a knack of giving opponents the impression he was not in their way and then, out of the blue, he was. For the Stamford Bridge stalwart this attribute was, at times, disconcerting and annoying.

Peter Osgood, a team-mate of Bridges for the last couple of years Barry was with the Pensioners, told me, 'Like Bobby Moore, I wasn't too quick over the ground, but he once told me, "Football isn't a race." The difference between two sides is often positioning, making yourself understand where you need to be, keep your wits about you, grasping what is going on right across the pitch. Dave

Sexton used to make the same point. When he was Chelsea manager, everything we did was about looking around you, seeing where people were, but also where they weren't. That is drummed into top basketball players in America. Possession means very little, it's about what you do with the ball when you've got it. The guy I recall being most aware of the use of space was Martin Peters. It was like most of his game was about that. They called him "The Ghost" because he seemed to drift in from nowhere, but he wasn't concerned so much with the player nearest him, he knew before a gap opened where it would be. I got a bit good at that myself.'

Bobby loved his first taste of international football, seeing it as 'terrific' (a word he used a fair bit). He was more than taken with the approach of the side's coach, Ron Greenwood, how Ron had helped him acclimatise to that initial outing as a youth international and that level football more generally.

Ron had a simple, overriding vision of how football needed to be played – 'Control, pass, run' – but his progressive ideas and theories about football engaged and excited young Moore. Greenwood's perspective on the game wasn't too far from Allison's, although mediated in a more didactic way. He also had solid ideals, a set of more complex principles, about football, much of which offered a firm foundation on which the likes of Moore could build an underpinning attitudinal disposition, looking toward a professional career. However, aspects of Ron's doctrine, that bled into other areas of life, soon became a bit too much for Bobby.

Greenwood was really Moore's first philosophy teacher, although at times it often lent a bit too heavily towards a species of secular theocracy (if that makes any sense). Ron's motivation and conviction was, similar to Allison and Fenton, built on the influence the great Hungarian national side had on him as a boy. His dad had worked at Wembley stadium, where England had been humiliated by the Mighty Magyars in 1953. This in itself must have been inspiring for the imagination and ambition of the teenage Moore.

Bobby sat with Greenwood on plane back to London and, as was his wont, constantly questioned Ron about his views, ideas, values and vision relating to football. For a time, Moore became a disciple of 'Saint Ron', hardly leaving his side when the opportunity arose, digging for knowledge and insight.

Bill Rush, a referee in the South East Counties League, ran the line for the England youth encounter with their Austrian counterparts in March 1958. Bill recalled the young Moore, remarking about his capacity to read the game and use this to marshal his players. Rush also drew attention to Bobby's marvellously well-timed tackles, comparing him to Scottish international George Burley of Ipswich.

Bill went on to remember the post-match banquet, at a hotel in Lancaster Gate. It went on to 1am, which meant some of the players faced a bit a challenge in terms of getting home. Seeing this, Bill offered a few a lift, including Bobby and Barry Bridges. He was impressed by how pleasant and good mannered the lads were.

Later Rush refereed a West Ham game in the Metropolitan League. Moore was a model in terms of behaviour and conduct, to the extent that Bill was moved to confirm, 'All the good things you read about him are true, because it's really the way he was.'

Bobby was in the England youth team that claimed victory in the British Championships – a competition, at that and senior level, which was once a traditional end to each season and the finale of each footballing year. England claimed the title by smashing Wales 8-2.

The pinnacle of Moore's England youth career was a tournament in Luxembourg that was widely taken as the European Championships. Bobby played sublimely and according to his fellow Hammer in that side, Tony Scott, he 'virtually took the team to the final on his own'.

England had disposed of the home side to move into the final four. The semi-final was played in a snowstorm, wherein Romania were put to an icy sword. This sent England and Bobby on to meet the Italians in final. He hit his 17th birthday the day before the game.

Many years later Bobby still had the telegram, printed on bright yellow paper with the Luxembourg coat of arms, sent to him from the Boleyn Ground. It read,

'Many happy returns. Sincere best wishes for a bright football future. All at Upton Park.'

Sadly, Bobby didn't get the birthday present he might have wanted; Italy won by scoring the only goal of the match in the 60th minute (their right-winger put it away). Bobby's fellow Hammer, Peter Reader, had stepped in for the first-choice goalkeeper, Chelsea's Barry Smart. That Italian goal was the only one that got by him during the whole of the tournament.

England's youngsters won 13 out of the 18 youth matches Moore played in, scoring 41 goals and conceding just 25, experiencing defeat on only four occasions. Bobby rounded off his England youth career at one of the great palaces of football, the Estadio Santiago Bernabéu, in front of the biggest crowd he had run out to up to that point. It was a truly exciting game. The atmosphere in what had been the Estadio Real Madrid Club de Fútbol up to 1955[9] was spine-tingling, and the impressive partisan crowd made it a heady environment for England's youngsters, not least captain Moore.

England going 1-0 down and coming back to take the 4-2 victory caused the Spanish spectators to applaud their guests more than the home side. Peter Bullock

---

9   The stadium is named after footballer and former Real Madrid president Santiago Bernabéu

was 16 at the time and the youngest player on the field, as well as being the only amateur in the England XI. He scored the two goals that got his side the result.

Prior to the game Bobby took a couple of opportunities to watch the Real Madrid senior team in training, showing once more that he was an avid student of the game and more than just another player. He was struck by the extent to which they played as a unit, constantly creating patterns in response to where play was at. Malcolm Allison had often talked about this, but he had never seen it realised in such a fluid and dynamic way. For Bobby he was seeing how football should be played – poetry in motion.

The glorious victory was a fitting farewell to this first stage in his journey as an international.

Greenwood and Moore were looking a winning combination. Having finished a fairly distinguished playing career, latterly with Chelsea and Fulham, soon after taking over the coaching at Eastbourne, Ron Greenwood was charged with responsibility for England's youth team. The young players back then were all ground staff boys with Football League clubs. Lancaster Gate believed if a coach from a professional club had taken charge of England's youngsters there would be a risk that they might lure the lads to join their side. Of course, Eastbourne was not in the competition for the nation's most promising young talent.

Ron had been involved with England youth at the national centre at Lilleshall, where he attended courses as a staff coach. He found it rewarding to work with the country's best young players. Clubs were able to recommend as many players as they wanted. Included were the likes Jimmy Greaves, Barry Bridges and Bobby Charlton. The programme concluded with a game between coaches and players; Charlton often didn't make the side, such was the talent on hand.

While with England's youth, Greenwood took in as much football involving young players as possible. One spring evening he found himself at Stamford Bridge watching London Grammar Schools play their Glaswegian counterparts. Bobby Moore, London's centre-half for that game, caught his eye.

The following season Bobby was at Lilleshall for the regular early selection course. Ron noted that he was playing at left-half. Later he told Moore that he had seen him at Stamford Bridge and had rated his contribution as 'brilliant'. As the chat continued Bobby let Greenwood know that West Ham saw left-half as his best position. Ron would eventually ask Moore to captain England's young lions at centre-half. Bobby responded by saying, 'That suits me fine.'

Moore was to become central to Greenwood's thinking about the development of England's best young talent, playing regularly in what was a consistently successful side. This was the beginning of the long association between Ron and

Bobby. Greenwood's next step would be to take over the national under-21 side. He was to continue placing his faith in young Moore, bestowing the authority of skipper on the Barking lad.

The gift of the responsibility of captaincy meant a lot to Moore, enough for him to take Allison's advice and delay signing professional forms until May 1958 to allow him to lead the youth team in the European Championships.

Bobby's 18 games for his nation's youngsters had been matched by no other youth player prior to Moore. This experience marked the start of Moore's next stage in his football education.

In late November 1957, following a 2-0 youth international victory over Belgium at Hillsborough which flattered the visitors, Ron Greenwood returned to the England hotel to get a phone call offering the him the job of club coach at Arsenal. Although he thought it might mean an end to his role with England, it was an opportunity he couldn't refuse. As it was his undoubted integrity was recognised and he continued to look after England's rising stars.

The Munich disaster happened just four days after Bobby had played a youth international for England against Yugoslavia, the country where United had played the European tie before the crash. Moore heard the terrible news while at Midhurst Convalescent Home in Sussex with Noel Cantwell; they were visiting Malcolm Allison, who was recovering from surgery after being diagnosed with tuberculous. Just as Moore's life was taking off, practically a whole generation of fine players were wiped out at a single stroke.

Most versions about Bobby picking up news of the crash tell how he was with Cantwell and Allison at Midhurst, the three of them being reduced to tears when hearing of the tragedy. However, Cantwell was to recall first hearing the news on the car radio driving back from Midhurst with Bobby.

Shortly after one of football's worst tragedies, West Ham, a side that had averaged 13th place in the Second Division throughout the 1950s, scoring on average fewer than 67 goals a season, would, during the 1957/58 campaign, score 111 league and cup goals and take the championship. West Ham clinched promotion and the Second Division title with their final game, winning at Middlesbrough. In the process John Dick scored their 100th league goal of the season.

West Ham were welcomed back to the First Division at Portsmouth on 23 August 1958. Around 7,000 of the 40,000 crowd were Hammers fans, a very high number of travelling supporters in those days. They went into raptures when Keeble and Dick scored to start West Ham off with a win.

When Allison came out of care the group of players in his 'set' held a party to welcome him back. It was an all-night bash at Malcolm's place. In the morning the

Bobby Moore's career with England Youth

Friendlies

Date	Venue	Result	HT	Attendance
2 October 1957	Olympic Stadium, Amsterdam	Netherlands 2 England 3		
	England: D. Gaskell, R. Collinson, D. Wright, D. Barber, Bobby Moore, J. Elms, K. Lewis, P. Vine, Barry Bridges, F. Beaumont, J. Mitten			
13 November 1957	Hillsborough, Sheffield	England 2 (Spence, Mitten) Belgium 0	0-0	7,801
	England: B. Smart, B. Smith, D. Wright, D. Barber, Bobby Moore, J. Elms, G. Mannion, P. Vine, A. Spence, F. Beaumont, J. Mitten			
17 November 1957	Stade Municipal, Luxembourg	Luxembourg 0 England 3 (Beaumont, Laraman, Bridges)	0-2	
	England: B. Smart, B. Smith, S. Farimond, D. Barber, Bobby Moore, J. Elms, P. Laraman, G. Mannion, Barry Bridges, F. Beaumont, A. Scott			
4 February 1958	Stamford Bridge, Chelsea	England 2 (Bridges, Hazelden) Yugoslavia 2 (Kovačević 2)	1-0	8,408
	England came back from two goals behind, but then missed a penalty with ten minutes left, Wright hitting the post			
	England: B. Smart, B. Smith, D. Wright, D. Barber, Bobby Moore, J. Elms, F. Twist, W. Hazelden, Barry Bridges, M. Tindall, A. Scott			

British Amateur Youth Championship

Date	Venue	Result	HT	Attendance
15 February 1958	Elm Park, Reading	England 8 (Hazelden 2, Twist 2, Bridges 2, Scott, Barber) Wales 2 (Williams, Edwards)	3-1	
	England: B. Smart, B. Smith, J. Bramhall, D. Barber, Bobby Moore, D. High, F. Twist, W. Hazelden, Barry Bridges, M. Tindall, A. Scott			
1 March 1958	Boothferry Park, Hull	England 2 Scotland 0		
	England: B. Smart, J. Bramhall, D. Wright, D. Barber, Bobby Moore, L. Cocker, F. Twist, W. Carlin, Barry Bridges, M. Tindall, A. Scott			

Friendlies

Date	Venue	Result	HT	Attendance
4 March 1958	Highbury, Arsenal	England 3 (Twist, Bridges, Barber pen) Austria 2 (Molzer, Skarelan)	2-0	4,677
		David Wright missed a first-half penalty		
	England: B. Smart, J. Bramhall, D. Wright, D. Barber, Bobby Moore, L. Cocker, F. Twist, R. Perry, Barry Bridges, M. Tindall, A. Scott			
12 March 1958	Burnden Park, Bolton	England 1 (Tindall) West Germany 2 (Heidner 2)	0-1	3,561
	England: B. Smart, J. Bramhall, D. Wright, D. Barber, Bobby Moore, L. Cocker, F. Twist, R. Perry, Barry Bridges, M. Tindall, A. Scott			
22 March 1958	The Oval, Eastbourne	England 0 France 1		
	England: P. Reader, J. Bramhall, D. Parnell, D. Barber, Bobby Moore, L. Cocker, F. Twist, A. Spence, Barry Bridges, M. Tindall, R. Collinson			

UEFA youth tournament in central Europe

Date	Venue	Result	HT	Attendance
5 April 1958	Ludwigsparkstadion, Saarbrücken	Spain 2 (Chuzo, Cartaña) England 2 (Bridges, Tindall)	1-1	
	England: B. Smart, J. Bramhall, A. Heaney, D. Barber, Bobby Moore, L. Cocker, F. Twist, A. Spence, Barry Bridges, M. Tindall, A. Scott			

Date	Venue	Result	HT	Attendance
7 April 1958	Ellenfeldstadion, Neunkirchen	East Germany 0 England 1 (Barber)	0-0	
	England: P. Reader, A. Heaney, A. Wileman, D. Barber, Bobby Moore, L. Cocker, F. Twist, W. Carlin, Barry Bridges, D. Parnell, A. Scott			
	Lee was sent off			
9 April 1958	Stade de la Frontière, Esch-sur-Alzette	Luxembourg 0 England 5 (Bridges, Tindall, Parnell 3)	0-0	
	England: P. Reader, A. Heaney, A. Wileman, D. Barber, Bobby Moore, K. McCarthy, F. Twist, M. Tindall, Barry Bridges, D. Parnell, A. Scott			
11 April 1958	Stade Municipal, Luxembourg	Romania 0 England 1 (Bridges)	0-1	
	England: P. Reader, A. Heaney, A. Wileman, D. Barber, Bobby Moore, L. Cocker, F. Twist, M. Tindall, Barry Bridges, D. Parnell, A. Scott			
	Dave Barber missed a penalty in the 63rd minute			
13 April 1958	Stade Municipal, Luxembourg	Italy 1 (Oltramari) England 0	0-0	
	England: P. Reader, A. Heaney, A. Wileman, D. Barber, Bobby Moore, L. Cocker, F. Twist, M. Tindall, Barry Bridges, D. Parnell, A. Scott			
	Three minutes into the second half, Peter Reader saved a penalty from Sandro Salvadore. England were runners-up in the tournament.			
	British Amateur Youth Championship			
10 May 1958	Clandeboye Park, Bangor	Northern Ireland 4 England 2	2-0	
	England: P. Reader, A. Heaney, A. Wileman, D. Barber, Bobby Moore, L. Cocker, F. Twist, D. Parnell, A. Smillie, D. Clapton, R. Bird			

Friendlies

Date	Venue	Result	HT	Attendance
26 May 1958	Stadion Letzigrund, Zürich	Switzerland 0 England 3 (Bullock, Hall, Twist)	0-2	
England: P. Reader, A. Heaney, A. Wileman, D. Barber, Bobby Moore, L. Cocker, F. Twist, D. Parnell, P. Bullock, D. Clapton, L. Hall				
1 June 1958	Gruabn, Graz	Austria 3 England 4 (Hall 2, Cocker, Smillie)		
England: P. Reader, A. Heaney, A. Wileman, D. Barber, Bobby Moore, L. Cocker, F. Twist, A. Smillie, P. Bullock, D. Parnell, L. Hall				
8 October 1958	Estadio Santiago Bernabéu, Madrid	Spain 2 (Dominguez, Cartañá) England 4 (Smillie, Twist, Bullock 2)		53,000
England: P. Reader, A. Heaney, A. Wileman, D. Barber, Bobby Moore, L. Cocker, F. Twist, A. Smillie, P. Bullock, D. Parnell, L. Hall				
Bobby Moore makes his record 18th and final appearance for the youth side				

job of getting some of the other younger players to leave fell to Allison's flat-mate Vic Keeble, the striker being the only teetotaller in situ and thus the only person in any kind of shape to do much of anything, although Bobby, who had popped out to get some milk for morning tea, looking a fresh as a proverbial daisy, helped him bring his team-mates round.

Prodigy

Bobby's career as a youth international encompassed his transition from a good youngster to him being viewed as exceptional. At the start of March 1958, he had been in the side that defeated Scotland. In that victory Barry Bridges looked the best player on the field by far, scoring both of England's goals. Tellingly, in the write-up in a national newspaper, Moore's first mention of any significance at that level, the hack assigned to the task appeared to be guessing what the 'R' in the 'R. Moore' on the teamsheet stood for when he scribbled,

'Ray Moore was always prominent in emergencies.'

An article from a practice match programme of 9 August 1958 marked Moore's progression,

Actually, we have no newcomers to the Hammers' colours on our professional staff, although three of them only signed pro forms during the past summer when they had attained the age of 17. All the trio gained youth international honours for England, and there is no doubt that Bobby Moore, Tony Scott and Andy Smillie have very bright futures ahead.

'Bobby Moore played for Barking and Essex Boys and then joined our ground staff on leaving school. He soon made progress in our A team, and after being selected for London youth first played for the England youth team at the age of 16. He has a total of 17 appearances for England Youth (a record for any one player) and skippered England during the latter part of last season (when they were runners-up to Italy in the European youth tournament).'

A week later, playing for the 'Whites', Bobby turned out in his first practice match, the second of West Ham's pre-season workouts. The report seemed to indicate it might have been quite a 'grounding' experience.

'There was an attendance of 4,500 at last Saturday's practice match – more than usual for this occasion. The increased "gate" certainly had value for their money – seeing no less than 11 goals scored in an interesting game.

'Several of our young players caught the eye, and their display was an encouraging foresight of our reserve talent. The Club Colours (consisting largely of our possible reserve team) won 9-2, but the Whites (possible A team) were not disgraced for they were up against rather more experienced opposition.'

At the end of 1958 a national newspaper organised a Young Footballer of the Year contest. Jimmy Armfield, then England's under-23 skipper, came out on top. The runners up were Bobby Charlton, Jimmy Greaves, Jim's Chelsea team-mate Mel Scott and Moore. By that time Bobby was no longer being named as 'The new Billy Wright', but hailed as 'The new Duncan Edwards'. Although he was still waiting for his chance in the West Ham first team, Bobby's quality was being noted practically everywhere else. But still, Ted Fenton failed to fully understand his rising star.

For the West Ham manager, a footballer had a few fundamental qualities. These included at least some level of heading ability, a range of pace and the ability to tackle in the traditional, 'robust' English way. He was literally blind to the 'fencing' Moore favoured, which allowed him to jog away with the ball and set up offensive moves. Bobby dribbling out of defence was another shocking habit that he had habituated, and Fenton deplored. Despite pleas, orders and demands to 'punt the bastard into row z', Bobby continued to insist on waltzing his way out of the penalty area.

Perhaps the most unconscionable 'Moorish trait' however was his apparent avoidance of heading the ball. A defender who was not having their brain regularly and almost constantly battered by the unforgivingly brutal balls of that period was, for Fenton, a contradiction in terms.

For the record

Nevertheless, Moore had been gaining prodigy status as he surpassed the record for England youth appearances, previously held by Barnsley Grammar School player David Wright. When Moore set the new record, he had skippered the side an unprecedented seven times. An added bonus was the newspapers had started getting his name right.

Unjustly the five European tournament matches (you can see the programme of 9 August 1958 is not entirely accurate on a couple of counts) for inexplicable reasons, did not count for caps, but that should not diminish his achievement. His caps were presented to him at a West Ham youth dinner by Ray Osborne, the FA youth section's chief official.

Reg Pratt, the West Ham chairman, awarded Bobby the Directors' Trophy as the club's outstanding youth player of the season. The big fat cherry on Bobby's cake was the Hammers' return to the First Division after 28 years. At the dinner marking this achievement Pratt said,

'Our juniors are now juniors in a First Division club and we expect a good deal more of them because of that.'

Reg didn't mention anything about himself doing a bit more.

All Bobby wanted at that point was a crack at a first-team game, but that relied not on Pratt and instead on Fenton, who continued to not really see much of a future for Moore at Upton Park. However, it would have been hard for Ted to dump Bobby following the accolades from club and country. So having done his time, not long after his 17th birthday, in May 1958, Moore was offered professional forms and £12 a week (what the FA stipulated was the maximum for his age at that time). A bit more wedge for sure, but during the close-season, like many in the football industry, Bobby took up temporary employment with a building contractor who supported the club. The work included labouring, digging the roads and mixing cement.

Well after his retirement Moore looked incredulously at young footballers in the modern game, about how they are seen to be full-time professionals, but are really only engaged for a few of hours on any given day. He was to ask himself if they might ultimately lose out. There is no such thing as training in the development of the will, nothing to wean someone on to the psychological endurance necessary for the repetition involved in skill acquisition. There is no equivalent to collaborative strength building a group might achieve lugging the heavy roller over an unyielding pitch. Where do the kids of the wealthy world of top-flight football learn the value of money, or what the life of those who pay to watch them might be like? And where is the sense of achievement, the mountain climbed that the likes of Moore had when he was finally rewarded with a professional contract?

Contrary to what seems to be common belief, Bobby being taken on was not straightforward. Fenton had not been totally persuaded that the Hammers needed the type of player he saw Moore to be. In fact, if Bobby hadn't been so well thought of by the other apprentices and the likes of Cantwell and Allison, the West Ham manager might well have let him go. Cantwell told me,

'Ted never said he wasn't going to take him on, but he did prevaricate. I don't know if this was just to wind up Malcolm, a demonstration that in the last analysis he, Ted, was the boss. In a way I'd hope that was the case, because by that time Bobby's class was obvious to anyone with an opinion worth listening to.

'But Ted was no fool. There really wasn't that much distance between him, Malcolm and myself in what we thought football might be or how it should be. Looking back, I think he handled Malcolm in the only way that was possible to handle him; giving him pretty much cart blanch. As I say, I don't think there was much difference between them when push comes to shove.'

The future assistant manager of Manchester United, Malcolm Musgrove told me that Fenton never really 'come off the fence' about Bobby, 'I don't think he saw what others saw in him, but he wasn't alone in that. But anyone who played with him understood he was a special sort of person and player.'

Fenton's position is hard to fathom at a distance. At the same point as he took on the captaincy of the England youth team, Moore led the young Hammers against his England team-mates in a friendly, although with seven youth internationals in their ranks, it was almost England v England. Nine of the West Ham side would advance to play for the Irons' first team. They counted in their number four players who would know the glory of FA Cup triumph at Wembley in 1964, and a couple of them would, at the same venue, lift the World Cup in 1966.

West Ham United 8 (Beesley 5, Smillie 2, Woodley 1) England XI 1
Upton Park, 10 November 1958
West Ham: Frank Caskey, Harry Cripps, Jack Burkett, Eddie Bovington, Bobby Moore, Geoff Hurst, Derek Woodley, John Cartwright, Mick Beesley, Andy Smillie, Tony Scott

This result just confirmed Bobby's class and leadership qualities. So all the more, even given the considerations I have already considered, it causes one to wonder what Fenton's problem with Moore was. Perhaps he was so trapped in his own era or ideas that he just could not make sense of Bobby, but I do think he was actually more insightful than that.

Ken Brown, who would play alongside Bobby throughout West Ham's 'golden 1960s', remembered the young Moore as being not too quick over the ground, 'He was possibly the slowest mover in our squad. When it came to sprints, he was always last.'

He was of course right, but he also told how 'there was no better captain' and 'he was a total one-off'.

Moore's experience in international football melded with his involvement with West Ham second string and A team. The success of the Colts side he led to victory in the Southern Junior Floodlit Cup Final in 1958 and winning an international youth tournament in Belgium was rounded off by the Hammers winning promotion. Despite whoever thought what of him, the dawn of his greatness was breaking.

Quirky Moore

For Moore, signing professional was more the end of the beginning of his career and a move into the demanding struggle for first-team recognition. To follow there were public trials, matches with the Colts and games for the reserves. Moore was very keen to become a *true* professional, to be more than just another bit-part player. He looked to emulate the likes Noel Cantwell and Malcolm Allison. This would not only encompass playing games. After matches Bobby would clean his boots assiduously, going to the trouble of putting shoe trees in them so that they would not lose their shape (something unheard in British football in the 1950s). His pristine habits and attention to detail underpinned what any profession might expect of its members – personal integrity, part of which is making every effort to act and present oneself in a dignified manner.

As he matured, Moore's unusual (in his era) attention to detail, extended more and more into his general demeanour and presentation of himself. Bobby was hardly ever seen off the field other than immaculately dressed and turned out. It has been said he had obsession for neatness. 'Obsession' is a heavy accusation; it turns meticulousness or perfectionism up to 11.

There is a propensity over the last few decades to use words such as 'obsession', 'trauma', 'depression' and 'paranoia' probably a bit too permissively. These are 'end game', and often not entirely secure terms, which lean more towards an accusation of pathology, malaise or malady than the moods, dispositions, inclinations and so on that are part and parcel of everyday human behaviour and personality traits.

For instance, an obsessive behaviour tends to stem from obsessive thoughts, persistent urges, intrusive mental images, or an unwanted emotional wrench that results in distress, anxiety, and disturbance of a person's usual life routines. It is not, for instance 'fastidiousness', which is about having high standards and/or attention to detail, which in some instances, jobs, interests, or life experiences more generally are often necessary qualities and/or appropriate attitudes. Who wants a 'couldn't-care-less' dentist, or a 'non-too-fussy' airline pilot?

Bobby had a tendency, although some said a 'compulsion', which might be thought of as a symptom of obsession, to arrange and order most things. The clothes in his wardrobe were organised as if for inspection. Shirts and jumpers were hung according to an arrangement from dark to light. His wardrobe was an exercise in classification and regimentation. For Tina, Bobby got something of 'aesthetic pleasure' in the storage of his clothes. Akin to this was his propensity for uniformity and precision to a detailed level. For example, before football shorts had any hint of design, Bobby had got his mum to cut v-shapes on the outside of each leg. This modification was exact in terms of dimension, placing and design. The first time Tina cut the v-shape in his shorts they split to the waist during a game. She lost that job and from then on Doris had a monopoly on that tailoring task.

Tina's mum, Betty, while being an indulgent parent, had demanded that her daughter's table manners should be exemplary. This predictably sat well with Bobby, who was pretty enamoured of Betty anyway. Looking to be correct in everything, he started to become very conscious of Betty's formal etiquette. This was a new discipline to him and, as was his habit, he watched, questioned and learned, as it was another opportunity to order things and do things 'the right way'.

As much as he was charmed and seduced by opportunities to organise routines, Bobby met the opposite with a level of incredulity, even at times horror. One such instance was when he shared a room with his Hammers team-mate Brian Dear. As Bobby was about to take a bath, 'Stag' (as Dear was known at Upton Park) casually asked him save the bathwater for him. Bobby didn't quite comprehend what the rumbustious striker was asking of him, and had to have Brian explain that he intended to bath in the same water Bobby would use. I think you might imagine Moore's response to that.

In Brian's defence he was born in Plaistow, the same area I grew up in. That practice was not unusual in that neck of the woods from wartime up to the late 1960s. I certainly as a boy would be put in my brother's bathwater, to be followed by my grandmother and then my grandad. My dad, for most of my youth, would use my mum's bathwater. It comes from the effort to save time and the cost of hot water, but unsurprisingly, for Moore, the very idea was off-putting. I'm not sure it was just distaste though, after all, these were the days of the communal bath post-match. What I believe Bobby found disconcerting was the context or setting of Dear's proposal, which for him, was out of the ordinary.

Wherever he went Moore took a travel iron away with him. This small detail is part of a catalogue of folklore about Bobby's fastidiousness, mostly emanating from piss-taking team-mates, about his actual, reported and supposed oddities. These behaviours have been mooted as confirmation of him suffering OCD – obsessive compulsive disorder – a vague and, over time and context, shifting set of apparent behaviours seen to be amenable to diagnosis and clinical treatment. This mythology included Moore's supposed habit of pressing his money, and before sleeping taking the trouble to stack loose change on bedside cabinets in architectural formations. Such tales were lined up with routines that he certainly did repeat; for example, tidily stacking his soiled kit after training, while his peers, uncaringly unconscious, just piled up the dirty clobber.

Albert Walker, the Hammers' kitman, who played more than 160 games for the club in the 1930s, loved Bobby as he routinely, post-match or training, scrapped the mud off his boots, characteristically using his socks for this work, as his peers just slung their boots into a huge dirty bin, leaving the necessary cleaning for someone else to do. I know which of these 'obsessions' I would see as more positive than negative. Moore's routines were more untypical than anything else and therefore seen as peculiar or a bit problematical.

Professional behaviour?

I have spent much of the last few decades concerned with defining, assessing and teaching, and promoting professional behaviour, expectations, duties, ethics and values. I have been obliged to judge and discipline the flouting of professional conduct and practice. The professional is a professional because they are not like non-professionals. I don't think this is the place to explain professionalism, but I do want to make the case for Moore's professional attitudes and his consistency with the same in his everyday life (which is what is expected of professionals).

Fellow England international and Manchester City star Mike Summerbee had it that Bobby was the only person he'd known who could exit a bath dry. Apparently, Moore could avoid a single drop of water falling on to the floor by flicking one leg out, towelling that peg off, and then stepping out on the dried leg, before drying the rest of his body. If ever you've slipped on a wet dressing room floor, you might see this as more sensible caution than anything else, particularly, in the case of a professional sports person, the slightest injury can lay you up for weeks. Professionalism does entail mindfulness of detail – the opposite is unprofessional.

This sort of attention can of course take one into some apparently eccentric expectations and routines. Bobby preferred towels folded in three, so one couldn't see each end. If he found that this hadn't been done correctly, much as was his role in football, he put matters 'right'. I'm not sure if anyone asked him about this though. My guess is that he might have had his reasons.

All this said, Tina has told how Bobby had a tendency to compartmentalise everything, seeing it as a consequence of not being able to deal with disorder. He would continuously be 'fussing about the house', arranging cushions and, if visitors smoked, he would trail around after them with an ashtray, making sure ash didn't fall on the carpet.

From the last part of his teenage years onwards, personal appearance and grooming became important to Moore, especially when he started to socialise in the orbit of Malcolm Allison. He wanted to learn how to look the part, to move up in the world, to fit in at the smart venues, to be stylish and respected. Even when apparently relaxing, Moore would be concerned with things looking 'balanced' and right. For example, he made the painstaking efforts when sunbathing to make sure the backs of his hands faced the sun so that the tan would be even and show up well against his stunning white shirt cuffs.

Looking at all this, one can draw a batch of negative conclusions. It's likely true that if one was to present some of Moore's behaviours to those convinced by pop psychology, one would likely be told this diligent and focused attitude might probably be a manifestation of compulsive habits; typically turning a personal asset into a psychological deficit (a lack, or malfunction). Such accusations imply firstly that 'the norm' is desirable (say piling your filthy kit up in a corner) and secondly that anything other than the bland pursuit of mediocrity and social conformity is in some way 'unhealthy' or 'sick'.

Pseudo/amateur psychiatrists might label Bobby's behaviour as typical of an anankastic personality – a need for neatness, perfectionism, desire for order often accompanied by a high level of conscientiousness. You could indeed read a selection of Moore's traits to be pretty indicative of this. But to go along with this is to follow a credo of 'ordinariness' from the church that is psychiatry. It's indicative of most inane incarnations of psychotherapy. At the time of writing the same thing is being applied to our kids, persuading them, us and anyone willing to listen that the majority of them are suffering from 'mental health problems', a euphemism for 'madness'. This has gone to a level that sometimes feels like mass Munchausen's by proxy.

Moore was not the only top football player with such foibles. Indeed, his fellow Hammer John Bond's mother, Lily Kate, was, not unlike Bobby's mum, a stickler for keeping things pristine. He would take his washing home to her, neatly folded, and she would return it to him spotlessly clean. Bond exhibited similar idiosyncrasies to Bobby, for instance lining up his wife's jewellery and when visiting friends' homes, as soon as they left a room, he would start straightening pictures and ornaments. I believe the spotlight of fame focused on Moore just brought attention to a sensitivity to pattern and regularity that one might not be surprised by in people who, from childhood, have been imbrued with strategies and tactics and who have cultivated a high level of special awareness.

Order is part of the life of specialists and professionals. I've seen similar traits to those associated with Moore in surgeons, musicians, dentists, police officers and engineers, especially in those tasked with inspection and regulation of services and performance. Of course, if your life hasn't been reliant on a disciplined observation of pattern, regulation and systematisation, then yes, the behaviour of those who have might well seem odd, or eccentric, but think how those taken as peculiar might see people who act more untidily, sloppily or 'chaotically'.

Taking a wider view, there are worse traits than tidiness, and there is actually more than a fine line between a taste for neatness and a life-ruling obsession for the minute ordering of the mundane routine of everyday existence. A more thoughtful analysis of Moore's comparative, supposed apparent, reported unusualness might understand the characteristics highlighted are concomitant with the foundations of his skill and success.

Moore was to admit that the standards he set himself were boundless, drawing a parallel with what it takes to be a top ballet dancer or concert pianist, seeking to perfect their performance by endless practice and rehearsal. I have occasion to be with some highly able bagpipers for example. You can be talking to them and they will be 'playing' their beer, almost unconsciously rehearsing the finger movement of a tune they are perfecting or learning. For sure, that can be a bit distracting, but while it might be the price to pay for excellence, is it 'sick'?

This question is turning to the other side of the coin, perhaps the side we need to particularly look at when eagerly making assessments of the behaviour of others (not just Moore). Bobby undoubtedly was influenced by his mother's customs related to neatness and attention to detail. He came at the rest of his life from this foundation. He had some success at school, perhaps partly facilitated by the same propensities, getting himself into the upper echelons of the educational tripartite system (I came in at the bottom end by the way) and doing well in his exams.

When Bobby began to shine at Upton Park, it was the basis of order, consideration of every element of skill development and professional deportment. That was the making of Moore. Without it, no Bobby Moore as we knew and know him; no 'General of '66' and no 'Legend'.

Any insistence Doris passed on to Bobby provided the fundamental building blocks that Allison, Greenwood and Ramsey worked with Moore to hone and expand. That this development, these fostered qualities, bled into Bobby's everyday activity in the world isn't surprising or 'abnormal'. A scientist will think and act rationally (scientifically); a priest might be expected 'live their faith'. The best of coppers will act lawfully. In short, the professions are more than jobs, and professional attitudes, values and ethics are what professionals live out in their everyday lives. And again, if you're not a professional, this might feel a bit strange.

However, if Moore had completely disconnected with the psychological propensities propagated in his childhood, much the same attitudes scrupulously nurtured in his professional life and routine functioning in the world, that would have been justifiably considered to be psychotic.

I often get told, in various ways, 'I am a different person in work than I am at home,' and similar comments. This boasting about effectively having a 'multiple personalities' is taken somehow to constitute a work/life balance or relative sanity. But there is only one person, at home or at work, or wherever; there is no 'different person' – to think that there might be is bonkers. For sure, we react differently in different contexts according to how we feel and what is demanded of us – but the 'I' who I am remains constant. If it doesn't, what might that say?

Moore's efforts relating to tidiness, presenting himself decently or correctly, and so on have been characterised as 'rituals'. His penchant to achieve order (as opposed to living in chaos) has been portrayed as a 'psychological need' rather than a professional attitude, more about an effort to propagate dignity and integrity than an uncontrollable urge. The neat storage of shoes, stacking kitchen pans neatly in cupboards, having the labels on cans facing the viewer and the like, are presented as examples of an 'over the top' attitude to order, as if the opposite (disorder) is in some undefined way, more desirable or healthy. No wonder in 2019 we put a scruffy, disorganised, mendacious, undisciplined, confused, chaotic, philanderer in charge of the country.

We are all too easily conscripted into this manipulative way of describing behaviour. I kick against it because I see it done to children so much – until they and their parents believe the negative prognosis, which at that point becomes a self-fulfilling prophecy. See Moore's tendency to fold towels neatly as 'fiddling' with them (something he has been accused of) and you are 'there'. He has to be a bit of a control freak – ergo, 'nutter'. This would be infamy if it wasn't so ridiculous, but we are doing this all the time to each other and our kids. It's not just Bobby who has been psychoanalysed without request or permission from an extremely negative and cynical perspective.

The current social obsession (and I believe it has all the features of obsessive thinking) with childhood 'mental health' is a broader manifestation of the same assumptions and accusations. The 'deficit model' of childhood responses to a mad world has much to answer for. The potential consequences, as yet unknown, fail to inspire optimism.

Maybe Bobby did do things that paid more attention to detail or order than was necessary, or perhaps he did them now and then, or once or twice. Maybe you or someone you love has one or two (or three or four) similar reactions to the world, but so fucking what? Who's it hurting? People have seen these things in Moore as humorous, but also as signs of 'obsessiveness' rather than say the actions of civilised consideration and adult responsibility taking – behaviour associated with his professional achievements and high level of performance.

The case for the impact of a professional lifestyle and training aside, Bobby's alleged 'fixations' could be understood as what in Plaistow we might have called 'ways' – slightly odd, elaborate, perhaps even endearing little oddities, and if anything, collectively that's what they were, not some pathological desire for manic neatness and 'order mania'.

Most people I grew up around had a sprinkling of such idiosyncrasies. I know I do – one of which is endlessly writing. I had an aunt who weekly would take the wain skirting off the walls so she could clean behind it. Certainly, for many of his generation, put together all of Bobby's quirks and they might seem a little much to the ordinary mortal, but he wasn't ordinary was he!

11

FACTS OF LIFE

Unselfconsciously, now and then, Bobby would tell of his love for Malcolm Allison. This sort of overt affection was not typical of Bobby, although in and out of football a lot of men and maybe more women loved Malcolm.

Allison had film-star good looks, somewhere between Cary Grant and Rock Hudson. A magnetic and charming personality, a lot has been said and plenty written about Malcolm, sometimes it feels most of it by me (see in particular Belton 2013b, 213c). Because of that it feels redundant to reiterate too much here, but Malcolm Allison is and was hard to say little about. He gave me a fair bit of time over the years, and it wasn't hard work to get him to talk about football, footballers and most interesting for me, the politics of the game. He had a way of looking and commentating on football that made you think about the wider world, yourself and the nature of things. The game was for Malcolm a prism through which life could be viewed and, to some extent, better understood.

Fearless: live more

At Upton Park, Allison was recognised as a belligerent character and thoughtful centre-half. He was a popular choice as the club captain. In that role it was he who organised the team, its strategy and the tactics to achieve the same. It's too easy to see him as a dictator, a bully even, but that would be a worse than superficial assessment. He welcomed debate, although his passion to question ideas and perspectives was often mistaken for dismissiveness, but most of his arguments concluded with smiles, and he was always listening. Malcolm cared about others and took it on himself to be the players' representative off the pitch, fighting their corner, particularly around payment. He resisted and created, he was certainly arrogant and stubborn but also innovative, wise and, at times, vulnerable.

Much has been written recently about 'positive manifestation'. I look at these, mostly paper-thin ideas, with a deal of scepticism, then I think of Allison as perhaps the personification of 'determined confidence' – that rare persona of optimistic realism, which includes a measure of pragmatism. The rational visionary will always risk being labelled as a cynic.

After his playing career Allison was as much associated with cigars and champagne by the general public as he was with football. He took, for a time, to sporting a fedora, which from where I was standing didn't really suit him. As a spectator of his character and behaviour, he seemed determined to enjoy the experience of living, perhaps in a way only those who have stared death in the eyes might. However, Malcolm's give-and-ask-no-quarter attitude in that pursuit seems to have always been prevalent in the spirit he exuded. But while the notion of 'compromise' didn't come to mind much when talking to him, the attention he gave when offered an alternative standpoint or asked a question was palpable; the man had a powerful aura.

Just as for Ted Fenton, Walter Winterbottom, Alf Ramsey and Ron Greenwood, the Hungarian showing at Wembley in 1953 was an epiphany for Allison. The sweeping aside and humbling of the entire class and patronage ridden English game's system in the space of 90 minutes was to ignite an abiding interest in the continental game and the creative imaginations of overseas coaches and players.

Deposed

Bobby was always to remember the angst of perhaps his greatest mentor's demeanour as Allison shook his progeny's hand before his baptism into the senior game against Manchester United. Like the rest of the playing staff, Moore knew, following long and life-threatening illness, Allison, in his own mind, was ready, and on the desperate side of eager, to return to first-team football and to play against elite sides like United.

While nothing appeared to be entirely set in stone until the day of the game, Bobby had lost sleep the night before the match, although not as a result of the prospect of facing the Red Devils. It was a sense of guilt and regret that his possible promotion would be an effective usurpation of Allison's shirt, snatching Malcolm's hopes of ever fulfilling his lifelong ambition of running out to ply his trade in the top flight. The hunger to pit his wits against the very best in the game had a great deal to do with the way Allison had fought back against and overcome the tuberculosis had that ripped into his body for seemingly endless months. However, Bobby's concern does indicate he suspected he had a good chance of being selected for perhaps West Ham's most significant test since the 1923 FA Cup Final. United, as a force in football, were a universe away from the relatively workaday challenges of the English Second Division game that had been the bread and butter of West Ham's existence for decades.

Having struggled to get to the Boleyn Ground on time for the kick-off, Moore dived into the innards of the stadium complex, ultimately rushing headlong into the dressing room and, as he did so, bumped into Allison.

Malcolm diagnosis had been confirmed in November 1957. Tuberculosis was a devastating disease at that time. That was the end of his season and for most, it would have signalled the end of any kind of athletic career, perhaps any kind of life at all. But Allison came back, applying himself to training in a way that staggered everyone who knew him and what he had been through. He worked every day, seemingly every hour, on each and every element of his game. He got back in the reserve team and looked strong, fighting to realise a lifetime ambition to exercise his intellect and judgement at the pinnacle of English football, something, for the best part of a decade, he had struggled to make West Ham fit to do more than any other one person at the club before or since.

Prior to the game with United, looking at shrinking options, Fenton told Noel Cantwell that he wanted his advice on the 'left-half situation'. Various versions of the story have been told many times since; the choice was stark. Noel did not have a closer friend in or out of football than Allison; Moore had, to a significant extent, been moulded by Malcolm, with a deal of collaboration with Cantwell, who liked the Barking boy a lot.

Cantwell was to tell that it was customary at Upton Park for the manager to ask the skipper for his opinion on selection, a level of inclusion Allison had taken several steps further by totally disregarding many of Ted's teamsheets. Noel remembered that Fenton had been undecided, and believed his manager was unable make the final decision. Ted had put it to his captain,

'Manchester United have got that lovely little player, Ernie Taylor, playing on their right side of midfield. What do you think?'

Noel decided to look at the matter as rationally as possible. He calculated that Taylor should be the fulcrum of his choice. Although a gifted player, Ernie famously had been well down the queue when pace was being given out. At 5ft 4in (1.6m) in his size four boots, United's inside-forward was a craftily beguiling performer, who had spent years at Blackpool supplying deft passes to his wing partner Stanley Matthews. He had moved from Bloomfield Road to Old Trafford following the fateful air crash in Munich the February before what would be Moore's debut game. Allison had played just two reserve matches in 12 months. On the basis of these considerations, it was clear to Cantwell that Moore should play, and that is what he told his manager, adding, 'He'll never let you down … play the kid.'

Fenton was visibly shocked. He would have expected Malcolm's pal to have opted for his mate. Cantwell was to recollect,

'I think he was surprised that I picked Bobby over my closest friend,' but Ted said, 'All right – thank you,' and the teamsheet went up with Moore lodged at left-half, wearing the number six shirt.

Despite his continuing doubts about Moore, Ted's rational self would have probably known his captain was right. The bonus for Fenton was, albeit perhaps not altogether consciously premeditated, that he effectively unloaded on Cantwell what was a crushingly disappointing decision for Allison, and what would have felt like a heartless slight by most of the team and their supporters.

Of course, Cantwell admitted it was a difficult decision. It was a case of, 'The sorcerer or his apprentice?' But he was honest and frank – he told Fenton that he believed Allison lacked mobility and plumbed for Moore.

Love

Not too long before Cantwell's fateful decision, Bobby had made the trip to Midhurst, Sussex, with the Hammers skipper, to visit Malcolm in the sanatorium. Sickness did not suit Allison. Frustrated, angry and upset, he didn't give his visitors an easy or comfortable time.

By macabre coincidence that was 8 February 1958, the day of the Munich air crash that had wiped out most of Manchester United's 'Busby Babes', including Duncan Edwards, another giant of a man who Moore had admired throughout his development as a footballer. Edwards had been a left-half and was already established in the England side, despite his relative youth. If that terrible tragedy had been avoided, come the summer of 1966, Edwards would have been 29, at the peak of his playing career, and pretty certainly it would have been him and not Moore who would have captained England in the World Cup. Indeed, if the fallen Reds had been in the England team that went to Chile for the 1962 tournament, Bobby probably would not have been given a chance to play at senior level for his country and perhaps England would have started their 1966 odyssey as world champions.

Bobby was shattered on hearing the terrible news. When Moore spoke to Tina, his then girlfriend, about the loss of Edwards, she really didn't have a strong idea of who the great man was, but although they hadn't been seeing each other too long at that point she did what she could to console her boyfriend and of course, over time, she would understand the significance of Bobby's feelings about what had happened. Bobby had found not only an attractive soulmate in Tina, but someone he could share not only his joys with, and also his sorrows. She could however also make him laugh, something the intense, shy footballer was to value.

Once you're in a relationship of any worth, you get to know and trust the other person and then your real self begins to be shared, and there was a lot Bobby needed to share. The image of the teenage Moore sitting looking at her and laughing because she amused him was something that endured in Tina's memory.

She was an extrovert, in that respect Bobby's opposite, and he took delight in that aspect of her character; it helped him come out of the shell of the essentially bashful young man he was.

Tina had a knack of seeing humour in most things, and while Moore as a young man was taken by the public as serious, self-controlled and reserved, he commanded a dry if nuanced sense of humour that could easily be missed if you didn't know him pretty well. The couple's love was maybe to a great extent founded on Tina's gift of giving Bobby an emotional place to relax and, often through a smile, to find, be and express himself in a way football couldn't facilitate.

We appreciate the light of love and joy because we experience the darkness of sadness and anger. Allison's anguish and a feeling of denied entitlement, when the fates seemed to have cleared the way for him to face United, could not be hidden or denied. He had vowed from his hospital bed to get better and do battle in the First Division. For Allison, the news that Moore was preferred over him was shattering. It not only deigned him the treasured prospect of a glorious return to fulfil what he saw as his destiny, his belief he had 'made it back', it marked the end of his playing career.

As Matt Busby and his patched-up army departed the 'Rainy City' of 'Cottonopolis', Bobby had been a professional for ten weeks or so. Allison had pathed way for him at West Ham. Of course the young man wanted to play, but he wanted the same thing for Malcolm, part of him convincing himself that, given his experience, the older man would likely do a better job, although he countered that feeling by, realistically, seeing himself as the future.

As Moore stumbled into the dressing room and with his place in the team confirmed, Malcolm was the first person he saw. Bobby was too embarrassed to look at him. In that awkward moment, the instant Allison's eyes met Moore's, during the disconcerting seconds of silence that crushed between them, Bobby was struck by a deep realisation of the gravity of the moment. The sadness and mortification of that sensation was always to stay with him, together with the discontinuity of the feeling of jubilation he also felt; his euphoria was in stark contrast with the angst of his friend and inspiration, his footballing father.

As Allison walked out of the West Ham dressing room Bobby thought that perhaps he could pass up the chance he had been given; being the younger man, his time might come again. He remembered wanting to give Allison the shirt and tell him, 'It's yours. Have your game. My time will come.' At the same time Moore understood that his selection to face United might have been the only opportunity he would get. He told himself he had been fortunate to get the nod, and, as he had it decades later, 'When the chance comes you've got to be good enough to take it.'

Bobby was distraught, but he understood Malcolm would not have wanted him to turn his back on the door that had been opened to him. Ultimately, he didn't doubt that he had to play in the way Allison had taught him, to 'be big'. Retrospectively, many years on, Moore was to conclude that there really hadn't been a choice – he had to grab his chance; Malcolm would have given him that advice.

Allison was an inspirational captain and leader of the Hammers; his influence in and around the club as a whole cannot be underestimated. Allison and Cantwell can be regarded as the founders of the 'Academy'; the mythical 'West Ham Way' emerged out of this seminary of the choreography of 'the working man's ballet'. Noel Cantwell was Merlin to Allison's Uther Pendragon and Moore's Lancelot, around a Round Table encompassed by the likes of Dave Sexton, John Bond, Frank O'Farrell, Ken Brown, Malcolm Musgrove and Jimmy Andrews – all of whom would later become highly respected managers and coaches in their own right. This was never a big group, but their intellectual progeny was to be men like John Lyall, Alan Curbishley, and the figures who would shape soccer in the USA and South Africa, Bobby Howe, Clive Charles and Johnny Byrne. In time, men of this ilk would warmly acknowledge the huge influence that Allison exerted upon them in those defining years of English football.

Moore was to name Allison as his hero, and the person who laid the foundations of his approach to the game, saying that he would have done anything for him and readily told how Malcolm was,

'The be-all and end-all for me. I looked up to the man. It's not too strong to say I loved him … he'd worked like a bastard for that one game in the First Division.'

Life

In all published versions of how Bobby came to get his first league match for West Ham, various versions of the above narrative have been reiterated. Malcolm Allison confirmed it when I met him. Noel Cantwell also corroborated this interpretation of events more than once,

'I remember taking over from Malcolm as skipper and we became Second Division champions. The game against Manchester United was on a Monday night. Fenton called me into the office asking who should play left-half, Allison or Moore. He didn't really want the burden of the decision. Malcolm was not a mobile centre-half, so I went for Bobby. Malcolm found out and we fell out. He resented me for a time, but eventually he told me that I had made the right decision.'

Bobby was to feel that he had been obliged to move into his mentor's place, denying Allison a game in the First Division and effectively finishing his career.

He was to always carry some guilt about this. Allison had taught Bobby so much; he had become a friend, as well as inspirational presence in Moore's young life. The former Hammers skipper and centre-half had helped transform tubby Bobby, the least talented of the ground staff boys, into a classy first-team player. Now Moore was the instrument used to turn Allison away from Upton Park. Others have verified that a place in the West Ham line-up was certainly between Bobby and Malcolm, but they question if it was between Moore and Allison.

Immediately after the game Bobby had looked for Allison back in the dressing room, but there was no sign of him. However, as the victorious players were taking the post-match communal bath, Allison walked in, directing what was to become his nationally recognised scowl at Cantwell, a novel experience for the thoughtful Irishman. Allison had a naturally deep, loud and assertive voice (he could hold a tune well) that gave the impression he was incapable of a whisper, so in the echo chamber of the post-match dressing room, when he bellowed, 'Thank you very much!' it resonated around in the resultant silence.

The naked state of both Moore and Cantwell likely made them appear and feel even more vulnerable to Allison's wrath as he loudly declared that he would have been capable of dealing with Taylor with his 'ankles tied together'. The experience left both Cantwell and Moore devastated.

Feelings were likely heightened because Allison's non-inclusion in the team, as the story goes, had not been confirmed until practically the last minute. But it appears that Fenton hadn't taken his chat with Cantwell to be in any way confidential as, well before the game against United kicked off, the rest of the playing staff were pretty much clued up on the way things went with regard to team selection. Cantwell wasn't the type to inflate rumour, so it's difficult to see him as the source of any leak. I can't think that he would have told anyone about the situation before he let his friend know. Malcolm already knew the score before Noel got a chance to break it to him. It might have come directly to Allison from Fenton however; Ted being armed with the back-up that Malcolm's friend Cantwell had made the call. That would have almost certainly been a double wound for Allison.

Malcolm's anger continued to be expressed toward Cantwell. It took weeks for the two men to resume something near normal relations. However, when the heat of emotion cleared and cooled a little, Allison was to let both friend and acolyte know the right decision had been made. I'm not sure about that, even though the Hammers' victory should have allayed any doubts, but it was a seminal moment, for West Ham and Moore, and also for the history of English and world football.

In hindsight Bobby told how he had wished things had been different, and that Allison would have played. Moore had it that that he could have waited longer, and that the game would have meant much more to Malcolm than it did, retrospectively, to him. Who can say what would have happened if Allison had played well enough to see the season out? Again, with Moore not a favourite of Fenton, he might never have progressed to first team football at Upton Park.

Allison remembered his feelings on that September day, but also the player he built,

'I was heartbroken for myself, but delighted for Bobby. It was a privilege and a pleasure to be in on the ground floor of his career. Most players could beat him in a training sprint, and his heading was weak. But he was a thinking man's footballer and knew exactly where to be for greatest effect.

'No matter how crowded the penalty area, he was always in command and could put in a wicked tackle if necessary. He was never ever a dirty player, but he was as solid as a rock and when he tackled it was with determination and a desire to prove himself the master of the situation.

'He also instinctively knew when NOT to tackle. You never saw him diving in and committing himself. You could count the number of times you saw Bobby on the ground on the fingers of a one-armed bandit. He realised he lacked pace, so worked at having a quicker mind than anybody else. He knew where everybody who mattered was on the pitch before the ball reached him, and knew exactly what he was going to do with it the second it arrived at his feet.

'I have never known such an inquisitive young footballer. He was forever asking questions and he was always looking to be with the older players and picking their brains.

'Bobby was not a natural born genius like a George Best or a Jimmy Greaves, but he had an instinct for the game you could coax and develop but not teach. He had an obsession to improve, even when he was established in the England team. A great role model and a smashing companion.'

Of course, Malcolm was hurt and upset when Moore was preferred over him. A proud man, who felt he had paid the price for his return, how was he not going to feel pain? But he never held any grudge against Bobby or Cantwell. Instead, for the rest of his days, Allison was to project his angst toward the football establishment.

In the last analysis Bobby was Malcolm's progeny and something of a living legacy. As he said to me, 'There was no one else I'd have chosen to take my place.' At the same time, what Moore effectively took from Allison was likely part of the motivation for much of what his mentor was to achieve in management. Those of us who achieve anything at all often do so to prove a point, to ourselves, to others and sometimes the whole fucking world.

Learning

Moore was to say, 'When Malcolm was looking finished as a player I looked to Noel on the pitch.' And it's likely, somewhere in Bobby's mind that started when Allison's illness had been diagnosed in September 1957 – exactly a year before his league debut.

West Ham visited Sheffield United on Tuesday, 16 September 1957 and came away after losing 2-1 to the Blades on a rain-soaked evening. The Irons' captain looked pretty much a shadow of the performer supporters and fellow players knew. He had fallen down a flight of stairs a few days earlier, but from the start of the 1957/58 season Allison had not been in the best of form. During that game at Bramall Lane, he was playing alongside Ken Brown. At half-time Ken recalled Malcolm was looking distinctly distressed, fighting for breath, having been plagued by a terrible cough, but he carried on playing to the end of the game.

At that time the Hammers, when obliged to take longer journeys, would stay over in a hotel before returning to London by train the next day. During the night Cantwell, who roomed with Allison, was kept awake by Malcolm's constant coughing. He was still coughing on the team's morning departure for London.

Cantwell was born and raised in Cork, Ireland. During his youth the city and region had seen appreciable outbreaks of tuberculosis. Noel recognised the disease, how it looked and sounded, and he feared the worst for his room-mate.

While waiting for the London train, Fenton told Noel he was concerned about Allison's form, hinting that he was thinking of not selecting him for the next match. Cantwell suggested that the manager send Allison for some X-rays. Noel remembered Ted agreeing and 'wondering if there was something wrong with his ankle'. Cantwell made it clear that what his mate needed was a chest X-rays

On the Friday Allison saw Dr Thomas, the club GP and, following X-rays, Thomas told Malcolm that he had a shadow his lung. Cantwell remembered how Allison, after getting the prognosis, was in tears, putting his head on Noel's shoulder, telling him Thomas thought he had TB. Ultimately undergoing long and complicated surgery, Allison had part of a lung removed.

Bobby had been at the Boleyn Ground to pick up his wages just after Malcolm's condition had been diagnosed. He was later to tell how he had seen Allison on the day the big man found out about his illness. The ground staff boy saw Malcolm, his back to the Boleyn Ground pitch, with tears in his eyes. The young man couldn't believe his mentor was crying. Although he was very familiar with him as a coach,

Bobby still didn't feel he knew Allison well enough to ask what was troubling the figure he looked up to so much. He recollected checking on Malcolm again after coming out of the office. Noel Cantwell was standing with his arm round Allison. This was an image that would stay with Bobby forever.

Malcolm made his comeback attempt, feeling he owed it to himself to make the effort. He got no help from the likes of Ted Fenton or Bill Robinson, but it's questionable how a man like Allison might have been helped in those days. However, he still had enough in him to give the hierarchy a bad time. He was to confess that he was probably not the easiest person to get on with at that time.

Allison had been performing pretty well in the games he had played for the reserve side before the United game. He had worked out that the selection was between himself and Moore, who he believed should and would ultimately make a mark. Yet he thought, 'But not yet, Bobby, not yet.' However, he also knew he lacked fitness, although felt he could have got away with that, thinking he would have been able to play decent long balls and cruise through the match. He had intended on allowing Taylor to play in his own half. As things panned out, the Hammers dominated for most of the match and that would have suited Allison. This reflects much of what Malcolm thought about football; he argued that the game should be simple. For him poor players made the game more difficult than it needs to be. I have found that probably applies not just to football.

Allison was to tell Cantwell how much his friend's decision had hurt him, but when he hung up his boots he was to become one of the most attractive and charismatic figures in the football of his era, perhaps ever. Working with Joe Mercer at Manchester City, Allison led them through a period of success the like of which club hadn't seen before. The Maine Road men were surprise Football League champions in 1967/68 (City had been 200/1 to finish top at the start of that season). They won the FA Cup in 1969, and then the League Cup and European Cup Winners' Cup the following year, with a side that included City immortals such as Colin Bell, Mike Summerbee and Francis Lee – all northern lads and not a single Brazilian in the sight.

Allison refused an offer to manage Juventus on the understanding that Mercer, by that time really more of a figurehead at City, would move aside and let him take over as manager. Ultimately Mercer was to refuse to make way. Their relationship collapsed and finally Allison effectively ousted Mercer, who took over Coventry City in the summer of 1972.

The conflict caused a lot of problems at Manchester City. The club were unable to get over the rift and Allison moved on to Crystal Palace where he completely restructured the side in an attempt to halt the club's decline. Jim Cannon, a defender at Selhurst Park at the time, was to say that Allison 'put Palace on the map'.

In the 1975/76 season Malcolm led Palace to brilliant victories against much bigger and more successful clubs, including Leeds United, Chelsea and Sunderland, taking them to their first FA Cup semi-final appearance. However, the side he transformed from the 'Glaziers' to the 'Eagles' were defeated by the eventual winners, one of the best Southampton teams in the history of that club.

The FA Cup run was also notable for the first appearance of Allison's trademark fedora hat during a third-round game at Scarborough, and his use of an advanced version of the sweeper system which, at the time, was a relatively innovative idea.

Later Allison took over at Sporting Lisbon and guided that great club to a domestic league and cup double in 1981/82. That would be the only title won by Sporting until the 1999/2000 season, and as such Malcolm is fondly remembered at the Estádio José Alvalade.

For me, it is a tragedy of history that Allison was never to be West Ham manager. One can only imagine what he might have achieved with Moore as his lieutenant. I suspect it might have been something like his accomplishments with Manchester City, but probably a more protracted success, maybe with Bobby becoming an assistant to his mentor after his playing days. Who knows, we may never have lost Mooro in the way that we did if the world and football had been a bit more logical and a lot less heartless.

'Memories
May be beautiful and yet,
What's too painful to remember,
We simply to choose to forget'

According to Malcolm Musgrove, the decision to field Moore was a bit more straightforward than the story more often detailed and elaborated in most anecdotal accounts, 'Bobby got into the side because Malcolm wasn't fit.'

Malcolm Pyke, a 20-year-old at the time told me, confirming Musgrove's understanding,

'There was a lot of paper talk about Malcolm Allison being due to play the night Bobby made his debut against Manchester United. But that's not true! Allison wasn't fit, he wasn't even included. There were three half-backs injured that night, Bill Lansdowne, Andy Nelson and myself. Bill and Andy took a fitness test and I was the last one to be tested. If it wasn't for that, I'd have played instead of Bobby Moore – and that's the God's honest truth! And then, Bobby didn't look back. Allison was nowhere near fit.'

That fitness test would not have taken place on the day of the match or on the previous Saturday, when West Ham had lost badly, going down 4-1 at Luton Town with Bill Lansdowne wearing the number six shirt. In those days Sunday was taboo in terms of doing anything much, so Pyke was likely to have been tested on the Friday at the latest. Whatever, he was sure that by the Monday evening he was ready to play, so whatever injury he might have had a few days previously appears to have been not severe enough to keep him out of the game against United.

Pyke's account was verified by Bill Lansdowne, who responded, 'Yes, Malcolm Pyke was right, I had an ankle injury,' although Bill has also said he 'was dropped to make way for Bobby', but wasn't too disappointed given the quality of the young man and 'it's not too bad being replaced by Bobby Moore'. Indeed, after Lansdowne left the club, Bobby wore his training jumper, embroidered with the initials BL by Bill's wife Pat. Andy Nelson, a reserve centre-half at Upton Park at that point, confirmed Pyke's understanding of the situation, saying, 'Yes, that has to be true.'

So, after Luton, it appears two or three senior players were 'maybes' for the next home game. That being the case, why the angst about on Moore's part about him specifically being taken as a 'usurper'? Bobby's anxiety about being favoured over Allison days before the game had been severe enough to cause him to suffer temporary insomnia. If there was reasonable cause for Moore's concerns, any fitness tests of other players feel irrelevant.

Taking all this into account, and that Cantwell, for all intents and purposes, practically managed Fenton, one might be forgiven for thinking that Bobby might have known days before the game that he was, pretty much definitely, going to play on that Monday evening. Indeed, Cantwell, being the intelligent strategist he was, would have avoided, if at all possible, dropping the bombshell, with almost no notice, on a teenager that they were going to face one of the best teams in the country.

All this doesn't mean too much at first glance. Bobby got his first game that evening and maybe that's all that counts, unless, of course, you happen to be Malcolm Pyke, who told me,

'When we got up [promoted to the First Division] I wasn't included in the first team side – that hurt. I did try. I was first reserve at Portsmouth, the opening game of the season. But I didn't get a look-in after that.'

Who knows what it would have meant for Pyke if he had been fit and had taken the field against Manchester United – as he insisted was actually the case? Pyke saw Allison as 'abrasive' and although he argued he had nothing against him, and didn't 'bother about' Allison, he did say that 'Big Mal' had 'his favourites'.

Moore, Allison and Cantwell had become very close over the years. John Bond, who Moore roomed with when he first came to Upton Park, was also a member of trio's wider circle at Upon Park. Several players of the 1950s have told me that West Ham was run by Allison, Bond and Cantwell, so the events surrounding Moore's debut may have been much simpler than the appealingly complex, romantic and heart-rendering, commonly told tale. As one player said, 'I think John Bond was in control at the time – he preferred Bob.' I'm not sure Bond would have taken it on himself alone get Moore into the team, but Bond and Cantwell together coming to such a decision is probably not beyond belief.

Like Cantwell and Allison, Bond had developed a liking and admiration for Moore. He certainly rated him. John was to describe Bobby as 'simplicity itself'. He elaborated,

'There were loads of people at the time, the likes of Bill McGarry, because they played wing-half all their lives, looked at Bobby Moore and thought he wasn't a good player. They couldn't see what a great player he was. Everything he did he made look so easy, as if it was nothing. He never did anything difficult in his life. Ron Greenwood said simplicity of that sort was genius.'

Situations around crucial selections and decision are always more complicated than often described or understood. The scenario, that evening so long ago, as frequently portrayed, has an almost Hollywood western quality. Fenton the inadequate town mayor, Moore the young hombre, Cantwell the sheriff and the John Wayne figure of Allison, swaggering away into the distance, hurt but with his pride intact, having 'done the right thing'.

This is not saying that anyone has lied. Anything above does not imply that. Life, history, the past are structures cobbled together by memories, and memory is no more than an impression, built on perception, imagination, hope, emotions and everything that happened before and after any given memory.

When I put Malcolm Pyke's view of events to Malcolm Allison the big man said,

'I'd just come out of hospital and I'd played three or four games in the reserves. Ted called Noel up to his office; he asked who he should play, Malcolm or Bobby? Noel went for Bobby. I think Malcolm Pyke has got mixed up with another situation. He probably played in place of me in another match.'

However, there was no sense of that from Pyke's attitude. He was energetically certain, carrying perhaps a little anguish, but certainly more than a modicum of understandable regret, believing at the time and decades later that he was indeed fit enough to play, and he had some justification for expecting to run out against United that evening when the fates were in full flight.

Although I have no doubts that he convinced himself otherwise, Malcolm Allison was unlikely to be close to match fit; there was and is a world of difference between taking a turn in the reserves, watched by a comparative handful of people, and playing an all-or-nothing competitive game with top-class opposition, under the gaze of a packed home crowd and the judgement of the national media.

A couple of reserve games would have proved very little about Allison's readiness. Noel Cantwell would have recognised that. This consideration, added to the inescapable reality that he had recently suffered a critical, life-threatening disease and undergone radical surgery, being reduced to a single fully functioning lung as a consequence, rationally makes one doubtful that he would have ever again been up to matching opposition of the stature of Manchester United.

I had the great pleasure of meeting Malcolm Pyke and talking to him at length. He was a really top bloke, a solid and able footballer in his day, clear-thinking, smart, funny, kind and sociable. I can't see any reason why he would be misleading or mistaken about this episode. He came across as a good, straight-talking person. So, throwing proportions of benefit of the doubt in the club's direction and Pyke's, there was the option of playing a maybe not totally fit Pyke against United. In the promotion season Pyke had played 17 of West Ham's 45 league and cup fixtures, he had played just four first-team games in the previous couple of seasons and would not be in the side at all throughout the Irons' return to the top flight. However, at Upton Park, by the last months of 1958, if we go with him being 'selectable', Smith being unavailable and Lansdowne crooked, in terms of recent first-team match-play, he was ahead of Allison, Nelson and Moore.

All that said, I don't doubt the right choice was made in the end. Moore was the future and the 'class act'. If anything, he could have been blooded in the first team a lot earlier. There's not an argument with any semblance of logic which could convince that Allison or Pyke would have been 'better' options. Perhaps, if guided by sentiment, Allison should have been given his comeback moment. Maybe stark 'natural justice' would have sent Pyke out to play at Upton Park all those years ago. However, strategy and tactics are the children of rationality and pragmatics, while not necessarily being eager bedfellows of particular takes on fairness or the vagaries of emotion. Moore was the right choice – in fact, in reality, he was the only choice.

To reiterate, I'm not here saying I doubt the veracity of Moore, Cantwell or Allison in relation to Bobby's debut game against Manchester United. Moore was indeed moving into Allison's place, not only on the field of play, but in terms of his influence on his fellow players and the club. While Moore's selection was not quite a crude usurpation of the crown, it was what a lot of us experience at the end of a career or job; someone else, often a younger person, stepping into the plimsoles we might have worn with distinction, and felt we were more than able to continue schlepping about in for just a bit longer, all be it in blissful denial. It hurts to have to vacate a beloved role, to know you will never again know the pleasure of undertaking it. It is hardly ever not going to feel, a least a bit, like the 'bum's rush'. In Allison's case it wasn't just a job he was departing, but a lifelong ambition. At the same time, if those taking over that role think anything of us, it pains them to have to be the 'supplanter'.

Looking at and writing about the flawed history of West Ham United (and all history is flawed), I have, more than once, used L.P. Hartley's words from *The Go Between*,

'The past is a foreign country; they do things differently there.'

Since I first called on Hartley's words, other writers looking at the Hammers have picked up on that quote, probably because it has a strong ring of truth about it. Although imitation is the sincerest form of flattery, the point is we all need our tales of romance, lost chances, and moments of courage. These parables are metaphors for and a source solace in our own lives. Therein lies our hope for consolation, redemption even, and it is this that makes up the history we 'choose' and the 'truth' we invest our belief in; we nearly always believe what we want to believe, mostly for justifiable reasons, often laced up in our need for self-protection and personal validation.

At the same time, memories shape experience more than actual events, and we, mostly unknowingly, craft our memories to fit the pictures of our experience we desire. Memory and actuality are related, but they are not the same thing. What I remember often tells more about me than the events I convince myself I remember. 'Truth' is both contextual and subjective, while memory isn't an immaculate video of the past. Maybe the best we can hope for is a kind of general understanding of or feeling about our lives and the lives of others. If I have learned one thing speaking to the people featured in this book (and others) it is, in the end, that the world will be much as we would have it be. To be human is to be biased.

There was a lot of loyalty and affection between Allison, Moore and Cantwell. Put yourself in Noel's and Bobby's position; the only people who had been at Allison's side from the start of his illness, and who had sat by his hospital bed, wishing they could do something, anything to help their friend recover. Would you have encouraged him to follow his hope, the very motivation that pulled him out of infirmity? That (literal) lifeline, that chink of light in the darkness, was a belief that there was chance for him to play at the level he had always dreamed he might grace. Would you have told Malcolm, after all his effort, that he never, from the get-go, had a chance of getting chosen for the match with United? Would it have seemed more protective, kind or caring to have gone along with his feelings, that he had been in with a shout, that his manager had wanted him to play, that the choice had been a difficult one, a close-run thing? We are inclined to live our beliefs and we tend to be saved by our faith – without the same, only the void remains.

What is for sure is that Allison was a big man in more ways than one. He managed to find a smile as he said to his young student, 'Well done. I hope you do well.' Bobby knew he meant it.

The only reservation I have was Fenton's alleged and/or apparent mixed feelings about the 'right thing to do'. Maybe history got a bit tangled and what he was asking Cantwell about was the choice between Moore and Pyke (there were two Malcolms in the frame after all), although that feels too much like clutching at straws. It could have been that Ted didn't want to be the one to effectively cut Allison loose, perhaps out of fear of Big Mal's wrath or the team's response, thinking that if it were seen as Cantwell's call everyone would have been more accepting of it.

If you push me, and I guess you have a right to, I think Ted knew that Cantwell would name Moore, and he didn't disagree, he didn't even try to make the case for an alternative. It was likely a forgone conclusion, especially after the poor showing against Luton just a few days before. Moore playing, logically and practically, had to be a no-brainer for everyone but Allison at that emotive point. I think there are strong indications that he was later to accept this, if not fully.

Can, want, should?

My time in the training and education of 'people managers' is that they are guided by three main pillars of decision-making:

- What I can do?
- What I want to do?
- What I should do?

In this sphere, emotion and sentiment are too often the main organisational drivers. These tend to override logic, so potential rational thinking is displaced and decisions made surfing on the cusp of a wave of emotion. This is the dominance of 'What I want to do?' and 'What I can do?'. This makes for very messy situations and wasteful circumstances, because decisions are premised on feelings and dispositions, which are often less than rational (they are more or less irrational).

The engine of the 'best' (the most efficient and effective) organisational action, is rational management, which is premised on 'good' judgements that are the product of sound evidence. While we might simply take management to be another word for 'control', its regulatory and systematised character is attuned to 'What I should do?'.

A 'good' manager is someone who has 'the ability to translate logic into action'. This is not throwing the baby of emotion out with the bathwater of sentiment; temperamental considerations are a constant in human relations. However, 'What I can do?' needs to be established within the parameters of 'What I should do?'. The potential and limits for 'What I want to do?' need to be defined within the parameters of 'What I should do?'.

Allison *could* have played. He, Moore and Cantwell might have *wanted* him to play, but given the relative circumstances of Moore and Allison, Malcolm *shouldn't* have played. If it was Cantwell who had the last word in the decision then he was a 'good' manager – he was driven by the obvious logic and evidence and not the flood of sentiment, where hopes, wishes and dreams risk destroying the rational means to reach organisational direction – which on 8 September 1958, at Upton Park, was to beat Manchester United, and not to give Malcolm Allison a game – the latter, relative to the club's ambition, would have been irrational.

Not for a second do I feel anyone thought they had a World Cup-winning captain on their hands with Moore at that time, nor was he going to be thought of at that juncture as being the man to keep John Smith out of the Hammers' starting XI. But it was more than apparent he was close to ready to get a start in what was England's premier division in 1958, if only as option behind Smith and for a while Bill Lansdowne.

I think what is for sure is that there was really only one choice for the left-half role on the evening of 8 September 1958, and that was the player who had proved his credibility over the previous couple of years.

Allison, who did more than anyone to create the side that were promoted in 1958, never received a Second Division championship medal. He, along with the rest of the team, attended the official celebration at the Café Royal in May, but it was only then that he found out that the Football League rules had it that players needed to be involved in 15 or more games warranted a medal. Malcolm had only run out in the league five times. He walked out shrouded in a mixture of embarrassment, disgust and sadness. That's something that *shouldn't* have happened.

BREAKTHROUGH

The spring and summer of 1958 was Bobby's breakthrough point; a sort of mini-run for 1963/64 and 1964/65. This was when the future finally emerged from the womb of potential. On 22 April 1958, Bobby was in the West Ham Colts side that met their Arsenal counterparts in final of the Southern Junior Floodlit Cup at Upton Park. The Irons had beaten Chelsea in the final of that competition in the previous season, 2-1 at Stamford Bridge, with George Fenn and Charlie Rowlands scoring.

The evening's programme introduced Moore thus,

'Bobby Moore, Played for Barking and Essex Boys and then joined our ground staff on leaving school. A London youth cap, he first played in the England youth side at 16 and a half and now has a record of 15 youth caps to his credit: skippered the England team which was runner-up to Italy in the European youth tournament over Easter. Has made several Combination appearances.'

The Floodlit Cup was a competition for youth teams. The ties were played on midweek evenings. It ran between 1955 and 1999 and was initially sponsored by the *Daily Mail*. For younger players the competition was only second in importance to the FA Youth Cup, players competing had to be under the age of 18 at the start of the season, but there was no bar to those who had signed professional. The first final of the competition was played at Upton Park in January 1956. Chelsea were the winners, beating the home side 2-1.

Offering a bevy of local derbies, over the 42 seasons that the competition ran (the 1973/74 event was abandoned due to the power strikes) it saw some of the best of Britain's young talent competing. In its early days, when watching games under floodlights was a novel and exciting experience, the Floodlit Cup drew comparatively high interest and some relatively impressive gates, literally lighting up the midweek of people's routine in those grey times, bringing some colour to the dark winter evenings in the era of black and white TV.

The Floodlit Cup also acted both as something of a showcase for the player market, and an exercise in footballing equity. Many youth sides in southern England competed in the South East Counties League and South East Counties League Cup from the 1950s, but it was often not viable for some of the clubs, based in more distant locations, to travel regularly for league matches. However, these sides were able to field teams in the more occasional Floodlight Cup as an alternative.

Before the 1958 final the young Hammers had also distinguished themselves in the international arena that season. Three of their number had done well for England in the youth tournament in Luxembourg over Easter, and several had been selected for other international games during 1957/58.

For Arsenal, 1958 saw their first appearance in the final. On the way the young Gunners had seen off Queens Park Rangers away 4-3 after extra time, Reading at home 2-1, and Charlton Athletic at home 3-0. The previous season the Highbury kids had been defeated 4-2 by their West Ham age peers in the semi-final at Upton Park.

The young Gunners had got to the final with the guidance of the former Arsenal professionals George Male, who was born in West Ham and trialed for the Hammers as a boy, and Alf Fields. They had experienced a successful season in 1957/58, featuring a fine showing in the South East Counties League in which they were sitting in third place at that point, just behind the eventual champions Chelsea and Charlton, and FA Youth Cup, getting to the semi-finals of that competition for the first time. The north Londoners met Chelsea in the last four, but were beaten in both legs, at Stamford Bridge and Highbury on the Tuesday and Thursday of the week before the game at Upton Park. The young Blues had played out of their collective skin for the opportunity to meet holders Wolverhampton Wanderers in the final. Wolves had defeated Manchester United, the team that had won the first five editions of trophy from 1952/53 (the Red Devils had defeated West Ham in the final of 1956/57). The 1958 final saw 13 nettings – the Molineux kids won by the odd goal.

The Colts' record that season was also a good one. In the evening's programme, credit was given to assistant manager Bill Robinson and 'chief scout' Wally St Pier, as well as a whole slew of others including Stan Wilcockson, Frank Wilkins, Jack Turner and Tom Russell. The person credited as team coach, Noel Cantwell, was the last to be mentioned. He was taken to be working 'in conjunction with' Malcolm Allison.

The programme for the final assessed that the Hammers' season had been 'middling' in the South East Counties League, but went on to state that several of the young professionals and ground staff in the team had not played in that competition owing to 'their Saturday engagements in other sides, with the result that the strongest XI' had not been available. Along the way, prior to the encounter with Arsenal Colts, the Hammers had beaten Aldershot away 3-1, Millwall at home 2-1 and Chelsea at home 3-0

In the FA Youth Cup the young Irons had won their first three games – only to lose 3-1 to Chelsea in the third round; as the Gunners went under to the Pensioners by the same score this seemed to indicate that the sides were evenly matched.

West Ham had beaten Chelsea in the semi-finals of that season's Floodlit Cup. The performance was all the more creditable as the Blues had fielded eight professionals in their XI (against the Hammers' two).

West Ham Colts: Stan Earl, Joe Kirkup, Harry Cripps, Bobby Moore, Bobby Keetch, Geoff Hurst, Derek Woodley, Andy Smillie, R. Keeble, John Cartwright, Tony Scott
Substitute:: Eddie Bovington
Arsenal: N. Coe, J. Sanchez, D. Robson, M. Everett, A. Young, W. West, M. Barber, R. Read, D. Clapton, R. Howson, D. Dodson
Referee: R.Hounsell (London)
Linesmen: K. Markham and M.E. Day

West Ham ran out in their traditional claret and blue kit; Arsenal wore blue shirts with white collars and sleeves, and white shorts.

A crowd of 4,500 saw a fast-moving match. The home side performed as well as they had all season against what was a solid Arsenal formation. The only error of the night in West Ham's defence was the one that resulted in the visitors' goal, while the home attack consistently ran their guests ragged. West Ham's wing-halves, Hurst and Moore, combined well, and did much to lay the foundation for what was the thrashing of Arsenal.

Moore opened the scoring. This was followed by a brace from Andy Smillie before the break. Arsenal pulled one back in the second half, but inside-left Tony Scott made it 4-1 before Smillie completed his hat-trick.

The Arsenal schedule appears to have taken its toll. In the South East Counties League, they ultimately finished fourth out of the 15 competing clubs. The Hammers took seventh place, just a point behind Millwall.

Christina Dean

As summer of 1958 was fading, Bobby met the first love of his life in a place where many of us who lived within a ten-mile radius of the same venue can say much the same thing.

More than a quarter of a century ago Ray Davies, lead singer of The Kinks, invited us to 'Come Dancing'. You might recall (or knock it up on YouTube) that the song had a fairground organ backing that made it pretty original within the genre of pop music.

Ray's lyrics were inspired by one of his six older sisters' Saturday night visits to the Palais club. More recently a musical (again *Come Dancing*) motivated by Davies's composition was premiered at the Theatre Royal Stratford, a five-minute stroll from what is now West Ham's London Stadium. Set at Ilford Palais in the 1950s, the production tells the story of the people who made the venue legendary; the young men and women who worked all week, in often hard and/or boring jobs so, come the weekend, they could dance the night away.

I first went to the Palais probably 15 years after Bobby met Tina Dean there. The glitterball was still turning and the girls continued to dance round their handbags. Unlike the generation before, there wasn't much trace of the 'cha-cha' on the dance floor, but reggae was strong and the sync dancing (sort of line dancing, but not as naff) was a popular response.

The 'Babycham Bar' had gone; Bacardi and coke was the fashionable tipple for the 'ladies'. I preferred what we used to call a 'Flying Angel' – Southern Comfort, lemonade and lime. You can now get it pre-mixed in a tin, which makes it about as exotic and tomato soup – talk about 'kill my vibe'. If I had that today, in between the 15 or so pints of light and bitter I'd down in a night, I would almost certainly kill myself.

I won't mention the 'black bombs' (or 'bombers') that used to pep up the evening somewhat. These bad-babbies were the drug of choice in those heady days within the 'cercle social' of adolescent roustabouts I knocked around with. We'd down 'em like sweets! Otherwise known as 'Duraphet', bombers were ultimately to be phased out and replaced by illegally manufactured 'blues' and eventually 'sulphate amphetamine powder'. Next to 'purple hearts' and 'dexes', bombers were the best known and most widespread drugs used by a generation of young people, especially those engaging in the capital's nightlife.

'BBs' became *de rigueur* in the 1960s after pharmacists uncovered a rare combination of amphetamines that caused euphoria, hyperactivity, increased awareness of surroundings, interest in repetitive activities, decreased appetite, as well as dramatic rises in whole-body metabolism. It wasn't long before partygoers got their hands on this powerful drug cocktail for the 'high' experienced, or what my brothers in self-abuse and I called 'getting totally twatted' (I did say I wouldn't to mention them!).

By the end of my teenage years the Palais had become pretty shabby, and the resort for the classier arsehole like myself was the Room at the Top, located in the penthouse of the former Harrison and Gibson site, just across Ilford High Road from the Palais. Revellers had to use an elevator to access the club. From my earliest visits there, before the erosion of its reputation as a destination for the 'trendy' (there's a word that will date you), I recall on two or three occasions seeing Bobby with few others, the likes of Rodney Marsh and George Best (by that time Mooro was at Craven Cottage). Mostly he would nod and/or wink at me, with a bit of a smile. Once, as the flash teenage gobshite I could be, I got in the lift with him and a few others, and said, as smooth as you like, 'All right Bob.' He put his hand on my shoulder and said, 'Hallo Brian! How's Jim [my dad]?' which massively impressed the girl I was with. I'm sure he knew that would be the case. Thanks, Bobby. No, really, THANKS!

As it was with my nights at the Palais, when Bobby and Tina were going there, it was nearly always packed with young people. The 1960s were still young when it was a haunt of serial nonce Jimmy Savile during his rise to fame – who the fuck was he ever popular with and why? As he was poncing about 'in' places, saying shit like 'What about that bear then?', 'Now then, now then' and 'A thousand thanks', like Satan's brain-damaged, geriatric harlequin, the general summation of him from where I and my illustrious age peers were standing was that he was an out and out, complete and total wanker of the first order.

By the time the early 1970s came along, the decade my age group made their way up Ilford High Road, the Burley Beelzebub had moved on, as had the stars who had graced the Palais in Bobby and Tina's youthful years, the likes Ambrose and his Orchestra, Gerry Dorsey (the bloke who would morph into Engelbert Humperdinck) and Kathy Kirby, who became a huge star by the 1960s (her and sister Pat lived opposite Tina's home in Ilford).

When Tina and Bobby were teenagers the Palais opened for an afternoon session at midday, offering cut-price entry of 6d (a 'tanner' or 'sprazy', 21/2p). I think it had gone up by 100 per cent (that'd be a shilling – 5p) when my mates and I got the bus to Ilford at that time of day, just before the currency was decimalised. We went in the hope of meeting girls, but I liked getting on the floor, unlike the majority of other young men. Like Bobby and his pals, most blokes stationed themselves in clusters, trying to look 'cool' (a word we didn't actually use in those days, it being considered a somewhat fey anachronism from the long-dead days of Cafe Bongo and the Beatniks) but only getting to the foothills of that state known as 'awkward'.

It is generally said that the teenage romance between Bobby and Tina, like so many in our manor, started at Ilford Palais, but really it only hosted their first meeting. While Bobby was smitten from the get-go, the mutual attraction kicked in later. As East Enders had done and would do for generations, Moore hung out with a group of other young men (in his case mostly junior Hammers) on the balcony that surrounded the dancefloor, gazing at the attractive girls below (and as a teenage boy ALL girls are attractive to some extent). Having zoned in on Tina, Bobby looked out for her for weeks before finding the arsehole to ask her for a dance. Anxiety about a knock-back, and likely the ritual extraction of the axiomatic urine that comes with such rejection from one's caring companions, made him hesitant – hey, we've all been there! Finally getting the gonads to rock up to someone you've been fantasying about for ages, something all your confidants know about, and then being unceremoniously told to 'piss off' is a tough ship to sail. Believe me, I know!

'Blue Moon' was playing when gorgeously east London, mid-century, 15 year-old Christina Elizabeth Dean, the pretty girl in the boat-necked long-sleeved dress, said 'yes' to Bobby. When that happens it's a shock. The seconds of realisation seem to last hours. The urge to ask 'pardon?', because you don't believe your ears, is powerful. You find yourself instinctively smiling, looking either insane or idiotic or both, but glad you had milked the Colgate tube before going out. The only thing in your head is 'she said YES!' In my case, together with nostrils full of Blue Blazer aftershave that I tipped on by the gallon (everyone else seemed to favour Brut, which for me ponged like a horse's armpit – if horse's had armpits – or maybe I just wanted to be different), this banished any hope of coherent conversation to the realm of the sublimely in vain. That's when the panic sets in and you are thankful that the music is so loud. Eye contact becomes the only obstacle left to overcome (I wrote that like it was easy!). My own top tip was to 'ask lots of questions'. Not *University Challenge* though (although I did a decent impression of Bamber Gascoigne). The inquisition might start with 'What's your favourite colour?', 'Least favourite day of the week?' or 'Second choice flavour of fruit gum?' – pretty good for openers, eh? The silver-tongued Don Juan of E13, me, but without the success rate.

Tina was coming up to her 16th birthday. She didn't know Bobby was a footballer. Her stepfather tried to find out if Bobby was kidding her about being at the Boleyn Ground, and not finding any record of him, concluded he was a wind-up. That had no impact on his stepdaughter as she knew nothing about the game, and cared even less. That said, the epithet 'Bobby Moore' meant little to anyone at that time, and nothing at all to the vast majority of young teenage girls. Like Ted Fenton, in the world beyond Upton Park Bobby was still just another football apprentice, nothing more.

The first dance done, the couple agreed to meet at the Palais the following Saturday. However, Bobby was much more besotted by Tina than she was with him. He waited all evening, but the blonde lass didn't show. That's a choker. You hang around, sometimes hours after the hands of the clock tell their dire tale. In those days, long before the mobile phone, you'd spend these endless minutes blowing on the embers of illusion that she'll turn up, having made a mistake with the agreed meeting time or place. Another hope was that she had been waylaid and so delayed by some unforeseeable incident. But the truth always lurked in the dark recesses of the adolescent 'watch and chain', beneath the thick teenage skull, whispering with venomous joy – 'you've been ghosted'.

However, the girl had told the young footballer she often visited the local record shop, so he made a point of hanging around the store, hoping that he might bump into her one day. He did eventually get lucky, although all he got was a tiny nod of recognition. Tina had, however, mentioned the boy to her mother, Betty. And so, a week after Tina had stood Bobby up, while mother and daughter were in a taxi, navigating heavy traffic along Ilford High Street, she saw Bobby sitting in a coffee bar. Turning to her mum she said, 'That's him! That's the boy who asked me out.'

Betty took a longish look and – unsurprisingly – being taken with the attractive, sharply turned-out young man, passed judgement saying, 'He looks nice. Why don't you invite him home for tea?'

Tina was to believe that the moment her mum saw Bobby she had known he would be right for her daughter and decided she would do what she could to bring them together.

Life had not been straightforward or easy for Betty. She had always worked; there was no other choice as she and Tina's father had split up when Tina was two. Thus, Betty raised her daughter as a single mum at a time when such a situation was largely harshly judged, poorly understood and almost totally unsupported. The most important men in Betty's life had let her down and perhaps that is why she was so keen to bring Bobby and Tina together.

Betty almost immediately took to Bobby, but the relationship wasn't so warmly greeted in the Moore household. Doris found dealing with Bobby finding love difficult. Perhaps, to her, it took something away from the close mother/son relationship they had. My father's mother was much the same – like Bobby and Doris, my dad and his mum were close. Like the Moores they were together throughout the war years, but with no other parental figure around, my grandad was fighting in Europe for the most part. My grandmother actively destroyed my dad's first engagement and was a constant source of unhappiness in his eventual marriage to my mum.

The child/parent relationship is a delicate balance. Too close, like my dad and his mum, too distant, as my mum grew separated from her family by evacuation; I suspect few get it dead right. However, as time passes, the older I get, the more I am aware that the years of conflict the generation before my own experienced has cast a long shadow.

According to Tina, as her relationship with Bobby developed, Doris felt her son was excluding her from his life. Retrospectively this made sense to Tina, for her Bobby could only have one passion in his life at a time, and he was totally enamoured by Tina.

During their courtship the couple usually saw each other six times a week. Tina recalled that Bobby was 'shy and unsure of himself, but he was a very determined man. He showed that in all aspects of his life … He always put a lot into whatever he did – like our relationship. Every hour he wasn't at football was devoted to us going out. He was wonderful. Very generous, thoughtful and considerate… At that time Bobby earned about £8 a week and the most you could get was £16 a week, so I wasn't terribly impressed by the fact he was a footballer.' Indeed, in those initial years of their relationship, Tina was earning more than Bobby.

That first serious relationship changes young people. Love is not only a 'many splendored thing', it is also all consuming. Certainly, for most young men, the affirmation of the reciprocation of devotion of a young woman can make a world of difference to their self-image and confidence, it can be the making of them. As such, perhaps West Ham, England and football generally have much to thank Tina for.

Europe

Not long after the Floodlit Cup Final, Moore was with the West Ham side playing in an international tournament in Belgium. Teams from several European countries competed, including some notable sides, such as Ajax, ARA La Gantoise, Beerschot AC, Duisburger SV, KRC Gent, Torino, TuRU Düsseldorf, Stade de Reims, and Torpedo Moscow. As the age limit was 19 the Hammers were able to call on another seven professionals to see them through the five-match programme.

International Voetbaltornoo Belgium, Stadion Jules Otten, 1–3 May 1958

Group games	Score	Date
Duisburger SV (Germany)	1-0	1 May
KRC Gent (Belgium)	1-0	1 May
Stade de Reims (France)	3-1	2 May
Beerschot AC (Netherlands)	2-0	2 May
Final		
Torpedo Moscow (USSR)	0-0	3 May

West Ham: Brian Rhodes, Harry Cripps, Joe Kirkup, Malcolm Pyke, Bobby Moore, John Smith, Andy Smillie, Harry Obeney, R. Keeble, Derek Woodley, Tony Scott

West Ham dominated the final. Moore and Smillie were foiled by the woodwork, while Harry Obeney's 20-yard rocket was inexplicably disallowed. Brian Rhodes was hardly troubled in the Hammers' goal, at one point eating an apple passed to him by a spectator. As was often the way in such tournaments in those times, teams drawing in the final shared the trophy and the bragging rights as competition winners.

The victories at home and abroad marked a seminal time for the future of West Ham, but also Bobby Moore. Confirming his performances for the England youth side, and Ron Greenwood's estimation of him, he showed himself to be a successful leader and a young player of growing stature.

This was why he would have been chosen to make his league debut against Manchester United a few months later. All the romance, mythology and emotion provoked memories cannot camouflage that his selection, given the choices open to West Ham that September evening so long ago, would have been all but a forgone conclusion.

CONCLUSION

Josephine Lawson was from Cumbria. She was trained to be a midwife, but also a general district nurse. With the Second World War in its second year, she made her way to Plaistow Maternity Hospital (a facility that was ultimately evacuated and later bomb damaged). She had a case book of births, detailing the ages of local mothers, if they were having their first or subsequent babies, and so on. She cared for mums for the two weeks following the birth of their children.

Josephine hadn't been in attendance when Robert Moore came into the world, but for the rest of her life she would have his and Doris's details in that case book. If we need proof that Bobby is mortal, that is it.

I have tried to make that point and not to turn this book into a eulogy to Bobby Moore, that has been done enough, but it's hard to steer totally clear of extolling the man. I hope the pages have given more of an insight into the person and how the figure of Bobby Moore came to be. But he was, like us all, all too mortal.

Jimmy Greaves told how Bobby had a wicked sense of humour. Playing for England, when given the job on introducing dignitaries to the team prior to kick-off, he often went along the line presenting the players by the wrong name. Jim was once introduced to a foreign dignitary as 'Tommy Cooper'.

Greavsie was to also tell how Bobby 'got me into more trouble than anyone, and I've known some villains'. He did have a distinctly naughty side. Despite reports to the contrary, he was no saint, and as you have seen, his genius bloomed from his ordinariness.

According to Noel Cantwell, Moore stood out at West Ham as being, 'An immaculate-looking player … Everything was clean, even his shorts and boots … It was as though he ran out on to the pitch just after his mother had ironed his kit – and at that end, he rarely looked different.' Cantwell was impressed how Bobby 'pulled his sleeves down and just played, even when he first started'.

Noel was the best man when Bobby married Tina and, in 1968, godfather to the couple's son, Dean. Cantwell, seen by some as one of the most talented left-backs in history, had an unusual way of running. His elbows seemed to be held out wide as he ran. He had purposely developed this style to deter opponents getting too close, making the task of robbing the ball from him more onerous. In action, you can see something of an adaption of the same thing in Moore. This is a physical example of the subtle but profound influence Noel had on Bobby.

Moreover, it was Cantwell, following Malcolm Allison's belligerent insistences, who had recommended Moore to Fenton in August 1956 when Bobby signed amateur terms aged 15. It seems Ted had thought about pulling rank on his captain, demonstrating who was in charge, by refusing to sign Bobby. However, Cantwell had urged and counselled otherwise. And it was Noel who made the final judgement on 8 September 1958, believing Bobby could handle Manchester United's Ernie Taylor better than anyone else available at Upton Park. His thinking was the little bloke wasn't quick, but he liked to run at defenders, so Moore's timing when it came to tackling would make him the best foil for the inside-forward. But more than that, Noel knew that Bobby's time had come. If Cantwell had wanted something else, Bobby would not have played.

Cantwell once said that he always found himself admiring how Moore 'would never get too tight on a striker until the ball had been played'. The Irishman told how Bobby would handle himself when close to an attacking player and a ball came over the top. Knowing he would be beaten in a race for the ball, 'Before the ball arrived, he gave himself five to six yards and then you would not realise how slow he was because of the position he had put himself in.' That propensity, finding strength from an acknowledged weakness, can usefully be replicated not only in football, but in the course of any career or life.

By the time he was in the last part of his teenage years Bobby had progressed from the fringes of east London, and from the status of nothing special, to playing for his country and in the strongest league in the world. Walking on to the pitch at Upton Park to face the mighty Manchester United, Bobby exemplified what young people can make of themselves, against all the odds, and despite other people's opinions. He did this by way of a gift bestowed to many a Cockney of his generation, the ability to endure and work hard – you have seen how that happened.

Bloody John Quigley

Following his debut in the Football League, it seemed Moore had done well enough to be retained in the side to meet Nottingham Forest five days later, the following Saturday.

Johnny Quigley pissed all over Bobby in the 4-0 drubbing. Moore admitted, 'I got the roasting of my life. I've never since been turned over like that. A little Scots fella called Johnny Quigley did everything to me. Turned me inside out … I thought, "What the hell am I doing here?"'

Born in the Govan area of Glasgow in 1935, Quigley was a talented midfielder in the Scottish tradition. He moved to the City Ground from Celtic in July 1957 and would score 58 goals in 270 appearances over seven seasons. Working under Billy Walker, he would win the FA Cup in 1959, when Forest beat Luton Town 2-1. It was his goal against Aston Villa at Hillsborough, the winner in the semi-final, that opened the door to Wembley for his side.

In the final, Forest were 2-0 up after 14 minutes but Roy Dwight, Elton John's cousin and the man who had scored the opening goal, broke his leg in the 33rd minute. Dave Pacey pulled one back for Luton midway through the second half. Forest had further personnel issues when cramp reduced Bill Whare to little more than a hobbling spectator. Quigley helped Forest hold on though, and they maintained their 2-1 lead to lift the trophy.

It was in 1958, during an encounter with Manchester City, that Jonny became the first Forest player to score a First Division postwar hat trick.

After struggling in the first half at the City Ground, as Moore jogged out after the break he heard someone in the crowd instructing the home side, 'Play on the left-half, he's the weak link.' This brought all his neatly repressed doubts well to the surface. Years later Moore was to admit,

'Bloody John Quigley! He saved his best performances for me! Turned us over again in a cup game in the mud when he was with Mansfield.'

The Scot was a fine servant to the Stags and between 1968 and 1970 he ran out over 100 times for the Field Mill crew.

Bobby was to say that Forest side were a decent outfit. They were on their way to the FA Cup Final and were sitting third in the league on the Saturday the Hammers wended their way to the City Ground. He acknowledged, 'We lost 4-0 and the way Quigley took me apart, it could have been 40.'

Bogey players abound in the annals of the Hammers, but on reflection Moore was to think himself fortunate to have ever got back into the first team. He confessed that at the time he had been a bit too full of himself, believing it would be 'a doddle' facing Forest. Predictably he took the lesson, making the point that he told himself that he was never again going to be 'turned over again like that'. Noel Cantwell confirmed Moore stayed true to his promise,

'He learned from it and I can't recall anybody else taking him apart in the same way. It made him work even harder on his game.'

The evening following the Forest game, Bobby had his first 'proper' date with Tina. On his way home, at Nottingham Station, he picked up a late newspaper (many such journals would produce two editions some days or every day of the working week, which for many included Saturdays). The report about his showing pulled no punches, and chucked in a few kicks just to nail the point home. Sickened by what he read, more out of remorse than anger, he ripped the paper up. He was to tell how if he'd had the money he would have 'bought every evening paper and torn them all up'.

Perhaps he might have been distracted wondering about his future career, but Tina was a stunning young woman (she has never lost her looks) with scant interest in football results. One can only imagine that was helpful. Sometimes we need people who can just listen and not 'helpfully' pick over our setbacks and supposed mistakes. My guess is just being with her helped Bobby cope with vicissitudes of fortune implicitly embedded in football, perhaps personified at that moment by his Glaswegian tormentor. Beauty can heal sorrow, and there are some things more important to young men than football, even Bobby Moore.

There's so much to learn every day and in every game

Following the Forest game, Ted Fenton, likely feeling vindicated in his initial opinion of Moore, consigned him back to the reserves, the youth team and the grey English winter. By the end of the 1958/59 season Moore had made 21 reserve team appearances, under the guidance firstly of Harry Hooper snr and then Albert Walker, two long-term servants of the club. But at that point Bobby was looking to his next challenge; to win a regular place in the West Ham first team and play First Division and FA Cup football. Somewhere in his mind too was likely something between a hope, a dream and an ambition to break into the senior England side. That's another story in the life and times of young Bobby, and the next one I will be looking at.

There were other compensations though. Bobby was soon able to buy his first car, a Ford Zephyr, in fire engine red (a colour he was to continue to favour in cars for the rest of his life). As the 1960s loomed everyone under 29 wanted to be driving that car. This was quite an event in Moore's life; a marker of success in the world. Young men of Bobby's years owning cars at the end of the 1950s, probably up to the start of the 1960s, was relatively rare, hence the association of youth of that era mostly with two-wheeled vehicles.

When Bobby went to visit his parents everyone knew because there was always a classy car parked out the front of the Moore family home. The local kids used to go up to the door to ask for his autograph. If they failed get it from him, then his mum would always get it for them later.

Bobby purchased the Zephyr from a friend of Tina's mum. The cash for the motor, as we tended to call cars in east London up to the late 1960s, was handed over at Lyons Tea Shop in Ley Street, Ilford. I had cousin who worked as a 'nippy' in there; waitresses who worked in the J. Lyons & Co tea shops and cafes in London, from the late 19th century, were called a 'Gladys'. It was around 1926, because the waitresses nipped (moved swiftly) around the tea shops, that they got assigned the moniker 'Nippy'. They wore a characteristic black and white maid-like uniform with the requisite headgear. My cousin recalled serving Bobby and Tina, who used to have fruit buns, a bowl of tomato soup and a cup of tea.

As Tina was to remember, Bobby turned up with the dosh for the car (£375 – that'd be more than £8,000 today) stowed in a paper bag. Typical of him, the wedge of notes was stacked uniformly (all the images of HRH's boat facing the same way) bound in rubber bands.

The Zephyr was to be cherished by Bobby, and never was it seen less than as spotless and as gleaming as he was. His next car was a dark maroon 375 Ford Consul, with a column change and bench seat. This was succeeded by a Triumph Vitesse. But he had higher ambitions and even as he drove the Zephyr for the first time, he was setting his sights on a XJ6 Jaguar.

In their first season back in the First Division the Irons were to do themselves credit, finishing sixth, two points behind third-placed Arsenal. The east Londoners were way ahead of both Chelsea and Tottenham. Bobby did manage a few more First Division appearances that season; a defeat at Turf Moor, a crushing 5-1 victory over Manchester City at Upton Park in the penultimate game of the term, and a loss at Elland Road. However, gaining more representative honours added to his reputation.

Relatively early in his senior career Moore summed up the philosophy and approach to football and wider existence that he began to build under the tutelage of Malcolm Allison,

'There's so much to learn every day and in every game. I know I can never learn too much. This is not only a rule for the game, but for life.'

It was his capacity to learn and translate yearning into learning, and that learning into action, that was to be recognised by those in a better place to do that than Ted Fenton; that ability was to save him and make him.

Will we see the like of Bobby Moore again? The state of football finance in the mid-1950s, out of which the West Ham youth scheme emerged, created the means for him to be brought into the professional game and, by the time he made his league debut, at the highest level. At this point in time, the same consideration, the economics of football, probably more disallows any historical repetition of the circumstances that gave us Bobby.

The current state of the relationship between money and the game might be translated metaphorically as a reincarnation of Dodge City. It has its Wyatt Earp and Doc Holliday figures, brave yet necessarily flawed enforcers, who just about manage to hold back the excesses of the milieu that are enacted by its Clantons and McLaurys (Abramovich, Sheikh Mansour, Khaldoon Al Mubarak).

At the same time, the game is full of parasites, creaming off as much as they can in the process, taking full advantage of the situation that teeters on the cusp of chaos. When, for instance, Abramovich withdrew from Stamford Bridge (and that was always much more of a 'when' than an 'if') the contracts and pay of the players remained, but the situation in Ukraine, and so world politics, the amount of financial resources Roman was obliged to leave behind, dictated the future of Chelsea and the whole of English football; it could have easily have been a disaster for the game.

The Premier League is a market with the character of a house of cards economically speaking, within which, at times, it is hard to tell the difference between sheriff and outlaw, as the dealing, ducking and diving fragments into a multidimensional drama that gets played out on the event horizon of an economic black hole.

Hence, in terms of the top echelons of the game, the days of the 'local football club' and the pleasant fantasy of the 'family club' have long gone, while the 'homegrown' player, relative to the past, is an endangered species.

As you take your seat in your local stadium of choice, you have been sucked into to ergosphere of an international financial maelstrom. The modern chairperson looks out on this prospect. The reward is to milk the stars; the danger is tumbling into the singularity and the certain destruction which will follow; Qatar 2022 is the Tartarus of the obscenity.

The last time I bumped into Bobby Moore he was doing a gig for a radio station. As usual I was surprised he remembered my name. I had not long before spoken to his long-time defensive partner at West Ham, centre-half Ken Brown, in connection with another book I was at that time putting together about West Ham in the 1950s. I mentioned that Ken had told me how Bobby 'knew without a glance where everyone on the pitch was'. Bobby smiled and asked, 'Do you ever stop writing?'

Typically, he deflected the chat from him to me. I do understand that. I know as much about me as anybody might know, but other people will tell me something I don't know about the world. If you are curious, if you, like Bobby, habituate wanting to know what's going on around you, that's what you are going to do. In a way it was the perfect answer to the question I never got to ask him.

BIBLIOGRAPHY

Books

Allen, M. *Jimmy Greaves* (Virgin, 2001)

Allison, M. *Colours of My Life* (Everest, 1975)

Baker, W. J. *Sports in the Western World* (University of Illinois Press, 1988)

Belton, B. *Johnnie the One: the John Charles Story* (The History Press, 2003)

Belton, B. *The Men of 64: West Ham and Preston North End in the FA Cup* (Tempus, 2005)

Belton, B. *West Ham United Miscellany* (Pennant Books, 2006a)

Belton, B. *Black Hammers: The Voices of West Ham's Ebony Heroes* (Pennant Books, 2006b)

Belton, B. *War Hammers: The Story of West Ham United During the First World War* (The History Press, 2006c)

Belton, B. *The Lads of '23: Bolton Wanderers, West Ham United and the 1923 FA Cup Final* (Tony Brown, 2006d)

Belton, B. *East End Heroes, Stateside Kings* (John Blake, 2008)

Belton, B. *Burn Budgie Byrne, Football Inferno* (DB, 2012)

Belton, B. *Bubbles, Hammers & Dreams*, (DB, 2013a)

Belton, B. *The First and Last Englishmen*, (DB, 2013b)

Belton, B. *Days of Iron: The Story of West Ham United in the Fifties* (DB, 2013c)

Belton, B. *War Hammers II: The Story of West Ham United During the Second World War* (The History Press, 2015)

Belton, B., *Nearly Reached the Sky: West Ham in Europe* (Fonthill Press, 2017)

Chetwynd, J. Belton, B. *British Baseball and the West Ham Club* (McFarland & Co Inc, 2007)

Crane, T. *They Played with Bobby Moore* (Tim Crane, 2014)

Daniels, P. *Moore than a Legend* (Goal Publications, 1997)

Dickinson, M. *Bobby Moore: The Man in Full* (Yellow Jersey, 2014)

Edworthy, N. *England: The Official FA History* (Virgin Books, 1997)

Emery, D. (Ed) *Bobby Moore. A Tribute* (Headline, 1993)

Fenton, T. *At Home With the Hammers* (Nicholas Kaye, 1960)

Football Association *The Complete Guide to England Players Since 1945* (Stanley Paul, 1993)

Greaves, J. *Greavsie* (Time Warner, 2003)

Green, G. *Soccer in the Fifties* (Ian Allan, 1974)

Giller, N. *Bobby Moore: The Master* (NGB, 2013)

Greenwood, R. *Yours Sincerely Ron Greenwood* (Collins Willow, 1984)

Kohl, H. *'I Won't Learn from You': And Other Thoughts on Creative Maladjustment* (The New Press, 1994)

Hugman, B.J. *The PFA Premier & Football League Players Records* (Queen Anne Press, 2005)

Irving, D. *The West Ham United Football Book* (Stanley Paul, 1968)

Irving, D. *The West Ham United Football Book No.2* (Stanley Paul, 1969)

Korr, C. *West Ham United: The Making of a Football Club* (Gerald Duckworth, 1986)

Lewis, R. *England's Eastenders* (Mainstream, 2002)

Lyall, J. *Just Like My Dreams* (Penguin, 1989)

McDonald, T. *West Ham United: The Managers* (FootballWorld, 2007)

McKinstry *Sir Alf* (HarperSport, 2006)

Moore, B. *My Soccer Story* (Stanley Paul, 1967)

Moore, T. *Bobby Moore: By The Person Who Knew Him Best* (CollinsWillow, 2005)

Morse, G. *Sir Walter Winterbottom: The Father of Modern English Football* (John Blake, 2013)

Moynihan, J. *The West Ham Story* (Arthur Barker, 1984)

Oldenburg, R. *The Great Good Place: Cafes, Coffee Shops, Community Centers, Beauty Parlors, General Stores, Bars, Hangouts, and How They Get You Through the Day* (Paragon House, 1989)

Oldenburg, R. *The Great Good Place* (Marlowe & Company, 1991)

Oldenburg, R. *Celebrating the Third Place: Inspiring Stories about the 'Great Good Places' at the Heart of Our Communities* (Marlowe & Company, 2000)

Palmer, J. (Ed.) *Bobby Moore: England's Greatest* (Athem)

Powell, J. *Bobby Moore* (Alpine Books, 1993)

Revins, R. *The Old Hammers – Personalities and Reminiscences of Boleyn Castle Silver Jubilee* (Stratford, London, 1933)

Roper, T. *West Ham in the Sixties: The Jack Burkett Story* (FootballWorld, 2009)

Stevens, P. *John Lyall. A Life in Football* (Apex, 2014)

Tossel, D. *Big Mal* (Mainstream, 2008)

Venables.T. *Venables* (Michael Joseph, 1994)

Journals/newspapers

Hammers News
Newham Recorder
East Ham Echo
East and West Ham Gazette
East London Advertiser Evening Post
Ex Magazine
Stratford Express

ND - #0268 - 270225 - C0 - 234/156/15 - PB - 9781780916323 - Gloss Lamination